T0113225

MARK VONNEGUT
The Eden Express

"His descriptions of his schizophrenic experiences are not only convincing from a clinical standpoint but are written in an engaging style, with an admirable lack of self-pity. His story is worth reading."
—Library Journal

"A remarkable book." *—The Atlantic*

"A searching, vivid account . . . of the inside of a schizophrenic breakdown, the struggle to recover, to understand."
—The New York Times Book Review

"A disarmingly open, engrossing, oddly graceful chronicle."
—Kirkus Reviews

"Mark Vonnegut's remembrance of what it was like in the 1960s is not only a memoir about his loss of political and social innocence, and ours, but a surprisingly good-natured trip through his own head."
—Los Angeles Times

The Eden Express

Mark Vonnegut

A LAUREL BOOK
Published by
Dell Publishing
a division of
The Bantam Doubleday Dell Publishing Group, Inc.
666 Fifth Avenue
New York, New York 10103

The trademark Laurel ® is registered in the U.S. Patent and Trademark Office.

ISBN: 978-0-4406-1393-0

Printed in the United States of America

146673257

The author maintains that all people, places, and events in this book are real and that he has depicted them accurately to the best of his ability. Before drawing conclusions, however, the reader is cautioned to bear in mind the fact that the author has spent considerable time mentally unbalanced.

Contents

Preface-Schizophrenia

Most diseases can be separated from one's self and seen as foreign intruding entities. Schizophrenia is very poorly behaved in this respect. Colds, ulcers, flu, and cancer are things we get. Schizophrenic is something we are. It affects the things we most identify with as making us what we are.

If this weren't problem enough, schiz comes on slow and comes on fast, stays a minute or days or years, can be heaven one moment, hell the next, enhance abilities and destroy them, back and forth several times a day and always weaving itself inextricably into what we call ourselves. It can transform only a small corner of our lives or turn the whole show upside down, always giving few if any clues as to when it came or when it left or what was us and what was schiz.

If it seems I tell too much here and too little there, I've honestly done the best I can. I honestly don't know which parts of what follows are schizophrenia, just my particular schizophrenia, living in our times, trying to be a good hippie, or whatever.

If I had had a well-defined role in a stable culture, it might have been far simpler to sort things out. For a hippie, son of a counterculture hero, B.A. in religion, genetic biochemical disposition to schizophrenia, setting up a commune in the wilds of British Columbia, things tended to run together.

1
Traveling Hopefully

It is a better thing to travel hopefully than it is to arrive.

—R. L. STEVENSON

June 1969: Swarthmore Graduation. The night before, someone had taken white paint and painted "Commence What?" on the front of the stage. The maintenance crew had dutifully covered it over with red, white, and blue bunting, but we all knew it was there. We sat there more or less straight-faced, listening to how well educated we were, how we were supposed to save the world, etc. Most of us were wearing arm bands to let the world know exactly where we stood on the war. "What a swell bunch of moral people," thought I. "With us on the loose, corruption and evil don't stand a chance."

To pass the time, to try to figure out where I was and get some sort of lead on what the hell to do next, I had written my own commencement address.

"Members of the class of '69, parents, faculty, etc., greetings. Here we are on a fine sunny June day to celebrate and commemorate the graduation of 207 fine young men and women from this fine institution of higher learning.

"One of the things I'm taken by when I look out on a group like this one is how hard people have tried to do nice things for you. The financial cost of your education alone is staggering, but it doesn't begin to tell the story. In a process that goes back generation upon generation countless sacrifices have been made in your name. The list is endless. It ranges from World War II to making do with margarine instead of butter. You've been given the best of everything from prenatal care to college professors. Your grandparents, parents, teachers, and others have burned a lot of midnight oil trying to figure out how to make life more pleasant for you. One of the things they came up with is a liberal arts education, which is what today is all about.

"By and large, you're not a thankful lot. A lot of you feel terribly cheated and that a liberal arts education is a pile of shit. You feel you've been conned into wasting four years of precious time. I don't find your bitterness entirely misplaced. After all, here you are at the ridiculous age of twenty-one, with virtually no real skills except as conversationalists. Let me remark, in passing, what fantastic conversationalists you are. Most of you have mastered enough superficial information and tricks of the trade to be able to hold conversations with virtually anyone about anything. This is one of the reasons you're such big hits at your parents' parties. Being a good conversationalist is really what a liberal arts education is all about.

"Well, as I was saying, your bitterness is not entirely out of line. For one thing, no one has the faintest idea about what you should do next. But lest you be too bitter, let me point out that knowing a college education is a pile of shit is no small lesson. There are many people who don't know it. In fact, probably most people don't know it. There is surely no better place to learn this lesson than at college. In any event, you can console yourselves by knowing that you won't waste time and make fools of yourselves later in life thinking how different it all would have been if only you had gone to college. Now that you have your degree, you can say what a pile of shit college is and no one can accuse you of sour grapes."

* * *

My girl friend, Virginia, was in the audience with my parents, watching me and my classmates receive our precious advice and shiny new degrees.

"Well, Virge" (which is what I usually called her), "I imagine seeing a moving ceremony like that must have taken care of any silly notion you might have had about dropping out."

She wasn't thinking that seriously about dropping out. She had only a year to go and had seen too many friends get hung up explaining, justifying, and agonizing over whether or not to go back. Dropping out was too much work. The most efficient thing to do was get it the hell out of the way.

Our plans were vague. We had been offered a place to stay in Boston for the summer. We hoped we could find interesting jobs and I'd find some way around the draft. Virginia would go back to finish at Swarthmore and then we'd see what came up.

Virginia. There was something about us that fitted together. Tumblers moved and we locked together. There were some dreadfully unhappy times, but we both needed other things more than happiness. It was those other things that we were all about.

Virginia, Virginia, Virginia, how did my life get so mixed up with yours? It was spring, my senior, your junior year. I was lonely. So were you. We started walking together and talking together, mostly me talking, babbling on like an utter fool, wishing you'd say more and trying to get up the nerve to kiss you. It wasn't like it had been with other girls at all. For one thing, you weren't pretty at all the way other girl friends of mine had been pretty. You were pretty but a weird pretty. Your legs were much too perfect to be quite human.

You were very different from other women I had been attracted to. Had I met you earlier I would have thought you were almost ugly, nose much too big and poorly defined, narrow, low forehead, cheekbones high and spread, but you carried it all with such grace and dignity. Most women seemed to be either attractive or unattractive and that was that. I have never before or since met anyone who was as beautiful to me when you were beautiful or as ugly when you were ugly. Your awesome range transfixed me, and always those legs which were too perfect to be quite human.

Everything about you seemed like a magnet. The house you rented with five other girls was the spawning of a new spirit. The five guys and I who rented a house a few miles away were all weird, but we were weird in a boisterous individual way that seemed sure to die as soon as school was over. There was a unity to your weirdness that went beyond all eating out of the same refrigerator, vegetarian communal meals, and heavy political raps, which were admittedly all new to me. I and most of my friends agreed with you point by point all down the line, but there was something beyond the points that was very different. In any event, I didn't waste much time hopping aboard to try to figure out just what this difference was all about.

Our first date, if you can call it that, came out of one of my increasingly frequent and doubtless unsubtle wooing visits to your house. We were all having a quiet cup of tea.

Everything seemed peaceful and nice. You went into the kitchen and suddenly all hell broke loose. Someone hadn't washed the dishes. Your voice was short and clipped, your face set, your eyes filled with total disgust. Everyone scurried around meekly, trying to stay out of your way. It was an impressive show.

During a brief lull in the storm, while you were just sitting on the couch glowering, I said weakly, without much hope, "How'd you like to go to a movie?"

The absurdity of my invitation was compounded by the fact that it was about nine-thirty at night. You just looked at me. Your look seemed to soften a bit, from hate to gentle contempt. I guess the humor of it got to you some. "Shit, I don't know," I started again. "I just thought you might want to get out of here for a bit. Maybe there's an all-night movie in Philly or maybe we could just go out for a hamburger or something."

"Ya," you said, or words to that effect indicating a bare minimum of acceptance.

"Well," said I, feeling not at all sure you'd accepted or what you'd accepted, "we'll go to my place and pick up some money."

"OK," said you, and we went out and got into trusty old Car Car.

On the way, Car Car was filled with dead silence. "Do you really want to go to a movie?" I finally ventured.

"No," you said, "not really."

"OK, how about a hamburger?"

"That's all right, I'm really not hungry."

"OK, I've got some beer at the house. It's really a pretty pleasant place to sit around. At least you'll get out of your house for a while." Silence.

"Well, here we are," I said, trying to be cheerful. You didn't say a word. You just got out of the car and walked in with precision and dignity. Well, I thought to myself, feeling more and more like an ass, is she really that pissed off about unwashed dishes? Does she want to be here at all? You gave me so little to go on.

"Want a beer?"

"No."

"Well, I'm going to have one," as I opened the fridge. "Some milk? Maybe some tea?"

Just a shake of your head. You just sat there looking at me. The contempt had pretty much left your eyes, thank God. But it was replaced with an aloof penetration that was equally if not more disconcerting.

With so few clues, I was on my own. Maybe I just imagined it, but I started to see something else in your eyes, a plea: Try to understand why I can't give you more clues.

Then you seemed to be bordering on tears. I put my arm around you and tried to kiss you softly, trying to tell you there was nothing to be afraid of, that you were safe from whatever was haunting you, that I liked you, that I wanted you to relax.

You avoided my kiss, half buried your face in my chest, and hugged me softly, not moving, not breathing. I stopped breathing too. We stayed like that for what seemed like forever. I tried again to kiss you. Our mouths just brushed and you buried your head again and hugged me a little tighter. Almost afraid you might break, I gently moved your head back from my chest, stroking your hair. I smiled and you smiled back.

In your eyes, I thought I saw a promise that some day, but not now and not to be pushed, you would make it all make sense to me. The same promise was in your hugs. My eyes must have promised something back. You took my head in your hands and kissed me. We became lovers.

Feminine ardor made me suspicious. The fact is, I couldn't take it. It was lots of different things. If a woman panted and moaned when I made love to her, I felt uncomfortable, sort of lonely. Maybe I was just jealous because I couldn't lose my head like that. Maybe I thought women were faking something that was supposed to make me feel good. Maybe I thought that they were fantasizing about an old lover or maybe Mick Jagger. All I knew was that I felt left out. With Virge there wasn't much trouble that way.

About a week after we had started living together, we were taking a walk by an old abandoned mill, a very romantic place. It was evening. She had been even more quiet than usual that day. But it was that silence that I was supposed to get used to, that I was supposed to understand and not worry about. Worrying about it proved something bad about me.

"I've been thinking about what's going on between us." Said very meaningfully.

"Huh?" Maybe I would have eventually got the hang of her silence if it had not so often been broken so ominously.

"I've been thinking maybe it's screwed up." She always got to bring the news, or at least write the headlines. The col-

umns were my work. That was one of our unwritten rules
from the very start.

I got the "Uh-oh" feeling in the pit of my stomach. Jig's up,
she's figured out my game.

"You're just lonely and want someone to sleep with."

It was all I could do to keep a straight face. Could she
really be that far off base? Did she really think it was that
tough for me to get laid? If only it was true, I thought. It
would be so much easier, so much more understandable.

I don't remember how I actually answered the charge. It
doesn't really matter. Nothing much changed between us. I
just got a little lonelier.

June 1970. By the time of Virginia's graduation I had beat
the draft with an uncanny schizophrenic act at my physical
and put in six months as a nine-to-five, work-within-the-sys-
tem do-gooder. I had spent the next six wandering up and
down the East Coast looking for friends and land to get a
commune going and hanging around Swarthmore with Virginia trying to figure out what we'd do after she graduated.

During spring vacation we went down to her parents' summer place in the mountains of North Carolina. Vincent and
seven other people came with us. A lot of grass got smoked.
Most of the people did some tripping. We went to a Blue
Grass music festival. Zeke, the beautiful half-Labrador, half-
Gordon-setter puppy Virginia had given me for Christmas,
got hit and nearly killed by a motorcycle and had to be rushed
to a Chapel Hill vet about a hundred miles away. It was a
strange, jumbled week. Somewhere in there Virginia and I
decided to head for British Columbia to look for land, as soon
as she graduated.

"We're going to British Columbia to get some land." A bit
vague, to be sure, but it seemed much more satisfying than
most of my previous answers to the question "What are you
doing?"

"I'm going to college" or "I'm working in Boston" just didn't
make it either for me or for whoever was asking. It didn't lead

to conversations either of us cared much about. Looking for land in B.C. was another matter entirely. Just about everyone, young and old, straights and freaks, wanted to stay up long into the night talking about that one.

Looking back on it now, what I find most amazing is how little argument we got from parents, professors, or anyone else. What few misgivings there were were vague, apologetic, and usually mumbled. I think the Kennedys, Martin Luther King, and war and assorted other goodies had so badly blown everybody's mind that sending the children naked into the woods to build a new society seemed worth a try.

Farewell, Cape Cod and Family. I spent a few weeks working around the Barnstable yard before heading to hook up with Virginia. The family was in lousy shape, but the yard I could do something about—cutting vines away from fruit trees, making minimal order out of the wild grapes, just generally cleaning up. And I put in a vegetable garden. It wasn't a very functional vegetable garden. It was more decorative. I made it in the shape of a teardrop, which no one figured out till later.

The day I left Barnstable to go down to Philadelphia, I took my old boat, whose floating days were about over anyway, down to the end of Scudder Lane and left it on the beach just above the high-water mark, facing out into Barnstable Harbor.

Car Car. My trusty '65 Beetle. Dead now. Sold for parts when I was in the nut house. It served me well. People said that it was only my faith that kept it running. It was the only car I've ever felt any affection for and I was the only one it would let drive it. Others would try from time to time, but it usually broke down within a mile or two and wouldn't budge until I'd come and talk to it.

I didn't always love Car Car. It was given to me brand-new by my parents at my prep school graduation. It floored me. I wasn't the son of a struggling writer anymore, an image I had clung to long after it was appropriate. I looked at the car and decided that it would render me good dependable service but that it was utterly devoid of personality.

My conversion crept up on me slowly. It wasn't until around 75,000 miles and three years later that we realized we were in love. Shortly after that its odometer broke, so how many miles of service Car Car actually gave is anyone's guess. When you're in love, numbers don't matter.

It was at around 80,000 miles that I drastically altered the interior. I took out all the seats but the driver's and made some plywood and foam rubber cushions to fit the void left by the seats. I upholstered them with some old curtains. This increased Car Car's carrying capacity and versatility immeasurably. Ten people weren't comfortable but it was possible. Two people could sleep in it. Two people and a dog was pushing it.

The primary reason I did it was carrying capacity. In its career Car Car carried a full-size refrigerator, a BSA 650, which I had to take apart some to get it all in, and lots of other stuff. If someone somewhere is keeping records of things carried in a VW bug, they should know about Car Car.

Waiting for Virge to graduate, in early June, I spent a couple of hours a day the week before heading west talking to Car Car and fitting it with an ice chest, drawers for silverware, a plastic sink, a water jug. I made use of every conceivable bit of space. It was Car Car's job to take Virginia, Zeke, and me and all our worldlies to the promised land. Car Car was going to be our home for a while.

"Car Car, I know I've asked a lot of you and you're tired. There's just one last favor. Take me home. I don't know where that is but together we can find it. Take me to Eden and when we get there you can spend the rest of your days turning to dust sheltering geese on their way to dust." From studying designs for different farm buildings I had decided that Car Car was more a goose shelter than anything else. That was where its aptitude lay. It seemed to like the idea. I envisioned it as sort of a memorial in Eden. A reminder of times past when we used to need cars, and a symbol that all cars weren't all bad. But as it turned out, Car Car took us to a farm that had no road access, so it never got to be a goose shelter. Maybe it was trying to say something. I renamed it "Moses."

Two of Zeke's playmates got killed by cars zipping around our block the week before we finally got going. I kept him inside or took him on walks in the fields. After a while it seemed as if the interminable farewells were part of a plot to get my dog killed.

Good-by, good-by, good-by for days, and then finally Virge and I were on our way to the promised land and whatever else came up.

One of the first things that came up was we got busted just outside of Pittsburgh. It was bound to happen sooner or later. My long hair and beard, my beat-up old VW, and the spirit of the times had all conspired to make me a cop magnet. I couldn't travel anywhere without getting stopped, questioned, and usually searched. I was usually clean. It was a little game I actually started to enjoy.

I knew a little about the laws of arrest and search and seizure. Once I asked, "Officer, would you mind telling me a little about your probable cause for this search?" "So you want to know about my probable cause, do you? Well, just look in the mirror, that's my probable cause." I wasn't always dopeless. Holding tended to wreck whatever pleasure there was to be derived from these little vignettes.

I had been stopped for some pretty flimsy excuses before and Trooper Suchadolski was no exception, but at least he had a new line.

"I thought you might be having some trouble with your vehicle."

"No, Officer, not really." Car Car was doing beautifully, cruising with an incredible load between fifty-five and sixty. I had slowed down some when I saw the trooper because I didn't have that much faith in my jury-rigged speedometer and didn't want to give him any excuse. My muffler did something a little funny over fifty-five, but he never mentioned it so that wasn't the problem.

He looked at all the stuff in the car. "Going to California?"

"No, Officer, we're headed for British Columbia."

He never caught on.

"Seems like everyone I meet on the road is headed for California. What's out there?"

"We're going to British Columbia."

Three months later. "I asked the defendant where he was going and he said he was going to California."

"Can I see your driver's license and registration, please?" All his concern for the condition of my vehicle was gone.

I opened the glove compartment and got my license and registration. He craned his neck, trying to see if he could see anything more interesting in there.

"What else you got in that glove compartment?"

"Not much." I rummaged through it naming some items. "A screwdriver, some pliers, some gum, a can opener, some more papers, and our first-aid kit." I had mentioned the first-aid kit last, sort of mumbling it. There was nothing really illegal in there but I knew he'd hassle us about it.

"Let's see that first-aid kit. What's in there?"

I did the same routine I had gone through with the glove compartment. It was like Twenty Questions. "Some Band-Aids, some gauze, some iodine, some adhesive tape, some scissors, a butterfly suture, and some pills."

"What sort of pills?"

"Well it's mostly just leftover prescriptions for one thing or another." Which was true. "We're going to be doing of lot of camping out and we might be pretty far from a doctor at times."

He wasn't impressed. "What sort of pills?"

If there had been some rule about how many questions he got I might have had a chance. But there wasn't and I could tell that this man's curiosity wasn't the sort that would stop, having merely exhausted the possibilities of my glove compartment. I knew he'd get around to being interested in what was next to my battery and I knew that's where I had stashed the tail end of my Jamaican grass, such nice stuff, and Virge's mescaline. I knew I was going to be busted.

I opened the vial of pills and poured them into my hand. "These little white ones are penicillin. The prescription is right on the outside of the vial, with the name on it and everything. These gray-and-red ones here are Darvon for pain. Virginia's got a prescription. These here are Bufferin. See the little B right on them? They're easy."

For some reason, he was attracted by the penicillin. There was more of it than anything else. He went back to his car to study his little drug identification book—which I saw later—and came back and told me that the penicillin pills were amphetamines and that they were illegal. He handed me a little piece of paper and told me to sign it. I just sort of looked at the paper and then back at him and then back at the paper. Someone had done a dreadful job of typing.

"It waives your right to a search warrant," he explained.

"I'm not so sure I want to waive it."

Three hours of constitutional debate and assorted other fun and games, culminating in a search that left Car Car's contents and innards in shreds. Later I was checked for lice and crabs and clunked into jail. I blew my one phone call on a bondsman who refused to handle drug cases.

The next morning I was able to talk the warden into letting me have a second phone call. I called my father, who called an old college buddy who lived in Pittsburgh. He got me a lawyer who sprung me.

What made my brief stay in jail such a bitch was that I kept expecting to get out in just a few more minutes. I didn't sleep. I just kept wondering what red tape was keeping Virge from getting me out. When I finally got out it was about two o'clock the next afternoon. It had been only eighteen hours, but it felt like years. Maybe I stretched it on purpose. Prison was an important part of life I hadn't had a shot at before.

So there I was, having done twenty years in prison mostly

in isolation, a lifetime of being harassed by sadistic guards. In my spare time, I was a Jew in a concentration camp.

Oh goody, a real-life experience, something to write about. Something to talk about, a good story. I wanted to be a good storyteller.

A good storyteller is a good teacher, an entertainer. Storytellers provide cohesion, myths, and expression for a culture. A culture was what I thought we were all trying to build. Either we didn't have one or we wouldn't have one much longer.

It takes a story to find out what you think, and it takes a story to be able to pass it on to others. That was something that Swarthmore by and large missed. They had some funny idea that you could communicate and teach without stories.

All hyped up on my real-life adventure, something new to digest, a new story to tell—"Out on bail" had a nice ring—I started telling Virge about what had happened in prison, what being locked up had felt like, what the guards and warden were like, some of the conversations I had had with the guys on either side of me. I started working on my story, checking audience reaction, finding out what I really felt about it. I told Virge I thought it might make a nice follow-up to the draft story. I was thinking of doing a book of generational incidents. The innocent years. The aptitude kid, disillusion, dope, the draft, dropping out of the forty-hour week —and now the dope bust.

Virginia was stony silent. At first I thought she felt guilty for being so dumb about not getting me sprung earlier. I guess it never occurred to her that they'd really only give me one phone call. I admit I never thought they'd really do that either. She had gone off with some nice folks we met outside the cop shop and got wrecked out of her mind on Cambodian dope.

"What's wrong?" I asked.

"I can't help thinking of how many million times I'm going to have to listen to you tell this story."

I thought maybe she felt that way because she was diddled

out of so many real-life adventures because she was a woman. It was me, the man, who got to be the hero. I faced the draft, I got busted even though it was mostly her dope. It was significant that I decided not to work at some respectable job but no one expected her to anyway. From that angle her bitterness made a lot of sense.

I said that maybe the last section of my generational collage should be a piece by her about why she hated my stories. I was looking for something to tie the whole thing together and that seemed like a brainstorm. She didn't say anything.

She gradually stopped seething but still wasn't much interested in hearing about what had happened in jail. We'd be at Gary and Cheryl's with ten hours of driving. They loved my stories and I loved theirs. I could hold out that long.

Between Pittsburgh and West Branch, Iowa, we were stopped three more times by cops. It was like someone was trying to give me more material. One guy was nice enough. He just wanted to tell me a taillight was out. In Indiana we were stopped for a "routine check." Since we didn't have that "holding" look in our eyes, the trooper let us go after a quick once-over. In Illinois the rear light and the fact that my plates were held on by wire instead of bolts cost us $25. And finally we were there.

West Branch, Iowa. Birthplace of Herbert Hoover. We arrived about 2:00 A.M. We had called ahead from Illinois to tell them we'd be showing up that night. Gary was waiting up for us and showed us to our room, where we collapsed for a solid ten-hour sleep.

The next day was spent catching up on each other's lives and talking about our coming adventures. Gary had just gotten a Guggenheim fellowship to finish his third novel. They were going to live in Morocco for a year. We played a lot of chess and talked about how strange life was getting and how something had to give sooner or later. What was going to happen next was anyone's guess. We had to find all the people we cared about and make a tribe of some sort and all take care of each other. We needed some answers and pretty quick. Gary was looking in his dreams and hoped to find some clues from being in Morocco. I'd check out B.C. We'd stay in touch.

Gary and Cheryl asked if I would preside over some sort of christening ceremony for their son, my namesake, Mark.

The next day was a perfect Iowa day. Mid-June, seventy-two degrees, blue sky forever, slight breeze, fields of young corn green forever.

Welcome to Earth, Mark Jackson. Welcome to Mark, Earth. Just one or the other would be a mistake. I figured fifty-fifty was probably the best way to play it.

We got a lot of nice things together—flowers, incense, candles, and an excellent bottle of white wine my parents had given me for graduation the year before. They had given me a red too, but I was saving that for when we found land. We had picked out some Bach organ music for background.

Gary set up his tape recorder to capture the whole thing. He had the labor and delivery on tape too, and was constantly writing letters to Mark and putting them away in a special place.

I was wearing a shirt that Virge had made for me out of linen with lots of different weaves, the closest thing to vestments I could come up with. We all sat in a circle, Gary and Cheryl holding Mark, some friends of theirs, Virge and I, all holding hands. We lit the incense and candles, threw the flowers around a bit. Anyone could say whatever they wanted, anything they thought would be appropriate to welcome young Mark to Earth. I remember Gary saying something about how we were silly enough to try to live our lives in peace and that he hoped Mark would join us when he grew up. I told him not to take anything anyone told him too seriously, since everyone started off as helpless little babies just like he was and everything they learned they learned from people who had been helpless little babies themselves. We all told him that for no particular reason we were very dedicated to him and that one way or another there were a lot of people who would do almost anything they could for him. I told Mark that if there was a God petty enough to hold the irregularities of our little ceremony against him, then He no doubt ran a petty heaven that Mark wouldn't want any part of anyway. We talked some about what a strange historical time he happened to be born in. I tried to explain a little about my being out on bail. We all drank wine and sprinkled some on his head as we passed him around the circle, kissing him gently on his soft spot.

Two years earlier, Gary and Cheryl had asked if I could legally marry them. That they saw me as their pastor probably had a lot to do with why I didn't go to seminary. I've always been a fan of priesthood of the laity and I thought maybe seminary would somehow spoil whatever fragile magic I had that made them and a few other people look at me that way. I didn't want to trade the substance for the badge, and besides, most seminary programs I check out seemed candy-ass one way or the other.

The day after our ceremony for Mark, I had to go back to Pennsylvania for a hearing on the legality of the search and arrest. My lawyer figured we could get the case thrown out in a hurry, but the cops never showed. Maybe we could get another hearing in a week, maybe not. I couldn't stick around that long, so we'd just have to wait till the trial, which was set for some time in September.

All that traveling, all that hassling for nothing, was a royal pain in the ass, but somehow I didn't mind. This foolishness was telling me I had made a wise decision: to get away from all that shit.

When I got back to West Branch, Virginia was barely able to say hello. She was rigid, almost holding her breath, one step away from catatonic. I had seen her in this state a few times before and I saw it a few times later, but it wasn't something you could ever get used to.

It was like walking in and finding someone crumpled up on the floor. "What is it? What's wrong? Say something, please."

But she couldn't say anything. She'd just sit like that, maybe nodding or shaking her head slightly. I'd go on frantically, "Is it this? Is it that?" Trying everything till I hit on something that would make her eyes a little brighter, her breath a little deeper. It was like charades. The warmer I got the more she loosened up, until I'd finally said what was on her mind. Then she'd gradually regain her ability to speak and go on as if nothing strange had happened.

What she wanted this time was to turn around, to head back to Boston or New York, get an apartment, and find a job. In a way I envied her. Turning around didn't seem like an option for me. If it was for her maybe she should do it. I knew what was back there and it was just too much nothing. There just wasn't enough hope back there. In my mind those bridges were burned and I had to keep moving till I found something that would either save me or kill me. I didn't even care all that much which. I just couldn't take any more limbo.

Boston. My job had been an interesting one. In fact you'd have to say it was unique. How many full-bearded, hair halfway down their backs, B.A. in religion, pacifist chiefs of police do you know? I was chief of a twenty-man detachment of special state police that provided the security for Boston State Hospital.

How did this come to pass? I had filed an application with my draft board to be considered a conscientious objector. I knew there was a good chance of their refusing my application, but just in case they accepted it, I wanted to have an acceptable alternative-service job going. That way they wouldn't send me to East Jesus, Nebraska, to empty bed pans and might even give me credit for the time I put in prior to their granting me my status.

A draft counselor at the Unitarian Service Committee told me about a Dr. Bliss who ran the adolescent unit at Boston State and had hired C.O.s before. I figured teaching English or something to screwed-up kids wouldn't be a bad way to spend two years and set up an appointment to talk with Dr. Bliss.

Dr. Bliss is a big man who smokes big cigars and smiles most of the time. It isn't a nervous smile like so many full-time smilers have, but still it made me wonder what the hell he thought was so funny. Part of what he thought was so funny was C.O.s. He wasn't a pacifist himself, which I think was the first thing he said to me. His thing about C.O.s was a loving paternalism that flirted with sadism. In his eyes C.O.s were sweet, well-intentioned, upper-middle-class kids who had been overprotected and were in need of a touch of real work and real life, with which he was more than willing to provide them.

After we had been talking and smiling for fifteen minutes or so he appeared to have a brainstorm. I say appeared because I'm pretty sure he had it planned from before he even met me, it was so much up his alley. His brainstorm, his prescription for my pacifism, was that I take on the job of reforming and administering the security force of the hospital.

"That would make you a chief of police." A still bigger smile.

"It sounds like the sort of opportunity I'm not likely to be offered again."

"Then you'd consider it?"

"Ya. I don't think I could ever forgive myself for saying no."

So we went over to discuss it with Dr. Leen, the assistant superintendent of the place. The whole security mess had just been taken out of the steward's office and dumped in his lap. He was dying to have someone to deal with it. So I was hired. A week later, I started my career as chief of police.

I was a very good chief of police. For starters, I cut crime. And I set up all sorts of reporting and filing systems so I could prove exactly how much I cut crime.

Special state police are a lot like special children. There were very few in the group who could have been regular state police and those who could have been were mostly young, working their way through college, or taking a second job they could sleep through. Had they been capable of being real state cops, they would have been fools not to. At Boston State, $130 a week was the top salary they could get and that was after five years. They spent a lot of their time on the job drinking coffee, bitching about being handcuffed by the Supreme Court, grousing about not being respected, avoiding any sort of work, and watching television. Being a security man at a state hospital wasn't exactly what you'd call a prestige job. They were looked down upon by just about everyone else working at the hospital. They didn't get to carry guns. They didn't even have uniforms before I got there. The hospital was plagued with breaking and entering, theft, muggings, the occasional rape, vandalism, and so on. What I was supposed to do was anything that would make these guys an effective security force.

What I did was mostly showmanship. I'd give the heads of different units of the hospital a call and tell them that I'd like to address their next staff meeting on security. I'd talk about what they could do to help make our job easier, and what things I was doing to improve security. It took them by surprise. Lots of people working at the hospital didn't even know there was a security force. Whenever there was a crime of some sort I always showed up with a Polaroid camera and took copious notes from anyone who was there. Everyone was impressed. I created the impression of motion and that was as good as the real thing. People became aware that there was a security system and that it was being reformed and run by this dynamic, earnest young man. No one had ever gotten a memo from security before. Now everyone got them all the time.

I got my men uniforms, a shiny new office, standardized procedures for handling and reporting incidents. I dressed up the patrol cars with flashy decals.

All my previous jobs had been manual labor of one sort or another. Landscaping, loading trucks, pumping gas, shell fishing, marine maintenance, things you couldn't really say much about one way or the other. But this was an adult-type job with adults under my charge and all manner of heavy social issues every day.

But the hospital was a depressing place to work. I got to know a lot of the doctors and very few seemed to think the hospital was doing the patients any good. It was just a dumping ground for human garbage. Regular hospitals are places you go to get well. A state mental hospital is where you're put if you don't get well.

Although I never took any psychology courses at Swarthmore, I had read a lot of psychology and was very much interested in it. In a way, being a religion major was a way to be a psych major without all the boring stuff about rats and statistics. Most of my friends were psych majors one way or another. We were all fascinated by psychological stuff, which is how many of us came to be called "heads."

My job didn't involve working directly with patients, but I thought about them a lot. I saw them as victims of our fucked-up, materialistic, impersonal, hectic, overmechanized, dehumanizing society. There wasn't much mystery about why these people were so screwed up. The mystery was why everyone else wasn't nuts too. But somehow I never figured it could ever happen to me, that I could some day be shuffling around in slippers and pajamas, bumming cigarettes and mumbling to myself. There were too many people who loved me, who would never commit me to an institution, whose love would keep me from getting that spaced out.

Another theory I had about the patients was that they had taken their very justified frustration and rage and turned it inward, thinking that it was they who were screwy instead of their society. My clear vision of what was wrong would keep me out of places like Boston State.

If all else failed my vanity would pull me through. I could never degrade myself that much. Maybe being crazy was being honest or right or enlightened even, but I could never stand to have people look at me the way they look at mental patients.

Szasz, Laing, and Jung were my favorites at this point. These people weren't really sick (Szasz). If they were acting a little strange it was a reasonable reaction to an unreasonable society (Laing). If they wanted to do something about it their best bet was a Jungian journey back to their individual and cultural roots. Most of the doctors at Boston State seemed to have similar notions.

Some of my special state police hated my guts so much they probably would have killed me if they'd thought they could get away with it. Most of them were sullen, devious, and small-minded. It was a bitch to get any work out of them, though all I ever asked was that they go out now and then and walk or drive around a little. Their union demanded my resignation because my job hadn't been properly posted. Most of them had seniority so there wasn't much I could threaten them with. But even if I had been able to fire them, had been able to offer decent salaries and attract better people, what would I have accomplished? Giving Boston State Hospital a crackerjack security force didn't seem like much in the face of the corruption and collapse of Western civilization. Some of my friends thought what I was doing was more harmful than good. I was humanizing and giving life to institutions that had to be utterly destroyed before the world could be set right.

But more than hassles with my men or ambivalence about what I was trying to do, the city—the noise, the cars, the rush-rush of unhappy, unfriendly people—was getting to me.

The draft board had denied my application for C.O. status and ordered me to take my physical. I went to it so hyped and furious about the war and everything else that I saw everyone there, including others taking the physical who for a moment talked lightly or smiled, as mass murderers. I wasn't terribly cooperative. Things got jumbled. I was given a psychiatric 4F, without even the usual letter from a shrink. My friends said I should get an Academy Award for my act. I knew it wasn't an act and thought some about what that might mean, but I was so glad to have beaten the draft that I didn't worry about it much. My victory also meant I could quit my job whenever I felt like it.

Virginia had gone back to Swarthmore about a month after I became chief of police. She came up for weekends now and then, but most of the time I was lonely and horny. I was living in a run-down house with Vincent, a couple of other Swarthmore people, and assorted passers-through. Everyone I lived with, everyone I saw on the street, everyone every-where seemed depressed. People didn't like what they were doing or have any idea about what they should do next. It was all just killing time till the sun went out.

Things were especially bad on the subways. There I was more and more desperately unhappy and self-conscious, sure the people could see how upset I was. Everyone except the occasional drunk was so lifeless. I started feeling that anyone who wasn't as upset as I was by the subways was guilty of not paying attention.

Sometimes I thought these strangers felt contempt for me, but more often I imagined their compassion. "You're right, fella, but what can we do about it." Contempt, compassion didn't make any difference. There was always the loneliness and the impossibility of doing anything about it.

I talked to my father about these feelings and he said that no one was watching that closely.

"I am. I do. Anyway, that doesn't help, that's the problem. Maybe if people paid more attention the subways wouldn't have gotten that way."

August September October November. More and more miserable, shakier and shakier, but still a damn good chief of police. Drinking more, not sleeping well, but there were so many good reasons to be upset that I saw my state of mind as more an asset than something to worry about.

Part of what I was doing was justifying what I had already made up my mind to do: split, chuck the whole city nine-to-five reformer bit and try to find some real answers to the nightmare life our society had become.

Another thing I was doing was confusing disability with virtue. It was easy to do since all the things that were disabling me were bad things. The frantic city pace, rush-hour traffic, callous institutions, war, racism, and greed were all from the same pot of stew. If enough people became disabled by it instead of just intellectually opposed to it, the whole mess would come to a grinding halt.

And it seemed to be happening. The gyre was widening. The center wouldn't hold. More and more blown minds more and more blown out all the time. With all our preconceptions blown away we would be forced to confront the full horror of what was going on.

Today a slight inkling that all is not as it should be. Tomorrow a crippling pain in the gut. Today I can't take rush-hour traffic. Tomorrow there'll be no more war. All the generals and fat-cat fascists will be home puking their guts out.

December rolled around. I had done everything I could think of to improve security within the present administrative and budgetary setup. I submitted a report on all I had done, with a list of proposals and options for future organization, and quit, stating that I had completed the job I was hired to do.

My boss wanted me to stay on as his permanent troubleshooter. The parking and garbage collection situations needed attention, too. But he was very understanding about the whole thing and told me if I ever needed a job to just come see him. We had spent many a lunch talking about my dream of finding some land and a life style that made sense. He hoped it worked out and said it was probably what he would do if he were my age.

Meanwhile, Back In West Branch. Virginia was coming out of her trance and thinking about turning around. It occurred to me that she might be just testing me, making sure my politics, dedication, and whatnot were in good shape.

How had I suddenly become the spark plug of this operation?
I had thought about getting land before, but tying it up with
communes, politics, and liberation, though I took to it like a
duck to water, was something I had picked up from her and
her friends.

One of the things that attracted me to Virginia was that
she had such a strong show of her own. I had looked forward
to a nice vacation from being the macho leader, but somehow
things had got twisted around and I was leader but not with
ideals that were really my own. From here on whatever happened would be my fault. Even if we turned around, by the
time we hit Boston she would be fuming with resentment at
the chauvinist pig dragging her around. She could rightly say
she hadn't suggested it. I had, in that weird charade, a milder
version of that which had produced the British Columbia
decision a few months earlier.

One way or another we decided to keep heading toward
Vancouver. We turned north. We had heard tales of people
being hassled by Canadian immigration on the West Coast.
There'd be a lot less hassle going up through North Dakota.
Maybe the Canadian cops wouldn't stop and search us every
hundred miles or so. Besides, Trans-Canadian Highway had a
nice ring to it, and the Canadian Rockies were rumored to
put their American counterparts to shame.

Minnesota, land of 100000000000000000 lakes. But more
than the lakes I loved the blue roofs. No one back East had
blue roofs. If we had flown to Vancouver we would have
missed the blue roofs. It seemed like just the right color for
roofs. It seemed like such a nice thing to do for the world,
have a blue roof. I wonder if living under a blue roof is different from living under a black or brown one.

Maybe all these people watch the same shitty TV shows,
eat the same shit food, use the same laundry soaps, underarm
deodorant, and razor blades, but they've got blue roofs.

This was what dancing lessons from God were all about,
blue roofs.

Through North Dakota and across the border to the Trans-Canadian Highway.

Some people from Swarthmore were doing summer theater in Helena, Montana. We had thought about stopping off there on our way out. It was nothing definite. Now it turned into a fight.

I don't know why I was so dead set against it or even if I was. We had made it into Canada without any problems. Going back through U.S. customs would be a bitch. Helena was several hundred miles out of our way. I wanted to get into the Canadian Rockies.

But all that, according to Virginia, was beside the point. She was probably right. According to her, somewhere back in the Dakotas or maybe even in Iowa or Minnesota or maybe from the very start I had decided to diddle her out of visiting her friends.

"I should have gotten out in North Dakota and hitched to Helena."

The fact was I liked having Virginia alone. It wasn't so much having a good time. It was more wanting something to happen and thinking it was more likely to happen if we were alone.

Zeke. Beautiful, noble Zeke never complained about driving in a hot car day after day, ten hours at a stretch and sometimes more. He was a good traveling dog as well as a good everything else dog. He was nine months old then, seventy pounds of grace and dignity and still growing. The only problem was that he still liked to sit in my lap when I drove. He was getting a shade big for that.

Virginia and I never gave each other gifts. Christmases and birthdays went by pretty much like any other day. Zeke was the exception. Just after I had quit my job as chief of police, just before the Christmas of '69, Virginia dropped a want ad in my lap. "Lab-Gordon setter cross puppies for sale . . ."

"If you want to do it, it's your Christmas present," she said.

I wanted to do it very much. I had been thinking and talking a lot about how much I wanted a dog, and Lab-Gordon setter was my dream combination.

We called the people up and the next day went to check out the litter. The owners lived on a small farm sitting incongruously in the middle of a tacky development with tiny lots. They must have been the last holdouts against the developers. A funky old farmhouse and barn, a corral, horses, and fields smack in the middle of cheesy plastic.

There were four pups left, three males and a female. I wanted a male. I didn't want the hassle of puppies and was hungry for male company. The biggest, healthiest-looking male was a complete extrovert, almost offensively so. Frat-rat blowhard, not much substance. His white markings were pure white. The smallest male obviously idolized him, and was obviously low on independence and imagination. Then there was Zeke, almost as big as his big brother. He traveled farther away from the group, seemed to be a generally more serious sort of dog. Whenever he did join the group he was the leader. His sister seemed to love him more than she loved his brothers.

I played with the litter for an hour or so, until it became more and more obvious that Zeke and I were meant to be.

"I can't say much about what lies ahead, pup, but as long as I eat, you eat. That's a human's word of honor for what it's worth."

Beautiful, noble Zeke. Looking out for Zeke's interests, making sure he got all the right shots, ate regularly, got enough exercise, learned about cars, was properly trained and brought up, gave my life an immediate purpose and meaning I was much in need of. But above and beyond all that, Zeke and I had glorious gleeful times together. We'd spend days just walking and exploring, howl along with fire sirens together, have endless mock growling, wrestling, yelling, biting battles. I never hit Zeke. The most I ever had to do by way of punishment was narrow my eyes slightly and say his name. He'd roll over contritely, begging forgiveness.

I suppose clinical psychologists could go on endlessly about why I became so attached to Zeke—increasing inability to form meaningful relationships with people, etc.—and they're probably right. I was desperate for something good in my life, but Zeke answered my desperation in a way I doubt that just any dog could have. I could relate endless tales about how smart he was, how graceful he was, how strong, noble, beautiful, and loving he was, and how everyone who ever met him, even dyed-in-the-wool dog haters, loved him too, but it's probably best to just say he was a true prince and leave it at that.

As for the clinical view, Zeke did mean a lot more to me than most of the people in this book. The utter trust, simplicity, and spontaneity of being with Zeke made most human relationships seem hollow, clumsy, and hardly worth it.

The Prairies. I was amazed. I had never seen anything like it. I was ripe for amazement.

More blue roofs and land that looked like no place I had ever been.

Big sky, seeing forever, no hills, no trees. Incredibly clean air. So dry. Little puddles of water every hundred miles or so, but mostly dry brownness forever. Lots of people were born, lived, and died here. New England would be big news to them. Gas station attendants were proud about never having been off the prairies, but I never talked long enough to any of the people there to really get a grip on it.

I didn't know it was prairie at first. I thought we had stumbled into a unique little area. I loved it. Something to write home about. Five hours of driving later I was a little less amazed. Apparently this wasn't very rare.

There was no place to camp, no streams or trees, nothing to attach the tarps to, no shade. Nowhere to hide. Our original idea of driving three hours a day and camping and fishing our way across Canada became hysterically funny.

When it's all so much the same there's nothing that's any different from anywhere else. Why stop one place rather than another? So on and on and on. It was a treadmill. I had driven ten hours to get exactly where I started.

We drove straight through, just stopping for gas and food.

The tension between Virge and me over whether or not to stop in Helena, plus the surreal effect of no water or green or change and being able to see forever, going forever, bore down on me. I hated the prairies. I became obsessed with getting to the Canadian Rockies.

When we finally saw them we were still a day's drive away, but at least then we were moving toward something we could see.

The first camp site we stopped at in the Rockies was loaded with freaks. Most of them had taken off from Amerika and all the things we had taken off from. Most of them were headed for Vancouver. Most of them were looking for land. There was a roof over some half-walls with smoky fireplaces in the center of the camp site, where we congregated and talked about what we had come from and what we thought we were headed toward. It was all very pleasant. Lots of talk about Vancouver being a cosmic magnet drawing us all there. Lots of expectations that something pretty funky was going to go down there if only because of the incredible influx. I began to worry about having so much competition looking for land.

We camped at a couple more places in the Rockies. Fished, hiked around and moved on, did more of the same through the rest of B.C., making only about 150 miles a day.

"It's better to travel hopefully than to arrive." We could have made it to Vancouver easily. It was a little after three. We had at least five hours of daylight left and Vancouver was only forty more miles west on a six-lane highway. But we turned off and went to Cultus Lake Provincial Park. "Easy striking distance," we said. It was one of the loveliest places we had stayed, with incredible mosses and huge mother trees. "That's got to be the biggest—no, that one over there. Look at the size of this one."

The next morning we dismantled our tarp house, packed

up, and headed for Vancouver. We got into town about eleven.

Vancouver, July 1970. All we had was the address of Sally, a girl I had known slightly and Virge had been fairly close with at Swarthmore: 77 West Seventh Street.

It was a nice little two-story house in a light-industry neighborhood. The front door was open so we called hello. Rosanne, whom we didn't know, was working out in a garden in the back yard with her little girl, Holly. Sally had gone up north with her boy friend but we were welcomed in. A little later Rosanne's husband, Bert, showed up. Of course we could stay there. Lots of people had been staying there off and on. Rosanne and Bert were ex-Americans from Portland.

The laws about homesteading and leasing crown land weren't heartening. There wasn't very much available and you had to be a citizen, which took a minimum of five years. The worst news was that most of B.C. was mountainous, with gravelly soil, not suitable for farming, and that lumber companies owned just about all of it. There was virtually nothing available on Vancouver Island. There were a few encouraging stories about people who had found nice places, but mostly it was depressing tales of squatting and being thrown out by logging companies.

We talked a lot with people who had been looking for the same sort of thing we wanted and we checked the want ads faithfully. Prices and the sort of thing that was available didn't seem to be radically different from the way they had been in New England. If anything, the prices were higher. Large tracts of completely undeveloped, nondescript wooded land that might be farmable when cleared, and then again might not, ran about $500 an acre. We looked for old farms around the city that maybe we could rent until we got more money together, but here again the pickings were slim. We even snuck an occasional look at the apartments available and the help-wanted section. Apartments were pretty expensive and the job situation was dismal.

After a couple of weeks Virginia started getting discouraged and talking about running out of money, etc. I tried to be bright and cheerful. The thought of what the hell we were going to do if we couldn't find some land was just too painful to consider, so I didn't. We had moved out of Rosanne and Bert's living room into a leaky cardboard shack behind their house. You could barely stand up in it. It was pretty dismal. We weren't making love much. That was another thing I just put out of my mind.

Day followed day. Getting to know Vancouver, reading the newspapers, smoking a fair amount of dope, doing odds and ends and occasionally driving around the country saying "Ooh, ah, isn't that nice land."

During one of our drives out around the city I noticed a sign saying "Ferries to Sunshine Coast." What could be nicer? The Sunshine Coast became the new focus for my hopes. I bought some beautifully detailed maps of the area and fell in love again.

The Sunshine Coast isn't really very sunny but I didn't know that then. It has slightly less rainfall than Vancouver, which is where it gets off calling itself the Sunshine Coast while having a typically wet Pacific Northwest climate. But I wasn't in a very cynical or analytic frame of mind. Sunshine Coast was paradise. It had to be.

Swifty and Bo, old Swarthmore friends, came north in a monster Pontiac Bonneville. They brought up some good California wine and some ancient Spanish brandy. I went out and got a beautiful leg of lamb. We had homemade garlic bread, French-cut beans, a huge salad, avocados with lemon and salt, and on and on. A feast. It was old times. We had done this sort of thing at college. Half the kick was starving for weeks on end to be able to afford it.

The next day we packed up the tarps, the ice chest, all the camping shit, and got on the car ferry for the Sunshine Coast, Swifty, Bo, Virginia, Zeke, and me. I was in high spirits, happy to be back on the road, back to camping out, building tarp houses. Away from worrying about Zeke being run

over. Out of the city, out of stagnation. On the move and
with old friends. The only thing I didn't like was that pig of a
car, which didn't corner for shit on those mountain roads, but
it was somehow appropriate to Swifty and even that made me
smile.

The end of the road was where we were headed. Highway
101 starts somewhere down in Panama, comes up through
Mexico and California, up to Vancouver, and then about a
hundred miles north of Vancouver it stops. If you want to go
any farther up the coast you have to go by boat. If I was going
to find what I was looking for, the end of 101 seemed like
where it would be.

There were two long ferry rides to get up to Powell River,
eighty miles above Vancouver. The scenery was spectacularly
beautiful. The Coast Range dropped right off into the water.
This was virgin frontier, unspoiled except for ugly scars left
by loggers here and there. Man was here but not many of 'em
and he was certainly not master. Back East you could drive
just about anywhere you wanted to go. Here there were vast
areas that you couldn't get to except by boat or float plane or
on foot. The idea that man could ever tame these savage,
proud mountains seemed remote. For the earth to reclaim
itself here wouldn't take much effort. A little shrug would do
the trick.

I wish I could say we got the land by some soulful means,
but the truth is we got it through a real estate agent. Now
Virgil McKenzie is not your standard-issue real estate agent
but we had no idea about that. His was simply the first sign
we happened to see.

It might seem to some that a real estate office would be a
logical place to start looking for land, but I had been looking
for a year and had never talked to anyone in the business. It
was somehow against the rules. I suppose what we wanted to
happen was we'd be walking through the woods and come
upon some old codger who would take an instant liking to the

wonderful young people and sell us his land cheap. We did a lot of tromping through a lot of land without much luck.

After we had been at the camp ground for a few days, operating on all the soulful levels, it started to rain heavily, making a mockery of my tarp houses. As much to get out of the rain as anything else, with deep misgivings Virginia and I went into the first real estate office we saw. It was Virgil McKenzie's. Without much hope I described what sort of thing we were looking for, how much money we had to spend, etc., fully expecting him to come back with "Yeah, you and everybody else and their brother."

We wanted a fairly large piece of land, something over fifty acres if possible, not too easily accessible, suitable for farming. With what I had and what Virginia had, and with the help of some of the other people who were interested in this sort of thing, we could get maybe $20,000 together.

It turned out he had something he thought might interest us. As he described it I felt my eyes get larger and larger. "There's this piece of land . . . eighty acres . . . used to be a self-sufficient farm thirty years back . . . hasn't been worked since then. Old boys used to bring in huge loads of vegetables and fruit . . . no neighbors. To get there you have to go about ten miles by boat and then back a mile or so on an old logging road. A year-round stream running through the property. Old fruit trees are still bearing." And the asking price—$12,000. I caught myself just before the drool came over my lip. Would we be interested in having a look? It sounded too good to be true. We made a date to go up in his boat and have a look at it as soon as the weather cleared.

Why had it taken us so long to go into a real estate office? Having done it once it seemed easy to do it again, and so to be good shoppers we went into a few other real estate places to see what they might have. There was nothing remotely comparable to McKenzie's deal. Completely undeveloped stuff that was accessible by dirt road, had been logged over, would have to be cleared, maybe had water, maybe could be farmed, was all about $500 an acre. Whenever I asked about anything cheaper they all shook their heads knowingly and talked about maybe some stuff way farther north by boat.

The next day there was a break in the weather. McKenzie and his son came to our camp site. McKenzie was the perfect boy scout leader. He hadn't been at our camp more than three minutes before he started giving us advice on our fire, where to find dry wood, and what kinds of stuff were best for kindling. From most people it would have been offensive but somehow from him it was all right. He was an ex-logger who felt funny about making his living as a real estate agent. We found that out as soon as he had exhausted his kindling talk.

We put the boat in the water and zipped up the lake, with Mr. McKenzie's folksy lore barely audible above the roar of his outboard.

We got to the farm after tromping a mile and a half on a soggy, misty, overgrown trail. The place was more beautiful than our wildest dreams. Lush blackberries ripening, apple trees with green fruit. Several acres of field still clear. A stream ran right by the old house. Mountains on all sides. If there was any hesitation in my mind I missed it.

"Of course there's no value in the building," McKenzie said professionally.

"Watch how you talk about my house."

We walked around for a couple of hours uncovering more and more marvelous things. There were little trout in the stream, old harnesses and hardware in a collapsed shed, a wine cellar with old casks, lots of garter snakes and friendly toads. Zeke loved it.

I guess deep down inside I had never really believed it was going to happen; that we would really find something, let alone something so perfect, so beautiful, so cheap. I breathed huge sighs of relief. Home at last.

Virginia said something about shopping around some more. I laughed. I honestly thought she was kidding. She smiled and had to admit it was a hell of a beautiful place.

Swifty said something about its being pretty tough to go out for a hamburger or a movie. I laughed at that too.

Bo said that all the folks back in California would be glad to hear that they had a friendly place to visit up in B.C. I smiled and nodded.

I didn't say much on the trip back to town. I just sat looking at the water rush by, feeling happier than I had felt in years and thinking that for the first time in years that happiness was called for.

The next morning I went to McKenzie's office to put down a hundred dollars, which he said would be enough to hold the place while we got the rest of the money together.

Twelve thousand dollars. I had seven, Virge had three. We would need a fair amount of money for equipment and food. Simon was on the way up and he was reported to have a bundle that made ours look pretty silly. He had sounded enthusiastic over the phone but he might chicken out. I wasn't very worried. The place was so gorgeous someone would want to come in on it with us.

Grace. Here I was in British Columbia, with Zeke and Virginia and our meager worldlies in faithful Car Car, having just found our glorious land to build an alternative on. I had just said yes to lots of suggestions. I was taking cues. From God? World literature? Some weird consensus? I wasn't sure. I was just staying open and saying yes as often as I could and this was where it had brought me. I felt that I was tuning in to something, something that loved me and would take care of me.

A lot of the principles I was operating on were lifted from my father's stuff. It came from other places too. It wasn't that I was trying to live my life by things my father had said in opposition to other things. It was just that his voice was a familiar one and seemed to be part of the larger voice that was worth tuning in to.

Somewhere along the line I had become a grace addict. When everything happens just right and it seems that someone or something is trying to tell you something, nothing is coincidence. You reach into your pocket and pull out the exact change, no more no less, and it's terribly important.

It's important that it appear nonsensical. A radio playing next to a TV with the sound turned off. There shouldn't be a connection but there is, and further there's a point or message to it, and further it's important and if you were operating on your priggish notions of logic you would have missed it. And you wonder what other goodies your priggish notions of what is and isn't connected have robbed you of.

Gifts from God? Who else would operate that way?

Exactly when this sort of thing first started happening to me is difficult to say. By the time I got to college it was the biggest thing in my life, and it became bigger.

It felt so good.

After my first few tastes I was pretty much hooked. I'd have dry spells, months without any or only piddling amounts of grace, but I never forgot about it or stopped wanting it. The grace experiences seemed to be cumulative. They didn't lift me up and then drop me down leaving me lower than they found me. They added to each other. The dry spells were just plateaus on an ever higher climb, but that didn't stop me from looking forward to the next jump while I was digesting my last one.

There was usually a sensual rush of warmth and well-being. Sometimes that was all there was to it. Just feeling good.

I was doing things just right. I felt graceful and beautiful. Life was graceful and beautiful. We were moving very well together.

The message part of grace was something I was never quite at home with. I was perfectly comfortable when it seemed like just a simple greeting. "Hi, Mark." "Hi, God." And that would be that. It wasn't a one-sided affair. I could start it. "Hi, God." And usually he'd come back, "Hi, Mark." Not always, but there were probably plenty of times He said "Hi" and I missed it.

It was when there seemed to be more to it that it bothered me. "Look, God, I don't ask you for motorcycles, don't ask me to go slaying infidels." I was never sure of what was being asked or what lesson I was supposed to be learning. I doubt that God really wanted me to slay infidels but He might have, the same way He probably still has somewhere in the back of His mind the possibility that I'm angling for a motorcycle.

I was never at the point of saying for sure that this or that was definitely the work of God. I just wanted to keep the possibility open. If there was such a thing as grace, I didn't want to cut myself off from it.

Somewhere back in my childhood someone told me about drowning sailors being kept afloat and eventually deposited on land by porpoises. More recently some marine biologists decided to check these accounts. What they found out is that porpoises simply like to play. The research concluded that porpoises probably take as many drowning sailors away from land as toward it. "I had no more strength left but I was floating toward a beach about twenty yards away. I figured I could just about make it when this fucking porpoise came along and . . ." There are some phenomena which you normally hear only one side of. Maybe when I found out the truth of porpoises and drowning sailors I should have started having second thoughts about grace, but by that time I was thoroughly hooked.

Hippiedom. I wanted to be a good hippie. For me and lots of other people a good hippie was something very worth being, if not the only thing worth being.

In a way I'm glad no one seems much interested in being a good hippie any more. It wasn't an easy thing to be. I hope the fact that no one wants to be a good hippie any more means the whole thing worked, that the world is slightly less the desperate, mindless, cruel nightmare of unawareness that gave birth to hippiedom.

Maybe everyone's part hippie now so that really good full-time hippies like what I tried to be aren't needed any more. It's what the good hippies wanted all along anyway. Maybe we could get doctors and lawyers to do the same.

A good hippie had no last name. It wasn't entirely my fault I wasn't a better hippie. "This is Simon, and Kathy, and Jack, and Virginia, and Mark Vonnegut." Some of the best hippies I ever knew introduced me that way. If they hadn't I probably would have found some way to work it in.

I had other shortcomings as a hippie. I didn't have too much trouble getting over the idea of private property, but the big problem was that although I did all the things good hippies do, I always did them with a twist and was too conscious and/or proud of that twist to be the hippie I would have liked to be.

While we were looking for land around Powell River we met Steve and Sandy. Two minutes after we said hello I loved them.

It seemed so right. I was getting off on the rightness of how I felt as much as on them. Why can't people feel like this toward each other more often? Two minutes ago we were strangers, now we're all warm and happy.

Steve and Sandy had just taken off from all the things we had taken off from. Just about our age. Looking for all the things we were looking for. They had a Chevy van instead of our Volks and a Malamute husky instead of Zeke. Steve played guitar instead of sax.

They were physically attractive more or less in the same way we were. Not dazzling, but no major improvements needed or wished for. They walked a lot like us, with the same loosenesses and tightnesses. Steve was athletic the way I was athletic, not a superjock but a respectable addition to any pickup game—football, softball, soccer—with no real preference. We probably would have split sets in tennis.

They seemed to have a pretty good man-woman thing. People who believed all the stuff we believed and were trying to make the man-woman thing work too were a pretty rare commodity. "See, Virge, we're not the only weirdos."

Sure, loving Steve and Sandy was narcissistic. A lot of positive feedback about what we were doing and thinking. Why not? Today Steve and Sandy, tomorrow Trooper Suchadolski.

I knew that everyone was my brother and even felt it from time to time. Even with Steve and Sandy it wouldn't have happened a couple of years ago. How could I ever get to Trooper Suchadolski without a few warmups with guys like Steve and Sandy?

A lot of the people into "alternative culture" had a hang-over of bitterness about the things they had fled. They had been snubbed one way or another. They couldn't play foot-ball, the cheerleaders wouldn't go out with them, they couldn't get decent jobs. They were looked on as ugly or failures. Mostly unfairly, mostly for petty reasons. The Amer-ica they were fleeing didn't seem to think they were worth much. So they were doing a very sensible thing, building a culture where their very real virtues and attributes had a chance, where they wouldn't be just so much shit.

The bitterness left its mark. There was the nagging doubt: If the America they were fleeing had opened up her arms to them a little more, would they be out in the woods believing in all the things they believed in?

It went both ways. Those whom America had been nice to, who hadn't been very shat upon, felt guilty about it. "What's wrong with me that such a twisted no-goodnik thing liked me?"

Steve and Sandy were golden. They could have made it. Physically attractive, top of their class. America would have gone out of her way to make them feel welcome. But here they were out in the boonies of B.C. in a battered Chevy looking for land to build an alternative of some sort.

They were golden no more. Cops dying for a chance to bust them, customs officials hassling them, America praying that they would come to a bad end: "The blacks, the mis-shapen, the dummies, the graceless, I can understand. But you I loved. You were my hope. I would have given you any-thing. Told you my secrets, shared my wealth. But now you couldn't drink my spit if you were thirsty."

Golden no more. What did it? Dope? The war? The long hair? Steve and Sandy had a few horror stories to tell around the fire but they were all recent. Timing is important. If it had been much earlier they would have had scars; much later and it wouldn't have happened at all.

Steve and Sandy were scouting the Powell River area for a home for their Buffalo tribe. That was part of why they were there. They were also there to get away from the tribe for a few days and think about things. Steve asked very gently about the possibility of the tribe's coming to our place. We said we felt a little weird about saying yes to a whole tribe. It would most likely swallow us. If he and Sandy wanted to join us that would be great. But a whole tribe? If we had a tribe of comparable size maybe we could work something out. Good hippies though we were, it seemed a bit heavy. A whole tribe?

Steve had reservations about the tribe himself, so he didn't push it much. He said he and Sandy were about to split off anyway. Just thought he should ask. They invited us to come spend a few days with the tribe while we were waiting for Simon. Swifty and Bo headed back to California.

The tribe was impressive. Twenty-some-odd people, five dogs, three recently acquired goats, three Chevy vans, two VW bugs, three huge tepees, $3600 cash (going fast), and miscellaneous in search of a home. For now a liberal Simon Fraser professor was letting them use some land he was holding as an investment right near the main road. So here was this bucolic frontier scene playing in stereo with a six-lane highway.

The Buffalo tribe had been born that spring at a party where they all took MDA and predictably fell in love with each other. They liked loving each other so much that they all vowed to not let it stop when the drug wore off. So they formed a tribe, dropped out of school, pooled their belongings, and headed for British Columbia. It's got to be the longest MDA trip on record.

After a few very pleasant days looking at what might be a preview of what lay ahead for us, Simon was due so we split. The day after Virge and I left, four of the tribe got busted with a pound of dope. That pretty much killed it. The Buffalo tribe scattered to the winds. Another courageous hippie venture bites the dust.

McKenzie called to tell us that the owner had accepted our "offer to purchase," which was what the hundred bucks and those papers I had signed were all about. All we had to do was come up with $11,900 in the next forty days.

Simon took longer than expected to show. He doesn't move terribly quickly. I didn't know that then. Steady like rock but not terribly quick. I didn't really know anything about Simon then.

Simon. Swarthmore Class of '69, just like me. I have a feeling he majored in either English or sociology. It doesn't really matter. Except for engineering, there was really only one major at Swarthmore, which was Swarthmore. Even some of the engineers were really Swarthmore majors. All the Swarthmore people in this book were Swarthmore majors.

Swarthmore's small. Everyone is supposed to know everyone. I knew who Simon was. I knew his name and we had some friends in common. But if anyone had asked me about Simon before the Powell River venture I couldn't have said much.

I think our first conversation of any length was at Swarthmore, just before Virginia and I headed West. Simon was heading West too. He was fed up with teaching junior high school in Philly and said he was interested in the land thing. I talked a bit about why I thought B.C. was a good place to look. He said it sounded good, maybe he'd head up that way after California. He said he might be interested in buying in if I found anything. I told him I'd keep it in mind. I didn't take him any more or any less seriously than any of the hundred or so other people with whom I had had virtually the same conversation.

Two and a half months after that conversation, I had found land, spectacularly beautiful land, land tailormade for our needs. I had tried to get hold of some of the other people who had expressed interest, but Simon's phone number in

California was the first that worked. He was enthusiastic, and if I didn't have any overwhelming positive feelings about him I didn't have any negative ones either.

I'm subject to occasional theological nightmares.

The one that leaves me in a cold sweat every time is, I arrive at the pearly gates and the first thing I'm asked is where I went to college.

Swarthmore people tend to form enclaves. They are often unable to live with, talk to, or sleep with someone who isn't a Swarthmore person.

All non-Swarthmore people in B.C. seemed to assume that all the Swarthmore people there had been very close buddies at Swarthmore. It wasn't true. It was especially untrue in my case.

I wasn't thinking about my dread of spending my life in a Swarthmore enclave then. I wasn't thinking about much except how happy I was that I had found land. Simon was a Swarthmore person but one more Swarthmore person does not necessarily a Swarthmore enclave make.

Simon finally arrived with Ted, another Swarthmorian. Simon seemed very eager, so we all headed up to Powell River immediately.

I was feeling a little jerky and clumsy about things. What was agreed to between Simon and me? Was he committed to buying in or just shopping? Was I committed to letting him buy in if he wanted to? Shouldn't we sit down and talk a few things over? What did he want the farm to be? How did we know we were compatible? There were substantial sums of money involved, not to mention all the spiritual and emotional stuff.

Maybe it was just another situation in which I was being klutzy and dense. What bad could happen? But how did he know I wasn't into some super-weird trip, that I wasn't some sort of Charlie Manson? I couldn't imagine any evil lurking in that Brillo-wreathed head with his usually smiling cherub face peeking through. It was a completely honest, unforced smile but I think it gave a lot of people the wrong idea. Simon could be mad as hell, but unless you noticed that he was trying very hard not to smile, it was hard to tell.

Is this how it's done? Somehow I thought it would be different! There we were making the heaviest decisions of our lives, and from the way we acted we might as well have been co-chairmen of the decoration committee for the junior prom.

Problem number one: How do we get up there? We hung around the Powell Lake Marina half hoping someone would offer to take us up. But we were going to have a boat eventually anyway, so why not now? We went boat shopping.

There was a notice on the laundromat bulletin board: "Two plywood boats—ready for fiberglassing—for sale." Marcel was the guy who had built them, a nice guy about forty-five or so with sad eyes. He hadn't found what he was looking for in Powell River. He was selling these boats he had made and heading back to New Brunswick.

The bigger one, about thirteen feet, was just right. Marcel said he'd help us with the fiberglassing and take the boat down to the lake for us. The next day was sunny and dry, a good day for fiberglassing. He had some blue fiberglass coloring around, so we added that to the resin and fiberglassed the boat blue. There wasn't a lot of blue coloring so the boat came out sort of an eerie blue, almost transparent in some places and opaque in others. We put her in Marcel's truck and followed it to the lake.

Hippies love to name things. Everyone likes to name boats. Watching our boat in the truck in front of us, we tried to come up with a name. "Blue Marcel" was perfect. The old gold-painted outboard motor that was thrown into the deal became "Moldy Goldy."

Moldy Goldy, who had shown some reluctance to be an engine back at Marcel's place, lost all ambition in that direction once she was placed in the lake on the back of Blue Marcel.

So now we had a boat but still no way to get up to the farm. Everyone tried to coax Moldy into pushing the boat. New spark plug. New gaskets for the carburetor. But all to no avail.

While we were trying to get Moldy interested in her old line of work we asked around about other outboards. Dick was a pilot for the charter pontoon plane outfit that flew out of the marina, mostly taking loggers to camp and back. He had an old racing Merc 25. No neutral, no reverse, just point it and go; racing prop and the whole bit. Sold. It was the perfect addition to our shoestring transportation corps. The racing Merc became simply "Dick." That was perfect too. I was naming up a storm.

Dick was an interesting engine. The throttle was open. We were running along fine at what we thought was top speed. But Dick, after sitting around for a while, was just warming up. We started going faster and faster. About halfway up the lake we had to run at half-throttle for fear Dick would tear the boat apart going too fast. Dick was fast. Dick wasn't all that dependable but that comes later.

It was getting dark as we docked. After considerable crashing around in the brush we managed to find the trail. The trail wasn't very well cleared, but one way or another we managed to make it up to the farm. Just enough fading light for a quick look around the place, then a full moon and aurora borealis. It seemed like a good omen even though the two phenomena were in competition. Two kinds of light. Simon seemed dumbfounded by the farm's beauty.

We spent several days up there, exploring and setting up a rudimentary kitchen. A beachhead.

Back down to Vancouver to figure out how one turned stocks into cash, get a chain saw, other tools and supplies, and the rest of our stuff.

Ted went back to California on his way back to New York and law school and all that. Virginia, Simon, Zeke, and I headed back up to Powell River with the two loaded cars.

Simon toyed around some with the idea of getting Ted to

stay. How could he go back there to all that shit? I remember
being slightly jealous and/or admiring. How could anyone
take New York or law school, let alone the two of them together? Why wasn't Ted incredibly depressed by the prospect? I mean, what hope was there in that? What joy? What
adventure?

One thing I noticed about Simon was that he was a very
different sort of man from me. Not better or worse but different. He was the sort of guy the football team used to make
fun of or just ignore. His fogginess, his athletic ineptitude,
was something I liked. I saw so much of my own athletic
carriage, my coordination and quickness, as a fraud. It was an
image I had sought and aspired to in a very conscious way for
very superficial reasons.

Being shrewd and quick seemed like bad things, part of the
typical American syndrome that had landed the world in such
shitty shape. I hoped that being around such a noncompeti-
tive man as Simon might help me drop some of that shit in
myself. He was well over six feet and quite strong. He just
didn't seem it.

When we drove in next to our old site at the Powell River
camp ground, the people next to us were pulling up stakes
and throwing everything into the trunk of their huge, beat-to-
shit De Soto sedan. It was dark and we could barely see each
other but somehow a conversation got started. Joe, Mary, and
their child Sarah had been traveling all over B.C. for about a
year looking for land. Money was running out and Joe had
just taken a job in the local pulp and paper mill. They were
giving up the dream for a while and moving into a little
rented house in town. Somehow it was decided very quickly
that we were friends. They told us we were welcome to stay
with them any time on our town trips, which we were to do
many times, and we told them that they were welcome up the
lake.

There was some more work to be done on the boat. The

way the bottom flexed with good old Dick pushing her along was pretty wild. I put another rib in Blue Marcel and gave it another coat of resin. While I was at it, I put another seat in, for comfort and a little more strength. Then there was always our eternal project, trying to get Moldy interested in being an outboard engine. It seemed like a good way to learn something about engines, which was one of our weak points.

While I was working on the engine and Virginia and Simon were off getting groceries, Vincent showed up. No one had any idea that he was coming or even knew where we were.

I was glad to see him. He was supposed to know something about engines, but I was so happy about the way things were turning out that I would have joyously welcomed anyone. The more the merrier.

I should know Vincent a lot better than I do. We were classmates for four years at Swarthmore, shared a house with four other guys senior year, lived together with assorted people in two separate places in Boston, and then again in B.C. He's average height, blond, blue-eyed, very pretty to look at, and might have been a decent athlete if he had realized he had a body. All I can really call to mind when I think of Vincent is someone walking around in a fog, bumping into things a lot and saying "I'm sorry." I didn't dislike Vincent, but I couldn't help wondering from time to time why he kept turning up. It was almost like he was following me around.

Fifty pounds of dried milk, thirty pounds of honey, fifty pounds of brown rice, twenty-five pounds of corn meal, pots and pans, the chain saw, some gasoline and an instruction booklet, lots of different kinds of flour, assorted vegetables, fishing stuff, axes, hatchets, machetes, a crowbar, hand saws, hammers. Millions of kitchen matches, sleeping bags, assorted clothes, buckets, plastic dishpans, a dish rack, twenty pounds of detergent, knives, forks, spoons, mugs, plates, bowls, a four-man tent, two tarps, fifty pounds of common nails, a book on carpentry, a few on gardening. *Stalking the Wild Asparagus, The Whole Earth Catalogue,* lots of novels and other books, some first-aid supplies and a book on that, a typewriter, my tenor saxophone, a beatup guitar, towels, mosquito netting, a wrist-rocket slingshot, twenty-five pounds of soybeans, fifteen pounds of lentils, two pounds of butter, four pounds of margarine and four of lard, ten pounds of assorted cheese, four gallons of soy oil, four of corn oil, four of peanut oil, everything Adelle Davis ever wrote, fifty pounds of dog food, several kerosene lanterns, five gallons of kerosene, thirty pounds of peanut butter, and miscellaneous. The boats were overloaded, with maybe half a foot of freeboard.

The boats. We had Blue Marcel and John Eastman's boat. John was a local we had met at the marina who was to be one of our protecting angels. Moldy had consented to run a little that day, so she pushed John's boat up the lake in her own leisurely way while Dick spun circles around her all the way up.

Had we forgotten anything? Well, if we had we could pick it up the next time we were in town. Who knew what the hell we'd need up there anyway? We had taken the big step. The others would become clear as we went along, just like all the other steps in this long, strange journey.

One step at a time, one foot in front of the other, has worked just fine so far. No percentage in changing our mode of operation now. It seems an awful lot like someone or something is doing a first-rate job of taking care of us. This whole project is a little nutsy—I mean, if you had told me a few years back. But look at the breaks we've gotten. Something or someone must have something in mind for us. Why fuck it up with overplanning? I think maybe whatever or whoever doesn't care much for planners, or maybe it's just that it finds them hard to cheer up. Whatever-whoever seems to need a little slack to work with. Well, we'll make damn sure it has plenty of that.

In late August '70 the farm became our home.

Our New Home and Family. Jack and Kathy signed on shortly after we got there. They were often referred to as the little people. Kathy was five feet tall at most and Jack hit maybe five-three. They had both lived in the same house I did my last two years at Swarthmore, but I still can't say I knew them very well. They were good friends of Simon's. Both were borderline blondes with blue eyes, but Jack with his scraggly beard was considerably more scruffy looking.

Kathy had a Wisconsin-farm-girl wholesomeness that years of heroin addiction wouldn't have put much of a dent in. She had cheerleader good looks and a soft Rubensesque femininity that contrasted sharply with Virginia's tallness and spare lines. If you were to pick out someone at the farm to call normal, it would be Kathy.

Jack was generally quiet, but it was a strong rather than a shy quietness. He was into Zen and mountain climbing but in a very nonflaky way. If there was anyone at the farm with feet firmly on the ground, it was Jack. He had a much more tangible reason for being there than the rest of us, too. He was our official draft dodger. Kathy and he had been together since their freshman year.

Sarah and Beowulf were the next additions to our motley crew. More blue-eyed blondes. Sarah was a close friend of Virginia's. She was beyond a doubt the driftiest person there, but drifty in a very lovable, loving way. She was very bright but just wasn't paying much attention. Whenever I said anything to her I always had the impression that I had just woken her up.

Beowulf was an unknown quantity Sarah had found in Oregon. He had a ramrod-stiff spine, a darting weasel face with eyes that never seemed to blink, and a wispy, almost-not-there beard. He made his own clothes and wasn't much of a seamstress. That and his stiff, machinelike way of moving gave him the look of a hastily thrown together puppet.

On our first town trip, we stayed with Joe and Mary and met Luke, whom they had found a few months earlier in the Kootenays, a mountain range about halfway between the Rockies and the coast. He came back up the lake with us and fit in like a charm. Physically and spiritually he was much more like me than any of the others, and I came to feel almost as close to him as to Zeke.

Vincent passed through for two or three weeks every couple of months or so, and other friends and strangers would drop in and stay awhile, but the above plus Simon, Virginia, and me made up the basic cast.

Shelter was the first order of business. There were two standing structures—a roof on eight-foot stilts with half-walls on three sides and open on the fourth that had sheltered a tractor in the old days, and the towering house that McKenzie had said had no value. We set up a kitchen in the smaller structure and set about redoing the house.

McKenzie was right about the house and we would have done much better to tear it down and use the materials to build new ones. It was strangely built; set on a foundation of dug-in logs with hand-split eight-by-eight uprights every two feet, it rose about thirty feet into the air, covered over with hand-split boards of every imaginable dimension, which were covered in turn by hand-split shingles called shakes. It was twenty feet wide and forty long, and consisted of two stories, each divided into two twenty-by-twenty rooms with thirteen-foot ceilings, and an attic topped by a leaky roof. The strangest thing about that building was that there wasn't a triangular brace anywhere. It swayed slightly in the wind.

What we proceeded to do didn't help matters much. We tore off the roof and added another story, topped with the most insane roof you could imagine. The first third of the house was covered by a slant roof that started at four feet and rose to twelve, facing east. The next third had the same setup facing west. The back of the house had twin peaked gables facing south. The damned thing looked like a pterodactyl learning to fly. The top floor, partitioned off with blankets into five little bedrooms, was sprinkled with a strange assortment of windows which we always kept an eye out for on the way home from town trips.

We rebuilt the front porch, which had collapsed, and

added a new one under the third-story gables. The work went slowly, partly because of our inexperience but more because we had to cut down trees and handsplit any lumber we needed. Three people working all day could split enough boards to cover what six dollars' worth of plywood would have done tighter and stronger. The wood we split was a bitch to work with. Right angles, straight edges, and so on don't just happen; each piece had to be whittled and fiddled with incessantly and still never fit quite right. Along with the major construction, there was cleaning windfalls from the trail, cutting and stacking firewood, and several other projects.

An average day: up with the sun; fetch water from the stream; cook breakfast, usually ground whole-grain porridge with honey and dried milk; work five or six hours; lunch, usually peanut butter, dried fruit, and honey; work another six hours; then all run down to the lake, tear our clothes off and splash around awhile; back up to dinner, which was usually brown rice and some vegetable we had brought from town. After dinner we read, wrote letters, made music, or just talked. Kitchen chores were shared by all, though I remember telling Virge, after a snotty comment about the quality of my cleanup job, that I'd get better as soon as she showed a little interest in the chain saw. The traditional male-female division of labor would have made a lot of sense out there, but we stuck as closely as possible to these newfangled urban notions of equality.

The cooking got a bit fancier when we brought in a big old wood stove (a full day's operation) and set up an inside kitchen. Then, if someone was willing to grind flour for an hour or so, we could bake bread and make pies with the apples and blackberries we had coming out of our ears. Occasionally someone would catch a trout or two or shoot a grouse with a gun John Eastman gave us, but mostly it was very simple vegetarian fare.

Nootka and Tanga, sisters from a Border collie-Samoyed cross, joined us in early September. Nootka was theoretically

Virginia's dog and Tanga Vincent's, but both turned out to be
generalized commune dogs. Samoyeds and Border collies
don't cross very well. Nootka turned out a lot better than
Tanga and had a certain impish charm, but neither was much
use around the farm and both were always underfoot, tearing
things up and general-nuisancing. Tanga was an outright foul
and obnoxious creature who should have been shot. Zeke's
nobility shone forth brighter than ever next to these canine
misfits.

It was a great life. I didn't mind the physical discomforts—
smoke in the eyes around the cooking fire, rain, cold, lots of
hard work, the outhouse, general dirtiness, being so far from
civilization, the mosquitoes, the impossibility of keeping anything clean or dry. I loved it all. The only thing that upset me
was having other people upset by this or that hardship. I
wanted everyone to love it as much as I did.

I was in great health, better than I had been in for a long
time, and in a good mood most of the time. I even cut down
my smoking some.

I think I was thinking less than I had in years. Maybe it was
just that thinking wasn't the only thing I was doing. I liked
thinking less.

Think think think. What a funny word. A funny sound, a
funny meaning. Almost as funny as funny. I think I've probably spent more time and energy thinking than most people,
but that's a very hard thing to be able to say for sure. I don't
even know very well what thinking is, let alone have a way to
tell who's doing it and how much.

Thinking something worth thinking. What would that look
like? That's the sort of thing I spent a lot of time thinking
about. If you want to get something, thinking might help you
get it. But I really didn't do very much of that sort of thinking
unless you want to stretch definitions. There wasn't very
much by way of things I wanted. I'd been spoiled rotten as far
as that went. I didn't even think that kind of thinking was
thinking. The kind of thinking I did was mostly a luxury item
and it wasn't much fun.

Some of my happiness, no doubt, was simple good old vanity. I had done what I had said I was going to do, and the pot was sweetened by having what we were doing be such a glamorous, romantic, noble venture. Through most of the early days I walked around with a giddy giggly cockiness bubbling inside, as if we were pulling off a particularly elegant jewel heist.

For years I had looked at wherever I happened to be and realized "I can't stay here." It wasn't a panicky "got to get out of here" feeling as much as just sadly realizing that for one reason or another it could never be home. There were lots of good reasons to be upset by the cities—noise, lights, bustle, misery—but my reaction had gone far beyond intellectual distaste and had been literally shaking me apart. My serious doubts about how much longer I could have held out added a great deal to my joy at having found a place I could stay, a home.

I remember Victor, an early visitor, saying "I think I have more mosquito bites than not mosquito bites." But the hardships were part of what we had all come there for, and there wasn't much bitching about them. Besides, we found that there really wasn't much that couldn't be done, it was just a lot harder to do. We were getting rid of the insulation, partly out of curiosity about what life would be like without all the insulation we were used to, partly out of guilt at what that insulation had cost, partly in the expectation that the insulation was about to be wiped out anyway by one or another of the disasters we saw in the apocalyptic smorgasbord of the future. We thought it was good for us.

What gave me more pleasure at the farm than anything else was playing my saxophone. After putting in a good day's work clearing brush or chopping wood, I'd get out my old tenor horn, climb up on the roof, and play my heart out. Sometimes I'd be all tense and jittery and my hands or mouth would fuck up, but more often things fit together like magic and I'd sit up on our funky roof on our funky house, looking out on the mountains, feeling completely at peace and in harmony with the world and like I could play forever.

One of the things that made it all so wonderful was the acoustical properties of the valley. It held the sound just enough to give each note a lingering resonance without giving it any echo. That valley was made for music, especially the tenor sax, especially my tenor sax. Wherever I had played music before, I always had to contend with other sounds—cars going by, the hum of an electrical appliance. The only other sounds at the farm were an occasional wind and the melodic babbling of the stream running over the rocks. Although I may have gotten higher and more excited jamming with first-rate musicians, I've never felt so completely and deeply satisfied as when I was playing duets with the stream.

The way I played music there was the way I wanted to farm, chop wood, cook, make love, raise children. Everything. A lot of it had to do with things I felt while I played. If only I could feel that sense of total absorption in what I was doing when I was doing other things. It was more than absorption, it was spontaneity, competence, a sense of grace and playfulness, of being in touch with an inexhaustible source of energy and beauty. It was a lot like playing with Zeke.

I was finally just plain playing music, playing music just for the moment. I wasn't practicing so that I could knock 'em dead at some later time. The music was finally an end in itself. Making the perfect music for the perfect moment for the perfect place.

Music there was all music could be. It did all music could do. There was nothing second-rate about that music. And maybe most important, it was ours. We weren't crammed into some stadium or concert hall. We weren't dependent on any electronic gadgetry. Our music fit in perfectly with everything else there. We had brought up a battery tape deck, a really good one, but there was something jarring or alienating about it. We only played it once or twice. It didn't seem to fit in.

Serendipity. One time only. Fantastic beauty now, and

then gone forever. There was something delightfully subversive about playing music that good that far, far away from New York City's recording studios and the like. Who would have thought that here, twelve miles by boat from the end of Highway 101, twelve miles by boat from our nearest neighbor and then a mile and a half by foot on that old abandoned logging trail, was where it was happening?

Simon had his trombone shipped from back East, Jack bought a flute, and Kathy unpacked her violin, which she played very well. Now and then we got some nice music going all together, but the sax and the trombone tended to drown the others out. The solo numbers seemed to work best.

We had been weaned on horror stories of frictions between communes and local people. We figured things would be different in Canada and weren't expecting real, heavy trouble, but neither did we expect the degree of warmth and help we got. There were some funny looks from folks who weren't exactly in love with longhaired people, but it was so mild compared to what we had learned to live with in America that it was almost pleasant when it happened. What hippie hating there was up there was strictly amateur.

Mr. McKenzie dropped in several times to check on how we were doing. He'd shake his head in mock disbelief and pain at the condition of the teeth on our chain saw and then sit down and while away the afternoon sharpening them right. A Mr. Palermo, who had lived up here helping his uncles in the old days and had a cabin at the foot of the trail, came by at least twice a month. He told us how they used the old irrigation system and what grew well where, and gave us all sorts of other invaluable information. There was a big-shot executive at the pulp mill who used to bring us huge plastic bags of seaweed, which we were particularly fond of for compost. Bea and Sam, who ran the marina at the foot of the lake, were constantly putting themselves out for us.

Several times when we went down to the lake to swim or

fish we found big boxes of dishes, tools, winches, rope, saws, all sorts of useful things. "Here's some stuff I don't need." John Eastman. He had spent most of his life living and working in the woods of B.C., or, as they call it, the bush. He taught us how to use the chain saw, how to fell trees safely, how to split shakes and planks out of cedar, the best way to season firewood.

If it hadn't been for the help of the locals, things would have been much tougher.

Part of their reason for helping, I think, was that the sort of life we aspired to wasn't that far removed from their own. The frontier was recent history here. Many of them had spent their childhoods in the bush. We struck a chord.

Being respected by them was important to us. That flattered them and they loved us for it. Not many people gave a shit about what they thought. We had use for lots of their experience and skill, too. Everyone loves to be a teacher, especially of some skill he thought no one would ever want again. We were willing pupils.

Unfinished Business. The Pennsylvania dope bust had seemed absurd enough when it was happening. It was so predictable, so pointless. I could hardly keep from saying "Come on now, I mean really, isn't this a bit much?" And now, four thousand miles away, next to a whole other ocean in a different country, it was hard to believe that Suchadolski and company were really on the same planet we were.

I considered not going. The idea of marijuana and mescaline being illegal was absurd enough. The idea that Virginia and I were supposed to travel several thousand miles to see whether or not they would put me in jail for possession of less than an ounce of dope and a few pills was too ridiculous. I wasn't worried about conviction—poor Suchadolski had made every procedural error in the book—but the idea of going all that way just to get let off on a technicality bothered me almost as much as the possibility of doing time. And what was the worst thing that could happen to me for not showing? I'd be in big trouble if I ever got picked up in Pennsylvania for anything, and I'd forfeit my bond. It was laughable.

There was lots to do at the farm. Getting the roof done before the rains started was the most urgent. But trial time was coming up, and Virge and I took a ride on the Trans-Canadian Railway.

Early September '70, just before getting on the train heading East: "I feel better than I've ever felt about life."

I meant it. We could afford to be philosophical about the trial and any other unpleasantness that came up. We had our alternative, the farm, our hot-air balloon. We could stand a brief descent to where those funny little antlike things scurried around. If it got to be a drag, all we had to do to get our altitude back was cut away a sandbag or two. They couldn't really hurt us. We were facing this last hassle out of politeness and not because they had any real power over us any more.

Vincent had left for California a week earlier. From there he was heading back East to pick up some stuff. Our plan was for him to meet us on the Cape. We'd spend a few days at his place in Vermont before driving back to the farm with him.

The train ride was a gas. Watching the deer and the antelope play, cruising effortlessly across the continent through some of the most beautiful wilderness anywhere. We brought our own food along—crunchy granola, super pumpernickel, cheese, nuts, fruit, salami, peanut butter—enough to share with other people. It took three and a half days to Toronto. Every day at sunset we'd go into the bar car and have a couple of beers.

It would have been awful to go back having washed out. If we hadn't found any land. But we had found land. Not just any land, really spectacular land. We returned with our heads high. The trial was just a silly interlude. Then I could get back to the good stuff, the real stuff. I had beaten a bigger, far more terrifying rap than the one I had to face in Greensburg, Pa.

From Toronto we took a buff to Bussalo and tried to get hold of Steve and Sandy. The phone number and addresses they had given us didn't work. We sent them a "Fuck, where the fucking shit fuck are you guys," etc., etc., letter scrawled on a napkin giving them some addresses and numbers where they could get hold of us while we were East. Got on a pitt to Bussburgh and called a girl I had gone to elementary school with who had told my mother that she and her husband could put us up for the trial.

Luxury accommodations. It was the first time we had slept in what most people would call a bed in about three months. Nothing against couches and foam pads, mind you, but this was something else. A great big old maple bedstead, a mattress, a room all to ourselves. After four days of buses and trains, after three months of camping, it felt great.

Amanda and Lou were first-rate hosts: good food, good drinks, movies. They expressed suitable indignation over the silly trial we had to go through.

Lou was in graduate school, another thing I had avoided like the plague. They were making a pretty good adjustment to all the things I had refused or been unable to adjust to. Had I been a pathetic hippie whose dreams were getting stale, coming back East to be tried for dope, I would have hated them.

The trial was a bore. I got off on a technicality but ended up having to use some political pull to get the judge to see it. Mine was the first case of its kind that hadn't been pled guilty. People said it was an important case that would change things. I couldn't get into it.

Hitching to Swarthmore was a bore. Being stopped by the cops and searched again and again was a bore.

At Swarthmore, talk talk talk talk talk. The shit is on the fan or very close. What to do about it? Was what we were doing good? Was it an answer? To how much? Working with the system? I had been through them all so many times. Boring. Spiced with a touch of astrology, the I Ching, or yoga, and diet. Was a bore. Was bored. It never went anywhere. Nothing ever changed. Maybe it was adding up. But how much adding up was needed? Boring, bored, bore. In the time I've been talking to you I could have cut a week's worth of firewood, shingled a hundred square feet of roof, and shot three grouse.

When the shakes started coming on the talk was torture. Dope helped some.

Virginia went down to North Carolina to see her parents and I headed for New York City, where Pa was spending more and more time.

Somewhere along the line I started falling apart. My elevation stopped working. My capacity for politeness and social grace deteriorated. "I have the farm to go back to. None of this shit matters. Repeat. None of this shit matters."

Earlier it had been "I have the farm to go back to so I can enjoy being back East, New York, etc." Toward the end it was "If I get really awful I'll just put myself on ice and ship myself back to Powell River, where life makes a certain amount of sense."

Time started meaning less and less. It just hung there. Where I was meant less and less. More and more meant less and less. Just getting back to the farm where things made sense became everything. Just getting back. Where there was work to do that meant something. Something to get my mind off my mind.

Feeling something gripping the pit of my stomach. Hands shaking. Social blunders. Getting confused about names. Stuttering some. Confusion about how long to shake hands. Getting please, thank-you, you're welcome, hello, and good-by fucked up.

Then the crying started. First just little tears falling asleep. Then bigger tears. Then having to get away and cry alone.

Always on the verge of tears, waiting for, dreading the question, "What's wrong, Mark?" Not being able to answer except by crying. Nothing they could do. "Just get me back to the farm. I cry a lot less out there." They hardly ever asked. When they did, my answer was usually a look or gesture that said "Why aren't you crying too?" And their looks seemed to wonder back.

Maybe because I had the farm I let myself go further than usual. The pressure of having to endure was gone, so I allowed myself to see the full horror. Knowing how many valleys there were like ours, why New York City? It didn't have to be this way.

Automobiles careening. Drunks careening, junkies, pollution, misery ad infinitum, all careening. Dinners at Sardi's, famous people, lots of talk. I fled up to the Cape for a few days.

Being alone in the big Barnstable house was strange too. A post card to Virginia: "I've decided to cash in a little public sanity for some inner peace of mind. At the going rate of exchange I'd be a fool not to."

A good nigger. Laughing and crying only with his own, just coasting through the rest. Putting in time, waiting to get back to the farm where life made sense, where there was no need to cash in public sanity for peace of mind.

Finally Virginia showed up with Becky, an old housemate. Happy to see them. I was lonely as shit and going out of my mind. Then Vincent, the eternal wanderer, drove in. We could get moving. We put my Evinrude motor, a potbellied stove, and other stuff in the back of his station wagon and went up to his place in Vermont for a few days.

Virge's brother was in the area. Some other people. It was all jumbling together. They all tripped. I didn't. They wanted to know why. I couldn't say. I spent a lot of time crying in the woodshed. No one noticed.

Finally, after what seemed like years, we were on our way. The tension in my head eased somewhat as we moved West, toward the farm, toward work worth doing. I stopped crying so much. Just the little tears falling asleep.

How do them folk back there hack it? Certainly not in my repertoire of tricks. Maybe it's a blessing. If I could have hacked it maybe I wouldn't have taken off, I wouldn't have found the farm. Lucky me. Unlucky them. Maybe if they weren't so tough they would have found a reasonable way to live. Maybe if people weren't so goddamned rugged they wouldn't have so much to be so goddamned rugged about.

It went pretty quick, driving straight through most of the way. Before we knew it, South Dakota, Wyoming, Idaho, like a flash. Washington, the evergreen state my ass, most of it's desert. Dead deer on every other car from Wyoming on. The Black Hills weren't black but the Bad Lands were some of the prettiest, most awful bad land I ever saw.

Three days after leaving Vermont, we crossed the U.S.-Canadian border just north of Seattle, drove straight to the Vancouver ferry terminal, and napped in the car waiting for the first ferry. The usual two ferry rides and a hundred miles of driving (five hours) later we were at the Powell Lake Marina. Luckily John Eastman was there and took us up the lake.

Two pieces of bad news: Beowulf, who was getting on everyone's nerves, hadn't split as he had promised. Jack had slashed his leg with the machete. They'd brought him down to the water in a wheelbarrow and then found that neither Dick nor Moldy had any interest in being outboard motors. They had broken into a summer cabin on the lake and waited there a few days hoping a boat would come along.

John took Jack to the hospital in his boat. It wasn't serious, but it so easily could have been. Bringing my reliable outboard from Barnstable had been a good idea.

The roof had progressed quite a bit. Vincent and I, the former foremen, surveyed critically and did a bit of chain-saw surgery. But all in all it looked like a good job.

Nice to be back. The next day was more work: no more tears, no more tangles.

The Good Old-fashioned Organic Way. A commune a little farther up the coast, rather than exploit animals or use any sort of machine, plowed their land by harnessing themselves to the plow four at a time. This was seriously discussed

at our place somewhere in between my first two breakdowns.
We eventually compromised on a roto tiller, the worst of both
worlds.

We hadn't taken to the woods just for a change of scenery
and a different way of life. The physical and psychical as-
pects of our adventure were inextricably intertwined, but the
head changes were what we were really after. We expected to
get closer to nature, to each other and our feelings, and we
did, but even these changes were relatively superficial. They
merely meant getting in touch with things that were already
there. We wanted to go beyond that and develop entirely new
ways of being and experiencing the world.

We had only vague ideas about the shape of these changes
or when they would happen, but we looked forward to them
eagerly. Since they would result from being free of the cities,
of capitalism, racism, industrialism, they had to be for the
better.

It was a lot like taking some new drug and waiting for the
changes.

"Is it happening yet?"

"I think I'm walking more with my feet than my head."

Push-ups and football were out. Yoga and frisbee were in.
Hamburgers were out, soybeans and brown rice were in.

Fifty-pound sacks of dried milk from a wholesaler were
better than quarts from the corner store but not as good as
from our own goats. Buying Canadian was better than American. Red Chinese work clothes were better still. Bartering
was better than cash but couldn't touch dump picking. Anything that could somehow be construed as counterrevolution-
ary was out. I had my problems digging Charlie Manson and
felt bad about it sometimes. Not that the people there were
heavy into Charlie's trip, it was just hard to have bad feelings
about anything or anyone that Nixon and company didn't
like. If it had come down to choosing between Nixon and
Charlie it's hard to say which way the farm would have gone.
It was a hypothetical situation, a not very likely one, but a fair
amount of our lives was tied up with hypothetical situations

—the revolution, ecological disaster, the last judgment, the breakdown of Western civilization, Armageddon.

Apocalyptic expectations, revolution, economy, as important as they were still didn't get to the root. The truth is we didn't really know what we wanted. Ego death, mystic oneness with all things, seemed like it might be what we were after but it also seemed pretentious. We were after something a little less flashy but no easier to describe adequately. The best model I could come up with was wanting more of my life to be like playing with Zeke.

I think most of us were fed to the teeth with the brand of rationality that had made up so much of our education. Western rationality had made a dreadful mess of a lovely planet, but it was more that this form of rationality had taken up the lion's share of our minds without giving us much in return. Rational truths were true enough, but they were mostly trivial, boring, and not particularly useful. We wanted to free some of our rational brain space to make room for other ways of being. Having rationally decided to become less rational, we hoped to find new, meaningful, exciting, useful truths.

Folk medicine, astrology, the I Ching, other things Western rationality held in contempt, were more training exercises than things we absolutely believed in. We trusted gut impulses more and more, our plans less and less, and found ourselves having gut feelings about more and more things, and getting more and more done and feeling better and better about what we did.

There were some spooky parts to it. Stubbed toes, strange clouds, how many snakes we saw in a day, all fit together and had meanings which we would be able to figure out some day if we paid the right kind of attention. Nothing was meaningless or disconnected. It would be easy to dismiss this as just some kink in a mind about to blow sky high, or mass hysteria, or hippie foolishness, but I still think we were on to something very real.

Maybe just being open to things being connected made us see more. Now I shudder whenever I find that sort of connectedness creeping into my life. Then I couldn't get enough. There's something happening there but I don't know what it is. Do I, Mr. Jones?

Town Trips. Powell River was a two-supermarket mill town. Its raison d'être was the world's largest pulp and paper mill, which used twice as much water a day as New York City and could be smelled as far away as thirty miles if the wind was right. The whole time we were at the farm, the smell only got up to us twice, but it was hard to forget it was there. Some neighbor for Eden. Blowing it up was one of our playful fantasies.

Sometimes we went two or three weeks without anyone going to town, and we would have loved to dispense with town trips altogether, but we were a long way from self-sufficiency. Fresh vegetables and building supplies were the usual reasons for going. While we were at it we did the laundry, picked up mail, exchanged books at the library, and paid social calls.

We never went down en masse. Town trips were seen as a royal drag, so two was the usual crew. Besides, with more than two people Blue Marcel couldn't do the trip in less than three hours.

There were no set teams. We went in all possible combinations. Who went was usually decided on the basis of who hadn't done town duty in a while and/or who had expertise on whatever tool or building material we needed and/or who had some medical or other personal business to see to.

Except for one solo desperation run of mine for tobacco, it was always an overnight affair. Considering Blue Marcel's speed, there was no other way to play it. We had a variety of places we were welcome to stay, including a commune on Prior Road about ten miles out of town; Joe and Mary's place in town; two abandoned loggers' cabins a few miles by dirt road from town that had been taken over and fixed up by three refugees from New York, and a few locals like John who were always willing to put us up. If we weren't in the mood for any of these, there was an old twenty-four-foot, double-end lapstrake boat with an unlocked cabin tied up at the marina. No one ever seemed to use it, so we slept there from time to time.

There was a short-order greasy spoon, the Thunderbird Restaurant, which we usually patronized on town trips. We called it the Works in honor of the house specialty, which was a hamburger with mushrooms, onions, peppers, cheese, bacon, lettuce, tomato, and a hot dog thrown in. At $1.75 it was the best deal in town. The Works also had one of the finest juke boxes I've ever run into, and it was conveniently located directly across from the laundromat.

After three or four weeks of bucolic peace, suddenly seeing cars, electric lights, newspapers, your own face in a mirror was always a little jolting. Sometimes it was a kick to see all the shit we were getting away from, but more often the hassles and ugliness made us want to get back to the farm as quickly as possible and work our asses off so we'd be able to cut town trips to once a year or so.

That town trips were more and more upsetting was a good sign. It meant that the farm really was changing us. We were more and more in tune with natural and divine harmonies and more and more sensitive to discordances we had once accepted as being part and parcel of life. Being out of it we now look back on our society and see that it was worse than our wildest condemnations.

Mercifully, the winter rains came a few weeks later than usual that year. We finished the roof in the nick of time. When the rains started, much to our delighted surprise that crazy goddamned thing didn't leak a drop. We were still short a few walls on the third floor, but most of that work could be done out of the weather under our magic roof.

You're not supposed to just bop across international boundaries and set up housekeeping without telling someone. Some of us were on long-expired two-week visas, the rest of us had slipped by with no restrictions simply by flashing lots of cash and claiming we were on a shopping spree. Shortly after the roof was finished, we decided it might be wise to become legal immigrants.

There wasn't much to it. First Kathy and Jack and then Simon, Virginia, and I took a ferry from Powell River to Vancouver Island and drove to Nanaimo, which was the nearest immigration office. There were a few pages of forms to fill out: education, jobs held, occupational plans in Canada, financial stuff. We shuffled money around to make each of us look very wealthy. Although the immigration people seemed less than thrilled with hippie farmers, their "objective" point system didn't give them much choice but to accept us. We all had maximum education points, fluency in French, which only meant you had to know as much French as the interviewer, which wasn't much, financial points, points for being in our early twenties, and assorted other points.

It was much like the draft process. We were constantly reminding each other to be sure we switched gears. It was a joke, but we had been so conditioned to be noncooperative and insulting to all forms of officialdom, these reminders weren't out of place. We all sat through fatherly lectures from our various interviewers about the foolishness of what we were doing, and were granted landed-immigrant status conditional on our passing a standard physical exam. We were given forms to take to whatever doctor we chose any time within the next six months.

Thanksgiving. The Canadian Thanksgiving had been a few weeks earlier. Up north the harvesting time, which is what the whole thing is supposed to be about, comes earlier. So there we were, immigrants celebrating a holy day of the old country in their new home. We were celebrating the start of new things, new hopes, a new home, just like the Pilgrims.

We invited everyone. Everyone we knew in Powell River, everyone from the other communes around, everyone we knew in Vancouver, friends in California, and anyone else we could think of. We had had visitors before, people from Powell River dropping in on us, old college friends, total strangers, and occasionally there had been enough people spirit and whatever for something like an occasion to take place. But this was the first time we had anything you could call planned.

It was open house, inspection time.

Luckily, most of the inspectors didn't show up. If everyone we invited had come it probably would have been hell. The logistics of food and bedding would have been hassle enough, but the bigger problem would have been playing to that many different audiences all at once.

We wanted everyone to dig what we were doing. I think even Nixon's misgivings would have hurt some. Whenever we talked about the farm or showed visitors around, our presentation usually varied considerably, depending on who it was we were showing off for. Too many types of inspectors might have blown a fuse.

The inspectors who actually did show up were important ones, the Berkeley crew made up of friends from Swarthmore and some other folk they had picked up along the way, heavy into radical politics, women's lib, the revolution and all. It wasn't like we would have given up and all gone down to trash buildings on Telegraph Avenue if they had not dug the farm, but it would have hurt a lot.

We passed with flying colors. We weren't copping out. We were on the same team. Brotherhood and sisterhood confirmed, alliances affirmed. Good feelings all around, we sat down to Thanksgiving dinner.

A few grouse done up as much as possible like turkey, lots of things with apples, rounded out with a few cheat items from town. It would be different next time around.

None of the Berkeley people liked Beowulf, which may have been what pushed things to the brink. In any event, the brink came a few days after they left.

It was one of those scenes in which everybody knows what's going down but nobody will say so. We were all sitting around the kitchen after dinner. Showdown. The issue was why people didn't dig Beowulf and what should be done about it. There were hours of half-completed sentences and pregnant pauses. There was talk about how feeling should be in the open. The truth setting you free. Honesty being the best policy. Nothing being bad as long as it wasn't buried. Things you think are hard to say being much easier if you just try. About three hours of this shit, everyone waiting, prodding, edging around, teetering, teetering. It was mostly Sarah doing the leading. She was in the middle. Beowulf was her man. We were her friends. That there was considerable friction between Beowulf and the rest of us was no secret.

Beowulf's name wasn't the problem—lots of people were into strange name trips—but his attitude about it was indicative. It was twenty-four hours a day I've Got a Secret. He was smug about his diet, posture, breathing, and lots of other stuff too, but what he was smuggest about was that no one knew his real name. He guarded his birthday equally zealously and let on that these twin secrets gave him enormous advantage. Add the fact that the vibes were never quite right for Beowulf to do much work and that he never really talked with anyone except maybe Sarah and you've got friction.

Why me? It seems so pointless, so unfair. It's not like I'm much more bugged by Beowulf than anyone else. I didn't get my way with the shape of the windows or the roof. If everyone else was so hot to have me not be chief of this tribe why do I have to play the heavy now? Simon, fucking free spirit, perfect hippie, the windows went mostly your way. Here's a chance to earn it. Or Virginia. You're the one who says you can't live here if he does. Or any of you other jokers who keep coming up to me and saying how Beowulf is bugging you.

More pregnant pauses, more pleading in Sarah's voice, more looking at me, waiting for me to finish these dangling thoughts, waiting for Taurus to give some nice concrete example to all these abstractions.

"Beowulf, you give me a pain in the ass."

I wish Sarah had been right. I wish I could report that after everyone leveled with everyone else, after everything was out in the open, all hostility vanished, everything was resolved and the whole room glowed with the good feelings of brotherhood.

Actually, I don't remember most of what was said that night. It was so much exactly what I expected I had a hard time paying attention. Beowulf wasn't the only target. But all the criticisms leveled at others seemed like weak gestures to make things look a little more even.

Beowulf had been saying he was about to leave anyway but he had been saying that for a while. Maybe that night made him decide to really go through with it, but all in all I don't think that evening changed the tide of history one way or the other. Mostly I was just depressed that the whole thing hadn't worked out as smoothly as we had expected when we left for my trial.

Within a week he was gone and Sarah had left with him, which was too bad. Sarah hadn't been much of a worker but was a good friend and a general up for everyone.

Luke. Sometimes I think maybe I liked Luke as much as I did to make up for how little I liked Beowulf. There were some superficial similarities, which made them easy to think of as a pair. They were the only non-Swarthmore people, they were both superfreaks. Freaks in different ways, to be sure, but neither could be accused of doing things halfway.

If I and the others disliked Beowulf because he wasn't from Swarthmore, why did we all love Luke? If Beowulf didn't fit in because he was such a superfreak, why did Luke, who was second to none, fit in so perfectly? The real answer was that Luke was warm and open while Beowulf was a tight-ass.

I doubt that there have been many who moved over the face of this earth as gracefully as Luke. I can't imagine anyone or anything resenting his existence. He is probably as close to a saint as I'll ever meet.

Move over the face of this earth he did. He was brought up

somewhere in New Jersey, spent a lot of time traveling around, settling for a while in various places in California, New Mexico, Oregon, and then British Columbia. Last word placed him somewhere in South America.

Apparently he ran a hotel in Berkeley for a while, but beyond that I know of no work, regular or otherwise. I doubt if he ever had or ever will have much money. When I met him he had nothing but a few pieces of clothing that were the products of inspired dump picking and the like. I never heard him complain about having no money or brag about it either. He appeared to have some sort of faith that whatever he needed would gravitate toward him and it seemed to work out that way.

I never saw anyone in any situation anything but happy to see Luke. I have a feeling he could walk in on Nixon fucking chickens and Nixon wouldn't mind. Luke wouldn't mind. The chickens wouldn't mind.

He just about destroyed my car one day. Town was upsetting him. He decided he had to get back to the farm, but our boat wasn't there and no one was going up the lake that day. I don't think he really thought that by some magic there was all of a sudden going to be a road to the farm, but he might have. More likely he figured that maybe one of those old logging roads might get him part way there and he'd walk the rest. He had a compass. Predictably, he didn't get far. The car was hopelessly enmired, and there was a big operation to get it out of there. But the curious thing was that no one, not me whose car it was or any of the other people who had to salvage the situation, was the least bit angry with Luke.

We were angry with the highway department for not putting a road where Luke wanted to drive. We were angry that there hadn't been a boat at the lake for Luke to use. We were angry that one of us or someone hadn't been with Luke to keep him from getting upset.

How Luke had managed to survive this long was always a mystery to me. He'd do things like throwing a flimsy boat together with a few pieces of scrap wood, cut another piece of scrap wood into a paddle, and just vanish into the wilderness. A few days later he'd reappear, smiling, on foot, telling us about how his boat had sunk about ten miles up the lake and he just sort of moseyed his way back.

There was a thing he said a lot that summed him up in many ways: "Nothing is poisonous." The first time I heard him say that was in response to my look of disbelief as he picked up the deadliest-looking mushroom I ever saw and ate it. Later, when I was learning about mushrooms, he slipped often enough to let me know that he knew pretty much all there was to know about them. It's typical of Luke that he was embarrassed by and tried to conceal this sort of expertise. He appeared to look at it as unnecessary garbage he had cluttered his mind with before he learned to trust. He wanted to believe he was picking mushrooms according to vibes, but he was always very careful about inspecting those we picked before letting them go into the pot.

Luke was organic to the nth. He was the hippie's hippie. He even had misgivings about agriculture. He claimed to have gone for months at a time eating nothing but wild food. It's possible; he knew more about edible wild plants than anyone I've ever met. Of course he claimed it was just vibes leading him to his next meal. Meat, of course, was out of the question.

Luke had a deep mistrust of even simple tools. The chain saw drove him up the wall. There was little love lost between him and most internal combustion engines, though for some reason he did have a certain attraction to Moldy Goldy and a few other things, like my car. There was nothing dogmatic or fashionable about his attitude. He just couldn't stand to be around anything he didn't love. That he loved my car was a great source of pride to me. In time I came to trust his instincts almost as much as he did.

He was probably the least manipulative, least conniving person I ever met. He wasn't perfect. He tripped over his own rhetoric from time to time. "The truth will set you free," and then a little lie. But there was no way he could have lived up to the things he said. He did it as well as it could be done.

Some of the best times of my life were with Luke. Town trips with anyone else were a drag. Somehow he and I used to get everything that had to be done in about half the time it took anyone else. Obstacles seemed to vanish. Then we'd get a jug of wine and go visiting. We'd sing old rock-and-roll songs late into the night.

If I were to pick out the high point of my life, I think it would be strolling down the beach in Powell River holding hands with Luke in the shadow of the stench-belching pulp mill, half-crocked on wine, the sun setting, and singing "You Are My Sunshine."

Hanging around with Luke, I felt the same flowing good feelings and lack of hesitancy that I felt with Zeke.

Luke loved the old lapstrake double-ender and could rarely be persuaded to sleep anywhere else on town trips. The outboard I had brought from Barnstable made Blue Marcel dependable but she was still only thirteen feet long and couldn't carry much. We asked around about the old boat and learned that it had been on the lake since 1917 and, more important, was for sale. At $175, a steal. Feather, weighing in at over two tons, became our heavy carrier bad-weather hope.

Unfortunately, Feather got to make only two trips for us. The first brought us our two pregnant goats, the second brought Simon's family up for Christmas. Then, since the engine was acting strangely, we decided to just let Feather sit till spring, when we could fix everything right.

Christmas. Another holiday, another occasion. A new set of inspectors, Simon's family. His sister, little brother, and parents all showed up to spend Christmas at the farm. Jet fare alone must have run over a thousand dollars.

Simon went down to Vancouver to meet them: neutral ground, so to speak. They spent a few days there, did some skiing, and then came up. The parents didn't spend much time at the farm. After about a day and a half they retreated to the Marine Inn back in town. It was probably the outhouse that did it as much as anything else. We all thought they were pretty good sports to come at all.

There were little awkward moments, like when someone passed a joint to Simon's little brother, but all in all it went very well. We enjoyed having them there and I think they enjoyed being there. They weren't tickled pink that Simon had chosen this way of life but they weren't foaming at the mouth about it either.

There were lots of the usual conversations you have with parents about this sort of thing. Throwing away a good college education. Don't you get bored? Money? What about working in the system? Would you fill in an absentee ballot if I sent you one? Dope.

Same conversations but with a difference. The difference was it was taking place on our turf and not theirs. We were the ones who could afford to be indulgent and polite about their screwy ideas. Somehow, watching their reactions to this new situation gave the farm a solidity and reality that the previous inspection by peers had only hinted at.

On the way to the farm with his family Simon had picked up a Christmas package from Barnstable addressed to Virge and me. Red and green DO NOT OPEN TILL CHRISTMAS stickers were on all sides. We went along with it and just let it sit there till December 25, in spite of our talk about moving Christmas back to the winter solstice, where it belonged.

When we opened the box, it was all I could do to keep from crying. The two little bottles of champagne had broken en route. The champagne had all evaporated but the joint letter from everyone was stained and the pages of the books were warped. Nothing but the wine was really destroyed, my Christmas stocking and my mother's rum cake were OK, but the accident seemed fraught with tragic symbolism. It triggered off thoughts of Christmas a year ago.

*   *   *

Each of us in the family knew that it was "the last Christmas." The last Christmas we would all spend together. The
last Christmas that would be anything like the Christmases of
the past.

Something was dying. It was more than Christmas. The
magic that had filled the Barnstable house was dying. Our
childhood was dying.

What was killing it? Father's getting to be famous? The
changing times? The fact that we weren't children any more?
Nothing goes on forever, but we didn't let it die gracefully,
we just had to try to squeeze one more Christmas out of it,
trying to pretend it wasn't happening, trying to make like it
wasn't the last Christmas, trying to be twelve again. It seemed
like we were compelled to play a cruel joke on ourselves and
insult what had been so precious and real with a farce.

I honestly tried to coast through it and maybe in another
mood at another time I wouldn't have taken it so seriously. I
could have played the game like everyone else and just let it
go. But this wasn't that time and mine wasn't that mood. I
was too upset, too desperate, too scared and unsure of what
lay ahead.

There we were, my family, my blood. Cousin brother Jim,
twenty-five, tormentor of my late childhood and adolescence,
my replacement as eldest son, two-time college flunk-out, no
particular direction, a couple thousand dollars in photo-
graphic equipment, his inheritance, shrinking fast. Cousin
brother Steve, twenty-two, three months older than I, Most
Popular Barnstable High School Class of '65, B.A. Dart-
mouth, teaching English in Barnstable High, his alma mater,
hating every minute of it, planning to quit but without the
faintest idea what he was going to do next. Cousin brother
Tiger with a year to go at U. Mass. No real plans but with a
pilot's instructor license and reasonable prospects, undoubt-
edly in the best shape of anyone there. They were my father's
sister's sons. We had adopted them when their parents died

when I was eleven. It was a real bitch at first but things
worked out.

Sister Edie, twenty, two-time college dropout, no direction,
hooked up with and apparently unable to get free from Brad,
a second-rate Charlie Manson. Sister Nanny, fifteen, very
unhappy about school and lots of other things. My father
having difficulties adjusting to superstardom, not wanting to
be a writer any more, very restless, not very happy about
anything. My mother going through menopausal stuff, wondering what the hell to do with her life with the kids all
grown and the marriage not in the greatest of shape. Any
myself, twenty-two, B.A. in religion, fed up with do-gooder
work in Boston, no plans and less hope for what the future
held.

Christmas Eve. Everyone got drunk the way they used to
get drunk, everyone talked the way they used to talk. It was a
sham. Christmas morning all the "kids" gathered at the top of
the stairs, waited for the "OK," and rushed down the stairs
squealing with glee.

It was Edie I talked to first. "Look, this is really a nightmare. I can't take it any more." We had a good talk. She
understood. If this was the last time we were going to be
together as a family, and it most likely was, then there were
real things to talk about, real things that should be said if our
being a family was going to mean anything. This manic desperation wasn't doing anybody any good.

After talking with her I felt a whole lot less lonely. Eventually I managed to have sober conversations with everyone and
the whole thing became less of a nightmare. That didn't stop
it from being the last Christmas, but I needed a family now
and not just something that was a family five years ago. And I
got it. Not that everything was all cleared up and everyone
had hope and direction, but at least we had love and not just
memories of a past love distorted by some twisted resurrec-
tion.

* * *

Right after Christmas Luke's rotten teeth reached the critical point. He claimed that he had been born with lousy teeth but I doubt that his speed days in Berkeley helped much. They were all crumbling. The only thing to do was to yank the stumps and put in some falsies. He looked awful. He was in constant pain. His spirits were deteriorating too. All those rotting teeth were poisoning him.

One way or another enough money was gotten together and all of Luke's teeth came out. Afterward he was in even more pain and couldn't eat anything, couldn't do anything but try to smile.

I never saw him recover. He left a few days after the operation. All he knew was that he was heading south. Some months later we got a letter from South America.

Although I only dimly realized it at the time, Luke's leaving broke my heart.

Maybe if I hadn't hunted grouse, or maybe if I had thrown the chain saw into the lake, maybe . . .

My love for Luke was important to me then. It was very important to me when I went nuts and it's still important to me. If at the last judgment I'm confronted with a list of all my sins, my defense will be that I loved Luke. Proof that I was capable of higher emotion, proof that no matter how many ugly things I might have done I knew beauty when I saw it, proof that I didn't have to fuck to have fun.

January 1971. A new spirit settled on the farm. We had arrived. Thanksgiving and Christmas had been confirmation rituals and we had passed both with flying colors. There had been a slightly disturbing tentativeness to the place before.

There had been pressure to work work work to get the house ready for winter. All of a sudden we noticed that winter was half over. The house still wasn't ready and no one was dying or even sick. It was too cold to work very comfortably. Fingers didn't behave; they dropped things all the time. We stopped trying to get the house ready for winter. It was cold at times, but we had our down bags and the kitchen could be made plenty toasty by revving up the stoves.

We had a big laugh about the whole thing. What had we been worried about? Local people were saying this was the roughest winter in years. If this was the worst winter could do to us, our survival was a piece of cake.

The die-hard regulars, Simon, Jack, Kathy, Virge, and I, settled in. We had time to look around and try to figure out exactly what it was we had. By and large, we concluded it was pretty good and would get even better. The hardest time had been a snap and was behind us. We had enough wood and enough food, so we just sat back, carved wooden spoons, knit scarves, wrote letters, read books, made music, and waited for our goats to have their kids.

2
Arriving

If God is one, How can I be Evil?

—C. MANSON

The central law of all organic life is that each organism is intrinsically isolate and single in itself. The moment its isolation breaks down and there comes an actual mixing and confusion, death sets in.

—D. H. LAWRENCE

Drugs. Most of the people at the farm were well-seasoned trippers. It hadn't rotted their brains or taken over their lives. It was just something they had done several times a year for the past three or four, something they enjoyed and felt helped them grow and understand more. From the way I looked and talked and the friends I hung around with, people who didn't know me well assumed that I had done my share of tripping. They were always a little surprised to find out that I had never dropped acid and that my sum-total experience with psychedelics was one mescaline trip, and that not until I was an old man of twenty-two and out of college.

I rarely admitted even to myself that I might be afraid of drugs. I just kept saying that feelings of love, beauty, peace, and cosmic insights could be achieved more lastingly and meaningfully in other ways. But the drugs were always there and more and more tempting, if only to find out what the hell everyone was so excited about. So one fine and sunny day, two weeks after graduating from Swarthmore, Vincent, his girl friend of the moment, and Virge and I headed down from Boston to the incomparable dunes of Sandy Neck to do something about Mark's virginity. Vincent had four caps of super organic mescaline.

Oh, well, thought I, I'm going to trip. Strange travel suggestions are dancing lessons from God. I had a slight feeling of anxiety in the pit of my stomach but I laughed at it. No one ever has a bad trip on mescaline. It's not like it's acid or something. What bad could happen anyway? Down the hatch went the little pill.

When's it gonna start? When's it gonna start? How silly. Here we are on an absolutely beautiful day, four beautiful people in one of the world's most amazingly beautiful places. What are we messing around with some drug for? What more could we want? What more could there be?

I never called it a "bad trip." Sometimes other people would call it that when I told them what had happened. "Bad trip" didn't really describe it. It wasn't saying enough. It was saying too much.

If you had a bad trip it was because you were a bad person. If you weren't a bad person, then at the very least having a bad trip indicated that work was needed on this or that part of your head; a lack of wisdom or something like it was at the root of your bad trip. People would always talk about what a terrible trip someone like Nixon would have and what a nice wonderful beautiful trip someone they really loved or admired would have. I found the logic appealing. It made sense to me that the drug somehow opened you up and that if you were somehow pure, everything would go fine, but if you were twisted and kinky, you'd have a bad trip. Finding myself on the other end of the stick, the end of the stick I had hoped to use on Nixon, Mitchell, etc., didn't lessen the appeal of the logic.

I was shaking, I was crying, I was scared. Not the whole time but for quite a bit of it. The only honest thing to say is it *was* a bad trip. And that thought became an obsession.

I was different from other people. That was the meat of it. Vincent, Virginia, and Gloria were all fine. They didn't end up crying, shaking, scared. For them it seemed to end after eight hours. They all felt a tinge of regret about it. "If only it could be like this all the time." The hell of it was that for me it was.

Had I had a rock-stable world to start with, I might well have enjoyed an extracurricular jaunt into psychedelic perception. But it was just too close to home and accelerated everything I was trying to keep a lid on.

It had really been acid. I was grasping at straws, something to make the fact that I was shaking, scared, crying, more reasonable. An honest mistake? It happened all the time. Mescaline was in big demand. Some bastard had sold Vincent acid as mescaline.

And the bastard got closer and closer, as bastards always do. It became Vincent and it wasn't for money. It was to show Virginia what a fucked-up person I was deep down inside. Maybe they had all taken dummy capsules and I had been given a whomping dose of acid. That was too heavy. In a switch I decided that yes, I had been deceived but I was deceived because they loved me so much.

They knew me better than I knew myself. They had given me this acid to straighten out my kinks, to make me see how beautiful I was. To make me love myself as much as they loved me. They knew I wouldn't have taken it if I had known it was acid. That was part of the stupid but charming thing about me that they were trying to help me with.

It went back and forth. Bad plot, no plot, good plot, no plot, bad plot, no plot, good plot. Back and forth, faster and faster, and then a few days later, after many cold showers and lots of staying in bed, it finally started slowing down and then went away. But the nasty fact that mescaline had made me crying, shaking, scared remained. It haunted me. If the good fairy had appeared and granted me one wish, it would have been a good trip.

It wasn't just the psychedelics that hit me differently. Enough speed to keep most people up one night spaced me out for three. Amyl nitrate—poppers—was a fine two-minute high that blasted me for hours. Lots of the time I couldn't even smoke grass right. Everyone else would get drowsy and mellow and I'd get activated and hyper. Grass was still pleasant for me so I smoked my share, but I couldn't help worrying about what the hell made drugs so different for me.

And then it happened. I got my wish. Just after Christmas, a year and a half after my mescaline disaster, I had a "normal" acid trip. I went up, got high, and came down just like my fellow trippers, Virge and a couple from the Prior Road commune. Unlike the mescaline, which had woven itself too well into the fabric of my mind, the acid let me tell when it came and what it was doing and when it went. It was a pleasant, giggly day, and a huge relief to me. The farm or simply the passage of time had cured whatever it was that made me so different from my friends.

Goats. The goats didn't like me. I knew it and it hurt. The goats didn't really dig anyone but they seemed to like me least. Maybe it was because I had played the heavy when we first got them. It was I who picked them up and took them away from their happy home, put them in the back of the truck, and held them there while we drove to the marina. They appreciated even less being dragged into the boat. In an attempt to make up I offered Martha a joint on the way up the lake. She just curled her lip menacingly.

I did my best to make friends. I'd bring them apples and other treats and hang around in their house not saying or doing much, just trying to get them to accept me. They'd accept the treats but I never got the feeling I was making much progress.

Alice didn't seem to mind me much, but Alice was stupid so her acceptance didn't mean a whole lot. It was Martha I really wanted to like me. Realizing that the deep hatred in her eyes went far beyond her and me, I started apologizing for all the awful things that people had done to goats. Man had taken a wild animal and bent nature to his selfish needs, distorting it horribly and making it dependent on him for its survival. Martha's was the hatred of all animals that man had messed with and the resentment of all life for what man had done to what could have been such a nice planet. I even started feeling some of this resentment from Zeke.

The apple trees were sore about it too. Before I had felt gratitude from these beaten old trees for my help in patching them up and making them healthy. I imagined sighs of relief and appreciation as I cut away the dead wood, scraped their bark, and bound their wounds. But now I felt unanswerable bitterness. Cutting firewood became unthinkable.

I'm getting ahead of myself. It wasn't till several weeks after the birth of Nancy that these feelings really got to me. When I had given up hope of ever having a close friendship with Martha or Alice, Martha because her hate was implacable and Alice because she was so dumb, I placed my hopes for a good man-goat relationship on their kids. I figured they'd be much happier here than their mothers, who had known other fields.

None of us had any experience with goats, and the woman who had sold them to us didn't have any exact dates, so we just watched Martha and Alice swell up bigger and bigger, expecting the kids to come almost any time.

One morning, as I was out feeding the goats and making small talk with them, I noticed that Alice was acting strangely. At first I thought there was something wrong. There was some strange tumor sticking out of her ass. Then I figured out what was happening and ran back to the house to alert the folks to the impending blessed event.

Jack, Kathy, Simon, Virginia, and I all charged out to watch the miracle, hoping there would be no complications, since none of us had the faintest idea what to do to help if anything should go wrong. Their little shed had a space between the roof and the wall, so everybody watched from there. Everybody but me. I went into the shed. I had heard about farmers holding cows' heads and comforting them while they gave birth. I wanted to be involved. It was Alice's first kid and I thought maybe she could use some moral support. There was room in there for other people but no one else came in. I felt

Virginia looking at me as if I were making some dreadful mistake but I tried to ignore it. After staying in there long enough so that it wouldn't look like I felt I had blundered, I made some sort of excuse and went out. The goats, of course, did fine without me.

In the middle of all this Vincent showed up. Wet and cold, he was warmly welcomed and hugged all around. He was even more distracted and fuzzy than usual. He had been unable to get a ride up in a boat, so rather than waiting for us to come into town or for someone to bring him up, he had attempted the overland route. No one had done that before. He had started up in the afternoon the day before and had gotten lost and had to sleep in the bush. There was a heavy snowfall that night. In the morning, soaked and half frozen, he made his way to the lake, where he was lucky enough to find a boat and some oars, and he rowed about four miles to our dock. I attributed his more than usual abstraction to physical exhaustion.

Vincent was just passing through, as was usually the case. The heroics and poetics of his getting to the farm notwithstanding, he wasn't staying very long. He was on his way to a farm in California, where some other people from Swarthmore had something beautiful going. Later we found out that whenever he was there he was on his way to where it was really at: in B.C. with us.

Since he was just passing through and really wanting to get down to California, why had he bothered to stop by at all? We certainly weren't on the way to anything but us. To get his dog, Tanga? To pick up some of his clothes or other stuff? When he left he didn't take Tanga or any of his stuff. Maybe to check us out one more time, giving us one more chance to make whatever magic Vincent was searching for happen? For whatever reason, within an hour of his arrival Vincent decided and announced he was leaving.

Virginia and I had been talking about taking a trip away from the farm for a while. The dreary weather had been getting to her. It was too wet and cold to do much outside and there wasn't much that needed to be done inside. There were people she wanted to see here and there. What was happening with the revolution, women's lib, the cities, America? She didn't want to get out of tune. She said she was getting too ego-involved with the farm and wanted to see what would happen to it if she weren't there. I had been feeling some of the same things. We had been talking about taking off for a month or so and coming back when there was more work to do on the place.

When Vincent started talking about going to California it seemed to Virginia like the perfect chance for us to take our trip. The people at the commune Vincent was headed for had been friends of hers at Swarthmore. They were supporting themselves with pottery and trust funds. They had wheels, kilns, the whole bit. It was exactly what she had in mind.

But if I was going to take a vacation I wanted to just head south and see whatever I saw, meet whoever I met, and let the winds and fates put whatever they would into my path. And if I was going to head for somewhere, I sure as hell didn't want it to be another fucking Swarthmore enclave.

I remembered Vincent's talking about our trips from the East together after the trial. He had said he felt that Virginia and I were ganging up on him. I didn't want that to happen again. I was pretty sure it was paranoia on his part, but real or not, it wasn't the sort of thing I felt like dealing with again.

The biggest thing was that I wanted Virginia to be on her own. She felt that she had been dependent on me for quite a while for direction, energy, decisions, etc., and she resented it. I wanted a commitment from her to the farm, to me, to a way of life. I didn't want her thinking I was dragging her around. If she got away from me for a bit she might make the decision and feel it was hers. Also, I remembered what a bitch she could be to travel with.

The next day we went down to the lake to see which boat and which motor we could get to work. The night before the water in the lake had dropped to such a point that Blue

Marcel's bow was on the ground and the stern had been pushed under water, submerging the Evinrude. We pulled it up and tried to get it going without much success. Dick, the old racing Merc 25, didn't show much inclination to run either. The logical thing to do was to wait until someone came up to visit us and then go to town with the motor and bring it back. Feather was there, but I really didn't want to run Feather until spring. She had an erratic engine at best, with a tricky cooling system that was a bitch to drain, which you had to do if there was any danger of freezing, which there was. But Vincent looked like he was going to piss in his pants if he didn't get moving for California in the next few minutes. One way or the other I was persuaded to get Feather going. To this day I hold Vincent responsible for Feather's death. I got the engine running in its sputtery old way and everybody was just about ready to get on board when the frost plugs blew. It was the beginning of the end for that beautiful old lapstrake that had been on the lake for over fifty years.

The death of Feather didn't faze our soulful wanderer in the least. He immediately set to work taking apart the Evinrude. "He's going to kill all our engines," I almost screamed, but I didn't say anything. Eventually he got the Evinrude running and was roundly praised for his mechanical competence and ingenuity, which bugged me even more.

Vincent wanted to head for town that night and I had to play the wet blanket, saying that it was getting dark and pointlessly dangerous. Bright and early the next morning Jack, Simon, Vincent, Virginia, and I set out. Simon was just going in to bring the boat back. Jack and I were going on to Vancouver to check out tractors and new fruit trees, and to get staple supplies. Virginia wanted me to come so that maybe I would change my mind and go with them to California.

We spent the night in an abandoned cabin outside of town. Virge and I awoke to the sound of Vincent warming up the car. He was being very patient. We had little odds and ends of business to take care of in town and Vincent just sort of tapped his fingers, putting up with us with the endurance of a saint. He hardly said a word to anyone. The funny thing is no one ever called him on it. No one asked him why he was so anxious to get going, why he was in such a rush. He obviously didn't have time to talk about it. He probably would have denied he was in any hurry or, more likely, just smiled sadly.

The seed catalogues were in the mail, so on the ferries down to Vancouver Jack, Virginia, and I figured out what crazy things we'd try to grow. Peanuts? It was great fun. Vincent just paced.

We stayed with Sankara, André, and Sy, three guys from Swarthmore who were more or less supporting themselves with a business called the Sunshine Movers. They had visited us at the farm a few months earlier and said we could stay at their Steven Street place whenever we were in Vancouver. It was the first time Virginia or I had been there, but Simon and Kathy and Jack had been there earlier.

The Sunshine Movers were a funny crew. I hadn't known them well at Swarthmore. They were in the class behind mine and were part of a vaguely intimidating gang of militantly apathetic cynics. They were into drugs but their kick was taking monster doses and not being affected by them. André was the only one I had ever managed to have a decent conversation with. Sankara seemed too cool to bother and Sy too bristly and hard. In any event, these were all just surface impressions and it was very nice to have a Vancouver base of operations again. Rosanne and Bert had moved on to Victoria.

Somehow we managed to keep Vincent from leaving for California without stopping overnight in Vancouver. I had lots to say to Virginia and she had lots to say to me. We were reaching a new point in our relationship, getting to know each other again, even maybe falling freshly in love. But it was a bitch to try to talk or anything else with Vincent revving impatiently in the background. In spite of Vincent's incessant, unspoken, single-minded racket we managed to get some good things said. She understood why I wasn't going. I understood why she was.

There was a sense of closeness between us. It felt so good that she almost decided not to go. But we realized that this was happening partly from our anticipation of being apart for a while, and our hopes of the good things that might come out of that.

The next morning while Vincent warmed up the car we hugged and kissed good-by. When they left I felt a huge sense of relief that Vincent and his move move move was finally gone gone gone and I hadn't blown up at him. I was looking forward to Virginia's return and dwelling on the promise of fresh love that was in our parting.

I had started to feel slightly nauseated when we first came down from the farm, but the morning Vincent and Virginia left, something was drastically wrong with my plumbing. The night before, Jack, our Vancouver friends, and I had gotten blown away on grass and developed a craving for ice cream. I went to the corner store and bought gallons of the stuff. I had a great time picking out flavors, staring at the carton, tasting it through the cardboard with my eyes. It took me quite a while and the man running the store was staring at me as hard as I was staring at the ice cream. In any event I ate an incredible amount of ice cream and the next morning my stomach was dead. It just stopped working. I gulped down air and burped it up to try to figure out what the problem was. What came up smelled like no burp I had ever smelled before or ever heard of. I just wasn't processing anything. Things were just putrefying in there. I tried to bring my stomach back to life with yogurt, vitamins, and intestinal flora pills, but nothing seemed to work. I swore off ice cream forever.

After a few days Jack and I had done everything that was on our list and a few things that weren't. We headed home.

We went to the bar at Lund for lunch and had a few beers and some fish and chips. I gulped down some air and burped it back up. The putrid taste was going away. Beer and greasy fish and chips were succeeding where yogurt and vitamins had failed. After a few beers I decided to give Barnstable a call, collect of course, doing my bit to defuse the new family fortune before it could hurt anyone.

The news wasn't really news at all. I had expected it for quite a while. Dad had permanently moved out and had a new woman in New York. How fucking typical. I thought we were supposed to be a creative family. They assured me that they were fine and strong and I assured them that I was likewise. We all said love love love and hung up.

Jack and I spent the night with the people at Prior Road. It was a pleasant evening, talking about farming, food, money, changes we were going through, possible cooperative ventures, creating closer ties between all the hip communities in the area. I remember a tall red-haired girl playing classical guitar and an ex-medical student stitching up a goat's ear. Jack and I passed around some dope and fresh cabbage— scarce items, much appreciated.

Then I lay back thinking about how everybody who came up to the farm usually spent a few days with the runs or stomach trouble. We guessed that maybe there was something in the water up there that some people's systems couldn't adjust to right away. But with me it was the other way. Every time I left the farm I seemed to get some sort of sickness. Maybe I had become addicted to something in the water or air up there and my stomach troubles when I left were withdrawal symptoms. I thought about Simon and how he talked about finding it harder and harder to function anywhere but the farm. The new life we were starting seemed to entail an unforeseen side effect, a fairly disturbing one: an inability to function in any other context.

I didn't get very far thinking about all this. My mind kept getting caught up in the same circles round and round. Everyone else was sound asleep.

The next day Jack and I borrowed John Eastman's boat, loaded into it the various goodies we had picked up in Vancouver, and headed up the lake. It was a nice clear day, the lake was smooth. My stomach felt almost normal.

Simon, Kathy, and Zeke gave us a joyous hugging welcome. There was still snow on the ground but it was melting away. It was only January but there was a definite hint of spring in the air.

The worst of winter was over and we had made it in good health and spirits. Life on the farm would get cushier and cushier. In a little while we could plant crops. The seeds were ordered and on the way. Our expenses would drop to nothing, and we still had a healthy cash reserve. We were home free, not a cloud on the horizon. I got out my trusty horn and played and played. It was like magic. I felt so good I almost started to cry. Home at last.

Eden. The next morning I was up at the crack of dawn. My stomach felt great, the weather was even warmer than the day before, the sky was an almost summer blue without a cloud anywhere. January? What had been a hint of spring was now overpowering. I fetched some water from the stream and then ambled around our idyllic home waiting for the others to get up and share this gorgeous gorgeous day.

It was really Eden, there was no other way to describe it. Our crazy gamble had paid off. I remembered all the things various people had said about how difficult if not impossible our dreams were. I couldn't help laughing. I had really done what I set out to do, and it had been so easy. In a way I almost wished it had been harder. I wouldn't have minded putting in ten or fifteen really bitchy hard years to feel this good. I had fully expected to and it would have been nice to feel I had really earned it. But it felt so good that earned, begged, or stolen didn't really matter much.

It took forever for the others to get their sleepy selves moving. And when they finally trundled down they hardly seemed to notice what a wonderful day it was. Just to make sure they didn't miss it altogether, I suggested that it was a fine day to drop a little mescaline. Everyone was game. Down went the little pills. I was fully confident that this trip would be as glorious as my first mescaline trip was horrendous. I was right.

After a big mug of coffee made in our new super-see-through Pyrex glass percolator and seasoned with goat's milk and honey, I went up to the roof, took my clothes off, and lay in the sun. It was the first time in many wet, cold months that that had been remotely possible. Jack came up and joined me.

We were lying there in a timeless state of peace and contentment when the sound of uncontrollable laughter came from below. I crawled to the edge of the roof. The scene I looked down on was a vision of heaven and peace on earth, harmony-between-all-things. Simon had baked up a batch of crackers and brought them out just as Kathy finished milking the goats. Simon and Kathy were laughing so hard they were crying as they fed crackers to the two nanny goats and the kids. The goats couldn't get enough; they were prancing around kicking their heels in the air. Zeke was watching the scene, wagging his tail in approval and getting an occasional cracker himself. They were all falling in a big heap of joyous people, goats, and dogs. Spring was definitely coming.

I climbed down, put on my tennis shoes and wrapped a blanket around myself, and went out to join them. Simon and Kathy saw me in my blanket and tennis shoes and started laughing even harder.

"Tennis shoes and a blanket, it's all I need. I can go anywhere," I said by way of explanation. Jack came down and we all lazed around on the ground talking about the sun and weather and laughing harder and harder all the time. We looked around at the fields, the mountains, the trees, the house. "This is Eden," I said. Nobody disagreed.

I turned to Kathy and asked, "Is there a struggle going on?"

"I don't know. What do you mean?"

"It's just that I was wondering why people work at shitty jobs, live in ugly places, hate each other, have wars, etc. It really doesn't make much sense."

"It does seem a little silly," she said.

"I've been waiting for this for a long time," Kathy said after a while.

"There's no reason why it has to be just today," I said. "If we want it to, life can be like this even if it rains or snows. It's all up to us. This is our God-given birthright. I'll be fucked if I'm going to let go of it."

"I was wondering when this would really go somewhere," Simon.

No doubt about it, looking around at the farm, at the people, at everything. It had really finally gone somewhere.

Kathy and Simon and I were crying and laughing for joy. It had really happened. Everything confirmed it. We were dumfounded with joy. Jack was holding back some. I felt sorry for him, but he'd catch on.

"Did you ever think it would ever really happen?"

"I damn near chucked it many times."

"Did you ever really doubt that it had to happen sooner or later?"

"What I wonder is why it took so long. Why now? What was stopping us before?"

"You know there's no going back now."

"About time. Life finally makes some sense."

"What a long, strange trip it's been." "Thank God we didn't give up." "Thank God we persevered." Everything that had happened before was like some bad dream, something that we could finally look at clearly now that we were out of it. "How the hell did we put up with it as long and as well as we did?"

It was truly a magic day and a magic trip, but the next day brought cooler air, with the usual total overcast and sprinkles of rain. The next day it snowed. Simon, Jack, and Kathy had come down some, but I was still a touch or so higher than I had been before the mescaline. I didn't see what was to be gained by going back to my pre-Eden days. I was having a swell time and feeling a little sorry for the others, having their Eden depend on some silly pill.

If only Virginia could be here now, so I could share this

incredible sense of well-being and saying by-by to all the shit in my life.

I had somehow conquered the evil little troll inside me that had given me so much shit and kept me from happiness. I had finally beat all the little shithead fears about myself. Fear that I was very different from everyone else. Fear that deep down inside I was a shallow fraud, that after the revolution or after Jesus came down to straighten everything out, everyone from hippies to hard-hats would unfold and blossom into the beautiful people they were while I would remain a gnarled little wart in the corner, oozing bile and giving off putrid smells.

Everything that had ever happened to me made perfect sense. I was sore at absolutely no one and nothing. Everything that had happened had happened just right. But where to go from here? As much as it was better to travel hopefully than to arrive, as much as I believed that and had lived by it, once you've arrived, you've arrived, and there's not much to be done about it.

I had thought about becoming a minister because there would be no way my job would ever be finished. As long as there was one unkind thought in my congregation, one unjust deed in my community, one unhappy person, the Indelibly Reverend Vonnegut would have his hands full. I loved Virginia because there was clearly so much wrong with our relationship, so much to improve that the prospect of arrival was an incredibly long shot.

Instead of learning, I was looking for enlightenment. Instead of security, I was after infinite inner peace. Instead of a job, I was out to save the world, I thought I had taken adequate precautions against the prospect of arrival but something had gone terribly awry. I had arrived.

Things were still unbearably beautiful. I got this giddiness in my stomach and walked around completely overwhelmed by the incredible loveliness of the trees and the sky and the moss, infinitely delicate worlds within worlds, and people's faces and the way they moved and my own body and what a perfect machine it was and the stove and the floors and our funky house. And everything fit together so perfectly. It wasn't just in the way things looked. It was in the sounds of the wind and the stream and the way things felt, the ground gushing ever so slightly under my feet, the way everything smelled. It's everywhere, it's everywhere. And it keeps getting better and better. And I think to myself, Look Ma, no drugs.

People are all charming and silly. The idea of purpose cracks me up. The only thing that puzzles me is why it took me so long to catch on. How did I manage to keep a straight face for as long as I did? I vaguely remember pain and struggle but it seems so remote, so unnecessary, so absurd.

The Face. And then one night, after several days of pure Eden, as I was trying to get to sleep, marveling at the fullness of each moment, feeling that I was living whole lifetimes within each moment, I started listening to and feeling my heart beat. Suddenly I became terribly frightened that it would stop.

And from out of nowhere came an incredibly wrinkled, iridescent face. Starting as a small point infinitely distant, it rushed forward, becoming infinitely huge. I could see nothing else. My heart had stopped. The moment stretched forever. I tried to make the face go away but it mocked me. I had somehow gained control over my heartbeat but I didn't know how to use it. I was holding my life in my hands and was powerless to stop it from dripping through my fingers. I tried to look the face in the eyes and realized I had left all familiar ground.

When I first saw the face coming toward me I had thought, "Oh, goody." What I had in mind was a nice reasonable conversation. I had lots of things I wanted to talk about, lots of questions it must have answers to. God, Jesus, the Bible, the Ching, mescaline, art, music, history, evolution, physics, mathematics. How they all fit together. Just a nice bull session, but a bull session with a difference. A bull session with someone who *knew*.

My enthusiasm was short-lived. He, she, or whatever didn't seem much interested in the sort of conversation I had in mind. It also seemed not to like me much. But the worst of it was it didn't stop coming. It had no respect for my personal space, no inclination to maintain a conversational distance. When I could easily make out all its features; when it and I were more or less on the same scale, when I thought there was maybe a foot or two between us, it had actually been hundreds of miles away, and it kept coming and coming till I was lost somewhere in some pore in its nose and it still kept coming. I was enveloped, dwarfed. No way to get any perspective on the thing at all, and for all I really knew it was still light-years away and coming and coming and coming.

My own insignificance again? Shit, I sort of wanted to learn something *new*.

"So you really want to go on a trip, do you? OK, punk, now you're really going to fly." Or words to that effect. Not words exactly, more like thunder.

The few times I tried to fight back I was left exhausted. It took everything out of me and didn't seem to improve matters at all. If anything they got worse. So I retreated and retreated and retreated.

I lay rigid all night listening to the sound of the stream, figuring that somehow by being aware of sounds and rhythms outside myself I could keep my own bodily rhythms going. Losing consciousness of something outside myself meant that I would die. Only by falling into step with rhythms of the outside world could I maintain my existence. I realized that this meant I could never sleep again.

A few days before, I had asked the I Ching who mescaline was. I guess maybe that was some sort of no-no. It seemed like a logical thing at the time. It seemed that the two should know each other and might have some interesting things to say about each other. I got pretty excited at the idea. I wanted to cast a horoscope of the I Ching, throw the Ching on numerology, meditate on mescaline, throw the Ching on astrology, ask mescaline about the Ching, and so on and so

one, matrix and cross-reference the whole show and see what
I came up with. But when this face showed up, I figured
maybe I had been messing around with something I
shouldn't.

I tried to think that the face was essentially benign and that
the fear I felt was due to fuck-ups in myself rather than any
malignancy on the part of the vision. But it was so hideously
ugly. But beauty on a physical plane is meaningless superfici-
ality. Isn't it? But green is such a bad color for a face. Red is a
bad color for eyes, and purple glowing wartlike growths tend
to detract from one's looks. Could this be overcome? Could I
learn to love the face? Tune in next week for the saga of
expanded consciousness and broadened concepts of beauty.

There was nothing at all unreal about that face. Its con-
creteness made the Rock of Gibraltar look like so much cot-
ton candy. I hoped I could get enough rest simply by lying
motionless. In any event, the prospect of not sleeping frightened me far less than the possibility of losing contact with the
world.

The sun came up as I was lying quietly, listening to the
stream. Everything seemed fine. I felt a little strung out but
figured I had passed a crisis point and come through all right.
I got up and started the morning chores, building the fire,
getting water, starting breakfast. As I got water from the
stream I paused and listened to it, smiled to myself, said,
"Thanks for last night," and carried the water back to the
house.

Everything seemed just as beautiful as before but somehow
the beauty was more solid, less trippy. I felt warm and good.
Well, I thought, last night I paid my dues. I faced death. Now
I can stay.

I thought about the things I had studied in religion, and
about how much more of it seemed to make sense now. I had
somehow touched what Jesus, Buddha, and others had been
talking about. Formerly confusing phrases out of various
scriptures came to me and each seemed perfectly beautifully

clear. I became aware of a harmony and wholeness to life that had previously eluded me. Disconnectedness was very clearly illusory.

Jack had told me that according to the Zen Buddhists, after enlightenment you go back to doing whatever it was you did before—selling shoes, farming, whatever. It seemed like pretty good advice, so I tried to keep doing all the usual things I had always done around the place, cutting firewood, pruning the fruit trees, feeding the goats. But things started happening that made it increasingly difficult and finally impossible to keep functioning.

Small tasks became incredibly intricate and complex. It started with pruning the fruit trees. One saw cut would take forever. I was completely absorbed in the sawdust floating gently to the ground, the feel of the saw in my hand, the incredible patterns in the bark, the muscles in my arm pulling back and then pushing forward. Everything stretched infinitely in all directions. Suddenly it seemed as if everything was slowly down and I would never finish sawing the limb. Then by some miracle that branch would be done and I'd have to rest, completely blown out. The same thing kept happening over and over. Then I found myself being unable to stick with any one tree. I'd take a branch here, a couple there. It seemed I had been working for hours and hours but the sun hadn't moved at all.

I began to wonder if I was hurting the trees and found myself apologizing. Each tree began to take on personality. I began to wonder if any of them liked me. I became completely absorbed in looking at each tree and began to notice that they were ever so slightly luminescent, shining with a soft inner light that played around the branches.

I've lost patience. I've lost my brakes. I'm willing to make sense as soon as the rest of the world does. There were lots of things I just plain wasn't going to put up with any more. A lot of what I decided to chuck was my old way of doing things, my old way of being, the big part of which seemed to be patience. I was patient with this and patient with that. Patient with Virginia, patient with my parents, patient with the farm. Patient with Nixon, patient with the pulp mill, patient, patient, patient.

I figured I had taken patience about as far as it could go and it didn't seem to be working. Nothing good seemed to come out of it. It seemed the more patient I was, the more I had to be patient with.

Sometime in the next few days I gave up food.

"Are you sure you're not hungry, Mark? You haven't eaten anything for the last three days." Kathy.

I remember trying to eat some bread to make her feel better. I really wasn't hungry. The bread had a sharply bitter taste. The texture was awful, sticking to the top of my mouth, almost suffocating me, sticking to my teeth and gums and making my whole mouth burn and itch. It made awful squishy sounds. I had to spit it out.

At the urging of others I made a few more attempts at food between then and the hospital, but it never went much better.

It had now been about a week of Mark acting more and more strangely since the magic of our joint Eden. Simon, Kathy, and Jack were getting more and more alarmed, but there wasn't much they could do except talk to me a lot and hope things worked out.

Zeke was more and more my closest companion. No matter how screwy and frustrating things were getting with people, Zeke was always there, always loving, always utterly understanding. He seemed to know that something was up and stuck closely by me, giving up his usual solitary jaunts. He was my guardian angel. His unfathomable wisdom, compassion, and protectiveness were slightly spooky, but they made me feel not half so alone or scared. The third floor, where we usually slept, was accessible only by ladder, which made it impossible for Zeke to get there. I moved my foam pad and sleeping bag down into the little library-sewing room off the kitchen so that I could always be with him. Even though I couldn't sleep, I lay down from time to time to get a little rest and slow things down a bit.

What to do while the others slept? I had read *War and Peace* and *Anna Karenina* a couple of weeks earlier and had started through Jack London. I had finished *The Call of the Wild* and a collection of short stories and was working on *The Sea Wolf*. About halfway through, the whole thing started getting too real. It was dualistic, good vs. evil, and the evil was just too real and the descriptions too moving and . . . and it had to be more than just a book. The pages and words would twist and blur in the really gruesome spots. I had to stop and catch my breath after every two or three pages. The closer I got to the end the worse it became. I was convinced that I really shouldn't finish the book, that if I did I would die or the world would end or worse.

Since reading was out, I got my old Olivetti and started banging out letters to old friends, to Virginia, to various members of the family. I was trying to clue them in about all the wonderful things that had been happening to me and all the wonderful new truths I had found. Unfortunately, the typewriter bit didn't work too well. I had trouble hitting the right letters and even more trouble seeing what was wrong about the wrong letters I had hit. One key was as good as the next. While there was a lot of truth to that, I felt it was only fair to the people who weren't quite where I was yet to make an effort to make myself as intelligible as possible. I switched over to longhand. I still had some of the same problems but to a lesser extent.

Seventeen pages to Pa, twenty-one to Ma, twenty-five to sister Edie, twenty-four to sister Nan, sixteen to an old professor, and so on. I was writing like the wind. The words just came like magic and they were all just right.

As far as talking with the people who were really there, I kept coming back to my old question. "Is there a struggle going on?"

"Is there a what?"

"Is there a struggle going on? I'm not really quite sure what

I mean by that. I'm just sort of curious as to what you might feel about it."

"I think I know what you mean but I don't know. It's hard to say."

"Oh, well," said I and tried to get away from the sticky unpleasantness in the pit of my stomach and back to the sheer beauty and glee of it all. But the question haunted me.

Is There a Struggle Going On? Why on earth would there be a struggle going on? Struggle means some sort of pain. What sort of sense can there be in pain?

"Do you remember the other day when I asked if there was a struggle going on?"

"Yeah."

"Well, I've been thinking about it some and I think there probably is a struggle going on."

"What do you mean?"

"Well, I'm not exactly sure. It's just something I feel within myself."

"That there's a struggle going on?"

"Yeah. And I think that maybe like it's important. That it explains a lot of things, that it's going on inside everyone and that maybe it's real important to figure out how to get where we really want to be. How to get enlightenment, liberation, salvation, whatever you want to call it."

"This struggle, is it in you or the outside world?"

"Both. There is no outside and inside. It's all one. Where do I end and you begin? What's outside and what's inside? We're all one. The struggle makes up everything. The struggle is between two opposites, good and evil, positive and negative, yes and no, whatever you want to call it. On and off. Everything is made up of an infinite number of ons and offs. Like computer language, where any piece of information is stored as a series of ons and offs."

Simon and I got into a discussion of enlightenment. The talk was going pretty good. There seemed to be an awful lot of yeses going around. And then he said something that struck me very strangely.

"You know, stuff like this is really great. I really think there's something here. I really think I might be ready to go somewhere to find a teacher to help me get further. You know, a guru or something?"

I felt betrayed. "Go some place? A teacher? A guru or something? Why? It's all right here. What more do you need? You want a guru? Shit, right here you have the woods, the land, the goats, the birds, Zeke, Jack, Kathy, myself, and God knows how many other incredible teachers, right here. You want guru, shit. I'll be your guru and you can be mine. What do you want to know?"

"I don't know. I just have the feeling that there are higher beings, people who really know about this stuff who could help me out."

"I don't know, Simon. There's something about the way you say 'guru' that brings me down. I guess I'm just reminded of priests, professors, psychiatrists, etc., and professional poets and musicians even. I just keep hoping that we can find a way to do all those things ourselves. You know, 'get it in the streets' type thing. If you're really dense you might need signs to point things out to you and a real official-type guru, but I think a big part of getting there is just realizing that everything you need is right where you are."

"Simon, what do you know about hypnosis?"

"I don't know. Not too much, I suppose. Why?"

"Well, it's something I've thought about some before and have just been thinking about more now for the past few days. I think that very possibly it's a big clue. I'm operating under the assumption that I'm pretty much like other people and that everything I go through, other people go through the same thing to some extent and vice versa. It seems to be the only sensible way to look at things but I guess it could turn out to be a horrible mistake. If I'm sinking I don't want to drag you along with me, Simon. That's one of the things I'm afraid of now, that I'm sinking and am going to drag you and others down into the pit with me. Am I making sense? I think this is all somehow tied up with hypnosis and that I'm explaining it the best way it can be explained. Did I ever show you a book I started writing a couple of years back? It was all about stuff like this. It was sort of a manual about how to operate with a blown mind. Well, anyway, what I'm trying to say is that if your mind is in the right space of openness and awareness you can listen to what I'm saying and get a lot out of it, whereas some deadhead would listen and think I was crazy. I think maybe that's what a lot of craziness is. People just not being creative enough listeners.

" 'Is the tea in the tongue or in the leaves?' That's a phrase that's been popping up into my mind about every fifteen minutes day and night for the last week or so. Maybe some part of me is trying to hypnotize me with it. Sometimes I think I'm being hypnotized by compost. I guess it's all pretty funny. Really, isn't it?

"One of the things I might be doing now or want to do in some ways is to ask you beg you to hypnotize me. I guess I'm afraid of losing control somehow and running amuck and so if you could hypnotize me then you could control me and everything would be all right. It seems ridiculous to worry about losing control. I have no idea about what losing control would look like. I've never really thought of myself as being in control. The whole idea of being in control seems silly to me, hysterically funny in fact, but nonetheless I think I'm afraid of losing control. So if you could somehow hypnotize me, I'd be much obliged. I don't want you to worry. I'm pretty sure everything will be all right. I can't imagine what really bad could happen."

Most of the time I was talking Simon just smiled and nodded and said something like "It's all right, Mark. Yeah, everything will be fine."

"Simon, I feel like something really new is happening. Like I feel more open toward you than I've ever felt with anyone else. I guess I've just broken through something and have come to some sort of realization about brotherhood and communication or something. It's fantastically wonderful. I'm really overwhelmed. I've really got nothing to hide. Ask me anything. This is what the revolution, yoga, religion, meditation, etc., is all about. We're reaching for paradise. Hot shit. I had a feeling we'd get somewhere some day and now I feel we're really on our way."

My Glass Slipper. There were times I was scared, shaking, convulsing in excruciating pain and bottomless despair. But I was never clumsy.

Most people assume it must be very painful for me to remember being crazy. It's not true. The fact is, my memories of being crazy give me an almost sensual glee. The crazier I was, the more fun remembering it is.

I don't want to go nuts again, I'd do anything to avoid it. Part of the pleasure I derive from my memories comes from how much I appreciate being sane now, but most of what's so much fun with my memories is that when I was crazy I found my glass slipper. Everything I did, felt, and said had an awesome grace, symmetry, and perfection to it. My appreciation of that grace, symmetry, and perfection hasn't vanished with the insanity itself.

It's regrets that make painful memories. When I was crazy I did everything just right.

There were "problems" but somehow they didn't seem like problems at the time. Tasks that required only minimal concentration—cutting wood, building fires, pruning trees, fetching water—became progressively more difficult and then impossible, but that seemed too silly to worry about. Even if I managed by herculean effort to think something was worth doing, I couldn't keep my mind on it. There was so much else going on.

I felt no lack of energy, in fact I had a supersurplus; but my hands, arms, and legs were getting all confused. I'd get all hung up in how perfectly beautiful one muscle was, exactly what it did, and get it to do it just right. But then all the others would go off on their own little trip. I nicked my ankle with the chain saw. I was losing my coordination as well as my concentration.

Ambivalence and disability. It was like something in me knew I would become unable to function, and got me ready by telling me ahead of time that it didn't matter.

I worried about not being able to go anywhere. Any unpleasantness, any threat, and I would collapse. The idea of cops horrified me. The idea of anyone but people who loved me utterly was terrifying. I was stuck at the farm forever. And soon that wouldn't be good enough.

I worried about not being able to communicate with people. They wouldn't understand. Yet so much of what I was going through seemed so right, so valuable, so much fun.

"Simon, I keep getting these awful rushes of fear, waves of total terror that leave me shaking and weak. I keep trying to figure out what the hell it is I'm afraid of. Last night I thought my heart was going to stop again. Now I'm keeping you up because I'm afraid to go to bed. It makes no sense. There was a big thing about fear in *Dune.* There was sort of a chant that went, 'Fear is the mind killer. Let the fear run through you . . .' I've been trying to do that but I don't think it's working. I don't know if I'm going to be able to beat this bitch.

"What am I afraid of? What bad can happen? Fear never helps. Maybe in some cases, like if I was being chased by a bear, being scared would give me a rush of adrenaline that would help me run super fast, but how many times have I been chased by a bear?

"It really helps to have identifiable things to be afraid of. Out here fear seems so out of place. If I was living in New York I'd have no end of things to focus fear and worry on. I'd just pick one according to what sort of mood I was in. But out here it's a whole other story."

* * *

The Letter from Virge. Whenever I think about that letter
I find myself thinking, the worst part of the letter was such-
and-such, but it keeps being a different such-and-such.
There are so many good candidates for the worst part of that
letter it's impossible to choose.

On the back of the envelope in a barely legible scrawl was
"This is a terrifyingly incomplete letter." Maybe that was the
worst thing. It set me up for a doozy. It also made it impossible to answer or deal with it. I should have sent it back un-
opened and told her to send me a complete one.

"Dearest Darling Mark." Since when did she call me
dearest darling?

"Some of this letter is just for you and some is for everyone. You decide what's what." Fat chance of that. I hadn't
been able to tell the difference between myself and the trees
for the past few days, let alone the people. Besides, I was sick
of things being just between us.

Open up and let the sun shine in, the truth will set you
free and all. I published everything. It seemed to be the only
way to deal with it. I had the feeling I was reading someone
else's mail anyway.

There was some end-of-the-world stuff. "This is the last
time I'll see California. The sunsets are all eerie colors from
all the pollution." She sounded very scared. Maybe that was
what the incompleteness was. She had found out something
about the end of the world that she couldn't put in a letter.

She and Vincent hadn't said a word to each other the
whole way down. It had been very tense and unpleasant. At
least I hadn't been there for Vincent to blame.

There was some description of the land and the farm
there. And then some stuff about going off pills and getting a
coil and feeling much better.

Then there was the part about having slept with Vincent. I
guess that was the part that was just for me. And being sorry
about hurting me and crying and shaking in Vincent's arms. It
came right after the part about the new IUD coil. "Well, I

guess you get a new machine you want to try it out right away."

Was I hurt? I really had to think about it. I found the idea of giving a shit about who puts whose thing in whose thing absurd and degrading. Was this some role she was making me play? If I wasn't hurt would she feel insulted, unloved?

Did she have the clap? Did she want to live with both of us? Was she pregnant? Had she reached some new insight about sex? Was that the incomplete part? She said she wanted to come shake and cry in my arms. Was this maybe some new position or something Vincent had taught her?

There was no way I could write back to her. She was maybe going to Colorado to see her brother, who was going to jail for political Weatherman stuff. She might be heading back up to the farm immediately. She might even fly. She might be going to visit some people in Berkeley. All I could do was sit and wait for her return. Wait for her to complete the letter. Maybe a day or two, maybe a month. Wait . . . Suspend time and wait.

Every year about this time for as long as I had known Virginia, there had been a "new horizons breakthrough time." Politics, drugs, sex, religion, food; a pinch of this, a dash of that. Usually nothing changed much.

OK. One more time, Virge, I'll play. You can call your shots but I've got a few myself. I'm in a big hurry to get the fuck out of the oppressor business. Let's see the new Virge. I hope you're ready for the new Mark. Let it all hang out. This train is bound for glory. The brakeman has resigned.

Fear and pain would be everything and then nothing. The highs weren't that different from the lows. Neither was grounded. Both had at best a marginal relationship to anyone's reality. My happiness and sadness was all out of proportion to anything that was happening. There were things to be happy about, but not that happy. There were things to be sad about, but not that sad.

Having their feelings make sense is how people get their

kicks. There was no way I could make my being that happy make sense just because of the farm working out, or spring coming, or my being that miserable and upset because of Virginia's balling Vincent, my parents' breaking up. There had to be more going on. I needed things to be that happy and that sad about. The dawning of an age of universal peace and brotherhood, nuclear holocaust, and the like fit the bill.

Time had gotten very strange. Things whizzed and whirled all about me with great speed and confusion. Then everything would stop. There was no more movement, everything was being frozen solid, life was being drained out of everything. I'd feel a scream building up deep down inside me when suddenly everything would spring to life and begin rushing around again, violently and pointlessly. The scream would come but there'd be no sound. It was all drowned out in the frantic rush of wings beating all around my head. I'd come to myself from time to time and realize that I was walking, half stumbling through the woods. I'd wonder where the hell was I going, what was I doing? I'd take handfuls of snow and press them to my face, trying desperately to get some sort of a hold on myself.

It kept running through my head that Virginia mustn't see me like this. Tears of desperation were streaming down my face. "I mustn't be like this when Virge gets back." And a voice within me wondered, "Be like what?" "Like this," I screamed. "Something's all fucked up. I'm all shaky and falling apart. Virginia mustn't see me like this. She won't be able to make any sense out of it. She'll think her letter did it. She's got to be prepared. Somebody's got to tell her what's happened to me. Simon or Jack or Kathy, someone's got to go tell her."

Several times the dogs started barking wildly. Someone must be coming up the path. And every time, "It's Virge, it's Virge!" and my heart would start racing furiously. "Oh, shit, I won't be able to take it. My heart will stop. She can't see me like this. I don't have any idea of what to say to her." I'd hear her coming up the path. Sometimes I'd even catch a glimpse of her through the trees. False alarm after false alarm. No one coming up the path. What the hell's wrong with those damn dogs? If I get this way just hearing the dogs bark, what's going to happen to me when she really comes?

I needed help, but still in the back of my mind was the feeling that I was crying wolf, that there was really nothing wrong. It would be terribly difficult for anyone to understand what was wrong because what was wrong was such a strange, elusive thing, the sort of thing it would be easy, almost logical to discount.

Communicating was just about impossible. My tongue and mouth weren't responding very well. It was only with the greatest difficulty that I could tell who was saying what and that I could make any sense out of words. I relied heavily on grunts and gestures.

I'd all of a sudden be sitting next to the stove, wearing the half-finished sweater Virginia had been knitting for me. There were knitting needles sticking out all over it and I was crying. Kathy was saying something to me. I had no idea what I was crying about. Then something would strike me as hysterically funny and I couldn't stop giggling. Then I'd find myself somewhere else wearing completely different clothes or no clothes at all. Time stopped being continuous; it jumped around with lots of blanks. The only way I have any notion of time then is from Simon, Kathy, and Jack.

They became seriously worried about me a couple of days after we all tripped but just kept hoping I'd straighten out. They made sure I was never alone, and talked with me a lot. There wasn't much else they could do. But time passed and things got worse instead of better. By the time Simon took me to town, ten days after our trip, I hadn't eaten or slept for at least four days. Something had to be done.

I got it into my head that everything would be OK if I could just see Virginia, that the problem was this indefinite waiting and not knowing. They seemed to agree, maybe it was their suggestion in the first place. I also thought that maybe all the strange things that were happening to me were her cries for help. She needed me desperately and we didn't have a phone. Simon and I would head out in search of Virginia.

Everything was trembling and glowing with an eerie light. One foot in front of the other, step two follows step one. Somehow I got dressed. "See, I can still function," I said to myself as I made it down the trembling ladder and into the trembling kitchen. "Everything's going to be just fine," I managed to say to Jack and Kathy. As we left I tried a reassuring smile.

One foot in front of the other down to the lake in my Day-Glo boots that seemed to be walking without me—gush gush. Just put my body on automatic, everything will be fine.

"Whose popsicle stand is this anyway?" Who said that? Did I say that? I didn't say that. "Simon, whose popsicle stand is this anyway? Did you say that? Zeke?"

"Whose popsicle stand is this anyway, Virginia?" Can she hear me? Where is she? Did she say it?

It was perfect. It was just right for our reunion. That's what I would say. "Virginia, whose popsicle stand is this anyway? Do you think it could be the sort of place we might be able to talk?"

Cut Off. Sometimes when people ask me what happened I just say, "Cabin fever."

Twelve miles from nowhere by boat, and such a laughable boat on such a laughable lake over thirty miles long, one of the world's deepest, over fifteen hundred feet in places, with monster winds funneling down that monster valley stretching back up into those monster mountains, monster logs floating around like icebergs, fogs, rain, sleet, snow, hail, monster electrical displays. It had it all.

If we disappeared without a trace it wouldn't be very remarkable. The remarkable thing would be that it hadn't happened sooner.

And even before we got to our laughable Blue Marcel there was that mile and a half on our cute little trail tenuously wending its way through the impenetrable undergrowth and monster trees with which the winds casually cluttered our way on a fairly regular basis.

And even if we managed to make it to the marina, where were we? In a parking lot with an odd-lot assortment of vehicles if ever there was one. We were constantly losing keys, and as if our cars weren't in lousy enough mechanical shape, the local version of juvenile delinquents used them as a spare parts department.

And even if we managed to get one of the cars started, the roads weren't much of a match for coastal storms, let alone the stray earthquake. And then there were the ferries, which didn't run in bad weather, were hard to get a place on in good weather, and had been known to sink.

And even after all that, and then more driving unreliable cars on mountain roads and still another ferry and more mountain roads, you ended up in Vancouver. Besides the fact that you could get more places more easily from Vancouver than from Powell River, it's hard to say exactly what's been gained.

One reason the whole thing seemed suddenly so difficult was the "me" factor. A few weeks earlier I could have counted somewhat on myself to work my way around whatever problems might come up. I could tinker a bit with engines, knew my way around a boat. But now all that was shot to hell. There were times when I was having enough trouble walking and remembering to breathe.

But just what was it I was all of a sudden so worried about being cut off from? At times it was very specific, like that I would never see Virginia or my family again. At other times that was the least of my worries; I wanted only that something somewhere had an inkling of my existence.

"Some day, Simon, we'll be able to laugh at all of this. Some day it will be very funny. I know it's funny now. But who would believe it? But I'm scared. I sure hope whatever it is that's happening has a happy ending."

Simon sounded worried. "Take it easy, Mark, everything will be just fine."

A happy ending, something nice. I hoped it would somehow be all over as soon as we got to town. Maybe getting away from the farm would do the trick. At least in town we could see newspapers, make phone calls, and try to put everything all together.

Maybe Virge would meet us at the dock and everything would be fine.

She would be there. The closer to town we got the more sure I was. Virge was waiting at the dock. Everything was going to be just fine. Or at any rate whatever was going to happen was going to happen.

Simon knew what was going on, he had to. I was counting on him not to let anything bad happen. Maybe I missed it and he had gone into town the other day and set everything up. I was crying with joy and gratitude. He had taken care of everything.

John Eastman's boat, which was already going very fast, seemed to pick up speed and leave the sound behind.

I felt myself losing power. I drew into myself to save strength. I lay on the floor of the boat, sinking deeper and deeper into myself. I was losing awareness of anything outside myself and then I heard the engine slow down; we were there. I lay still on the floor of the boat and heard someone come running down the dock. Vincent was talking very excitedly to Simon. I could just barely make out what he was saying. He asked where I was and I heard Simon say that I was on the floor of the boat in some sort of a state. I caught only bits and pieces of their conversation and felt myself slowly losing the battle to maintain consciousness, but I could tell from their conversation that Virge was in about the same state in the back of Vincent's station wagon. I groaned louder.

Apparently shortly after Virginia and Vincent made love in California, Virginia had begun acting stranger and stranger much the same way I had, and then had become unable to do much more than grunt and groan that she had to find Mark.

The old rock-and-roll song "One Last Kiss" started playing through my mind along with wondering whether this was very good or very poor poetry. I felt myself being picked up and carried and then put down again. I could feel Virginia next to me but I couldn't move or speak. Slowly I began to feel a warmth where our arms and legs were touching. The warmth began to spread through my body. I felt life coming back to me. I tried to open my eyes but I couldn't. So I just lay there trying to send Virginia warm thoughts and picking up the love she was sending me. "It's all going to be all right, it's all going to be fine," we said back and forth without words. "Don't worry now, it's all going to be all right, love." "I know. I know."

The warmth from where our arms and legs had been touching spread over my whole body and became everything. Time and place meant nothing, there was just being next to her and a deeper feeling of peace and joy than I had ever known. How long had we been lying like this? I had no idea. It could have been minutes or years. It was infinite. It was enough. It was a happy ending.

Then through the warmth I heard Simon's voice, "Mark, are you all right?" I nodded very slightly. I started thinking about Simon and Vincent and Jack and Kathy and everybody I had ever known and everybody Virginia had ever known and what effect our miracle of love must be having on them. Easily as good a story as Jesus, I thought, probably better in a way.

The warmth started to fade. I became aware of cold and damp and little aches here and there. I heard the sound of an engine. I found I could open my eyes. Simon was looking at me worriedly. There was no Virginia beside me, just a soggy coil of rope. We were no more than halfway down the lake. I smiled at Simon and tried to reassure him that everything was going to be all right.

What could I tell Simon? It was just about impossible to say anything above the roar of the engine. Had it all been a dream? I looked around. Everything was zipping past us at incredible speed. There was still some light and the sky and the water, the sounds, the colors, everything was plastic and water all flowing together and too real or unreal . . . "I want to go back, Simon. Let's turn around," I screamed, but my voice came out all funny. It was too fast or I had said it backward or something. I couldn't make my voice sound right. Simon looked at me helplessly and shrugged his shoulders.

"We can't go back now, Mark."

"Help, pleh, pleh!" What's happened? Why can't we go back? What have I wandered into? What have I dragged Simon and God knows who else into?

And the mocking hateful contempt of the face a few nights earlier, "Now you're really going on a trip."

"Trip pirt, help pleh," as the sardonic wind and its accomplice, the Day-Glo water, rushed by in an eerie chuckle.

Simon handed me a carrot, which seemed at first like a strange thing to do but then as I bit into the carrot lots of things came back to me. It all made sense. The sound of chewing on the carrot was the same sound I had heard the night before while I was groaning in agony after I had tried to explain to Simon what was going on and begged for help. Simon had gone upstairs and explained to Jack and Kathy what had to be done and they had made rabbit-chewing-carrot noises and hypnotized me into believing that I was a rabbit. What a perfect choice, I thought, remembering my father doing *Harvey* in the Barnstable Comedy Club and everything else I could remember about rabbits. By giving me the carrot, Simon was starting to bring me out of my state. Hypnosis was being put on ice: a way to keep me from exploding, a way to help me last until I could find Virge.

That Simon had hypnotized me was very reassuring. He was in control and would make sure nothing bad happened. I had no real idea of how long I had been in that state. It was possible that Simon had kept me in something like hibernation for weeks or even years, waiting for Virginia to come back so he could bring me out of it and get us back together for a happy ending after which we would all live happily ever after in Eden. Since he was bringing me out of it all the danger was past, it was all right for me to come back to life. Virginia was waiting for us in town. Otherwise he wouldn't be bringing me out of my trance.

The trance slipped away as I ate more and more of the carrot. I felt strength and power spreading through my body. After my long sleep I was coming back, rested, stronger than ever before. I roared into the wind.

More than Virginia would be waiting at the dock. Simon had probably gotten hold of my mother and father and all the people we knew in Powell River and on and on. It was going to be the damnedest party anyone ever saw. A coming-out party, out of my hibernation that had gone on for God knows how long. A party to celebrate Virginia's and my coming back together. I envisioned some sort of pagan wedding. What a story. What a love. What an ending. I hugged Simon with joy and unfathomable gratitude for what he had done for me, but he looked back at me with that worried look in his eyes. I calmed myself down and decided to just wait for whatever happened. Maybe there's still more to this journey. I hoped for the best.

The sun went down just before we reached the marina. There was no one waiting there for us. No one at all. No Virginia, no Vincent, no parents, not even a stranger, let alone a brass band. Well, what did you expect? I thought to myself, laughing at all the wild fantasies I had had, still half expecting lights and fireworks to come on any minute and "Surprise, surprise!" from gathered friends, everyone I had ever known hiding in the shadows, or at least Virge and Vincent.

What funny, funny things have been going through my mind. I chuckled going over and over the things I had thought. What a funny thing for a mind to do. What a good story. "Well, we made it," I said to Simon, smiling. He smiled back, looking much relieved. Everything was going to be all right.

Town. We checked the mail. I even did the combination to show Simon I was all right. There was nothing of particular importance in the mail. I noticed some new psychedelic hip posters in the post office, which seemed slightly ominous to me. They looked out of place. Government posters advertising "Get it through the mail" or some such thing. I shook it off. I didn't want to think about it.

We went to the Works to get a little something to eat. Sitting there sipping coffee, feeling warmer and safer than I had in quite a while, still a little shaky but pretty sure everything was going to be all right, and then something new.

I started falling very deeply in love with the waitress and everyone else in the place. It seemed that they in turn were just as deeply in love with me. It was like something I couldn't get out of my eye.

I didn't understand it but I recognized it. There were all those little things that had happened occasionally between me and lovers before, but never this strong, never so lastingly, never with so many. I was completely in love, willing to die for or suffer incredibly for whatever they might want. A rush of warmth and emotion, spiritual and physical attraction, a wanting of oneness, a feeling of already oneness.

When I looked at someone they were everything. They were beautiful, breathtakingly so. They were all things to me. The waitress was Eve, Helen of Troy, all women of all times, the eternal female principle, heroic, beautiful, my mother, my sisters, every woman I had ever loved. Everything good I had ever loved. Simon was Adam, Jesus, Bob Dylan, my father, every man I had ever loved. Their faces glowed with incredible light. It was impossible to focus, to hate, to fix. They were so mobile, all moving, all changing. They were whatever I needed and more. I loved them utterly.

I worried about how complicated this could make my life. Maybe it was enlightenment but it brought up not inconsequential problems of engineering. Who sleeps with whom was one, but there were lots of others. Like what if two people I loved wanted me to do different things? Who would I spend time with, who would I talk with, who would I dedicate my life to? If I loved everyone there was no way to focus any more, no reason to spend time with anyone in particular.

What would Virge think about all this? I had somehow fallen in love with Simon, Jack, Kathy, the waitress, and assorted passers-by more powerfully and completely than I ever had with her.

I worried about what my eyes might be doing to other people. Was I making them fall in love with me? Was I hypnotizing them? I started keeping my eyes down. This thing could easily get out of hand if it wasn't already.

Falling in love with everyone I see. Oh, Christ, what will those jokers from the Pentagon come up with next, the fun-loving boys in biological-chemical warfare? If the Marines walked in that door with submachine guns and gas masks I'd probably love them too. I'm certainly not in any mood to fight anybody. Maybe it's the Russians. Not that it makes much difference. I wonder where the bastards put it. The air? The water? The food? I wonder if this stuff is supposed to be fatal or just debilitating. I wonder if there's an antidote. I wonder how much longer I'll be able to wonder about it or anything else. Better get my wondering in while I can.

I wonder if there's been some sort of mistake. I wonder who's trying to do what to whom.

Dogs and cats and even sometimes little children get into rat poison. War involves civilian casualties. Lots of them, usually more than military casualties. Middle-class white kids get into heroin. Luckless bystanders stop bullets all the time. Bullets and rat poison and heroin all work as well on the unintended as the intended, that's the way they are.

I understand that good old American technology has developed a scanner that can discriminate on the basis of race as to whom it kills. It has something to do with the pH factor in sweat. I suppose one way to fight back would be to put something in American underarm deodorants. Something like hexachlorophine or aluminum chloral hydrate might do the trick.

The ideal thing would be something that automatically rewarded good and punished evil. Something like what we had hoped acid was. You wouldn't have to worry about where to put it.

Maybe the Germans are putting something in the VW's they send over here. Sore about World War II and all. Maybe the Japanese are doing something with transistors. Inscrutable chaps, and after Hiroshima who could blame them? Sometimes I think it's timed to go off some day, sometimes I think it's going off all the time.

Who's trying to do what to whom?

Maybe it's freaks vs. straights, male vs. female, white vs. black, young vs. old, East vs. West, etc. The fuckers couldn't hit each other to save their lives, but every round's a direct hit on my little head.

Eternal vigilance is the price of freedom.

Insanity is the price of eternal vigilance.

Holy shit, is my mind running. This coffee isn't even cold yet. The same song is still playing on the juke box. I'm thinking about a million miles an hour, spinning fantastic webs. It's a gas. Cramming whole lifetimes of thinking in between sips of coffee.

That stuff about where to put it, mistakes, and all doesn't begin to tell the story. There's so much more there. It's like I've discovered some sort of shorthand. I've got these little microdots of thinking. I just go "dit" and I've got years of thinking and then "dit" and another big hunk. Fitting it all together more and more. And it's not just my thinking. I'm tapping huge pools of other people's thinking. "Dit" and I've got the whole Bible. "Dit," all of Freud and then "dit" and the relationship of Freud and the Bible in one "dit." It goes forever in both directions. I'm getting closer and closer to having it all in one "dit." I get it from time to time but can't seem to hold it very long but I'm holding it longer and longer. And then one "dit" is all I need. Everything is in it utterly distinct but still in just one "dit."

The same song is still playing, my coffee's still warm. Simon is sipping his coffee. Simon, the waitress, and everyone else is glowing softly with incredible beauty. I'm content forever. "Dit." Content forever? But it's not forever, it's just now. Now I'm content forever. I'm content forever at this moment of time but what about the movement of time? What happens next?

If I could just be content for now. Now. I don't care what happens tomorrow because I'm already content about it now no matter what it is.

No matter what it is. It could be dreadful and here I am content about it. I have an awful feeling something awful is happening or I wouldn't be feeling this way. All these strange things that have been happening to me must be clues of some sort. All these things I keep trying to laugh off.

"Simon, I have this awful feeling I'm kissing everyone good-by forever. It seems very sad. 'It's been very nice. You were really swell,' they seem to be saying. 'Good-by. I love you too,' I seem to be answering. 'Good night. Everything will be just fine.' Even strangers. Words aren't necessary. Just glimpsing people going by in cars, they're all saying, 'Good-by Mark, we all loved you.' 'Gee whiz, everyone, I loved you all too. It's really been great. I wish we could do it all again.'

"Simon, the time will come when you too will have to leave me. Don't be sad. It's meant to be. I love you, Simon, you've been wonderful, solid like a rock."

"What do you mean, Mark?"

"In time it will all make sense, Simon, be patient. I myself am not sure yet how it ends. But be patient, it will all become clear. We have a very strange and difficult journey but nothing is asked of us that we cannot do. Remember that."

"Sure, Mark."

"Thank you, Simon. Have faith. You will be remembered."

"Well, let's pay the check and get out of here. We still have to find a place to crash."

"Well, sure. Let us pay the check. I suppose it is time for us to leave this place. Do you have money, Simon? If you do not have any money, Simon, I have money. We do not have to worry about money. There will always be enough. Have faith. We will also not be afraid. Everything will be all right."

"Well, let's go."

"Yes. Let us go."

Across the street to the Marine Inn to use the pay phone. I tried to call my family. It took forever to get the operator. Terrible agonized electronic screeches coming through the whole time. There was no answer. No answer at the Barnstable place? It happened, but not often. I'll try again tomorrow. I went to the bathroom while Simon made a call to his sister in Cambridge.

The fluorescent light in the bathroom was just about to die. It was stuttering like a strobe. I watched my arms and legs stutter through space. "Maybe the light is fine and it's me." My breath, my heart, my everything started stuttering.

Mirror, mirror on the wall. There was usually something slightly unexpected waiting for us in a mirror after two or three weeks at the farm, but what I saw this time was totally other. For starters I looked at least ten years older and twenty pounds lighter. There were lines in my face that I had never seen before. My beard seemed much longer and fuller than I remembered it. I was entranced. There was a depth of feeling I had never seen before. An authenticity, a wiseness, an utter lack of games. I was awed. It was somehow what I had always wanted to see in the mirror but I still had trouble believing it was really me. That face was real. It was not a face that cried wolf.

How long have I been here staring at myself? The strobe was freezing me. What if the door's locked? What if I open it and there's nothing there? What if they're all dead? What if I'm dying? What if this is how it ends—in a plastic bathroom that could be anywhere? What if, what if, what if when I open that door I don't know where I am? Where am I?

I threw some cold water on my face. One foot in front of the other, one moment in front of the other. It'll all keep going. Somehow I got to the door. Somehow I opened it. Somehow Simon was waiting in the lobby. Somehow I was in Powell River, British Columbia, Canada. Somehow I shrugged it off.

"Goddamned light."

Simon and I headed out to Car Car.

"Under no circumstances can I be locked up, Simon. I cannot go to jail."

"Relax, Mark. No one's going to lock you up."

"I will be all right, Simon. I just need a little time. Getting locked up would ruin everything."

As soon as I started driving I felt much better. Things were still very strange but driving felt good. I loved my car, it was running beautifully. Driving along deserted Highway 101 at night. Up the hills, down the hills, round the corners. Everything was fine. I could do it forever.

It was taking forever. "My life certainly has gotten very full lately. It seems there's more happening in five minutes now than used to happen in years. Maybe I've just never really paid attention before."

I turned on the radio. The only things I could get was some station from Detroit playing old rock songs. All my favorites. "Shop Around," "Momma Said." The DJ kept talking about memory lane. "My Girl," "Dream," "Take a Message to Mary." He was playing exactly the songs I would have played had I been in charge of some "end of the world" radio program. It seemed strange to be able to pick up a Detroit station and nothing else, and that clear as a bell. One radio station left, wrapping it up. "Golly gee, fellas, that's sweet. Just for me."

Simon seemed to be nodding off. I looked over at him. What an angel, a big, bearded Pooh bear with a Jewish afro. I guess I had been hard to keep up with of late. I wasn't the least bit tired. I could go forever. Driving the car, listening to old songs forever, I couldn't imagine anything that would feel better. I had it down pat. Something else might not go as well.

I hadn't slept for what was probably only days but seemed to stretch back forever. It was like a whole other existence. "Oh, yes, I remember back when I used to sleep." I dreaded sleep. I was afraid that face would come back. Besides, I was having such a good time being awake.

There was some very good reason for going to have a beer at the Lund bar. I didn't know what it was but that made it an all the better reason.

Magic, wonderful, wondrous things happened when we went to have a beer at the end of Highway 101. It was apparently just the right thing to do.

The most wondrous of the wondrous things was what happened between us and a local guy about our age who came over to buy us drinks like he was pulled by some cosmic magnet. The big thing about him was how cheerful he was. He couldn't stop smiling. We couldn't stop smiling back. Here was a perfect example of lots of the things I had been thinking and trying to explain to Simon: how pleasant life could be, how we were all one, how nothing bad could happen.

He used to work in the mill. He had just quit that afternoon and was out celebrating. We congratulated him. We got to laughing, telling stories, slapping each other on the back. There were some ESP-type things and cosmic messages, but the big thing, the thing no one could argue with, was what a wonderful time we had, how famously we got along.

This was the way life should be all the time. This was the way life could be if everyone stopped worrying about all the silly things they worried about. This is what Jesus wanted. We were all in love.

The bar was closing. We hugged our new friend good-by and Simon and I went and pissed on the tippy-top last little bit of pavement of Highway 101.

On to the Prior Road commune to crash. I had put it off as long as I could but everything was closed and Simon was very tired.

We were always welcome at the commune. It was a kindred place with kindred people and kindred dreams.

Was Virginia there? It was possible. There was a red Microbus in the driveway with California plates. We opened the door. It was dark. There were a lot of people crashed on the floor.

Softly, "Could we crash on the floor?"

Softly, "Sure."

If Virginia was there she didn't say anything. Maybe she was, maybe she wasn't, but I wasn't going to make a big deal asking around. Besides, this was maybe her last night with Vincent or whoever she was with before she came back to the farm and me. I felt like an intruder, so I just lay down trying to be as unobtrusive as possible.

The sound of very gentle lovemaking came to me while I lay there, and a soft female voice: "We should have done that a long time ago." Was it Virginia's voice? I listened closely but there was no more. Everything was quiet.

A Half-Dream. I am in heaven, where the senselessness of pain is clear. The feeling is of peace and fullness. There's a slight giddiness just below my chest. The magic place of no shadows. Then a sharp pain in my foot, a small bump on the sole, between my toes, like a plantar's wart. Around it tender and sore but there is no sensation in the bump itself. Picking at it. Little by little I separate it from the surrounding skin. It's a plug about a quarter-inch across. I pull at it. Pain. It seems to have some sort of roots reaching into my foot. I adjust to the pain and continue to pull at it. It starts to come. The pain very intense but strangely almost pleasurable. Amazed by the size of the thing and how I hadn't noticed it earlier. I've pulled about six inches of foreign growth out of my foot, and there's no end in sight. A feeling of relief, making my foot all warm and tingly; the more I pull out, the higher the warmth and relief spreads. I pull another six inches and panic for a moment. What if this is all there is? What will be left once I get this thing out? But the gentle strong feeling of warmth and relief reassure me I am doing the right thing and I continue extricating this foreign growth from my system. After each six inches or so I rest, basking in the warmth and relief, letting each part of my body feel its new freedom, past my knee, up to my thigh. There seems to be a particularly tight concentration around my groin that makes it feel all the better when I pull it out. Down my left leg, until my left toes turn warm and free, and up my torso, bringing peace and warmth to my belly and my lower back. At my solar plexus the resistance increases again. I feel the roots pulling on my heart and stop, but only for a moment. "I've gone this far, what the fuck." Feelings of warmth and strength make me weep for joy. I can feel the root tentacles being pulled through my whole body: out it comes, more and more. I am ecstatic as the peace passes up my throat, over my mouth, and through my nose to the top of my head. Ecstasy.

That's what all the rushes of fear and pain were. Just getting free of the shit. Nothing but nothing is going to turn me around. Pain? Fear? Fuck 'em, this shit has got to go. I've seen heaven and nothing's gonna turn me around. What is it that wants to turn me around and make me crawl back into believing all the sham about pain being unavoidable, utopia impossible? I'm a freight train, baby, don't give me no side track, no. I want your main line, baby. Climb aboard the Eden Express. This train, this train is comin' through. THIS TRAIN IS BOUND FOR GLORY.

It was mostly out of politeness I had held off for so long. Not wanting to make other people feel lonely, not wanting to have people look at me funny. I had been convinced that something like the Eden Express existed for some time.

I stopped being polite because the things that had predicated my politeness were simply no longer true. Time was the big thing. We were out of time.

Do Not Go Gentle into That Good Night. Thank God I screamed. I came within an ace of waiting too long but at the last moment I got my shit together and came through in the clutch. What would have happened had I not screamed out I wasn't sure. It would have been the death of something. Maybe just the end of me and a few friends, but maybe the end of the world or worse. But I did scream. I didn't go gentle into that black night, blackly into that good night, or goodly into that gentle night.

"STOP—FREEZE—NOBODY MOVE A MUSCLE. IT'S HAPPENING!" I reached out and grabbed Simon's arm. My eyes were closed. I was in a cold sweat. "DON'T ASK ME HOW I KNOW. THERE ISN'T TIME. JUST DO AS I SAY. I KNOW. THE RAIN HAS STOPPED." It was only fair to give out a few clues, enough so that they would know that I *knew* and do what I said. The rain's stopping definitely had something to do with it.

It might seem strange to tell a roomful of sleeping people to not move a muscle, especially a roomful of sleeping people you didn't know. But it made sense. It made more sense than anything else in my life ever had. It wasn't a night like any other night, or sleep like any other sleep.

Maybe there's not really anything extraordinary going on at all, but then again maybe these feelings are right. In any event, it's best to cover all the bets. If nothing's going on, someone will correct me.

There was nothing to lose by acting and possibly a great deal to lose by not acting. So I acted.

"It's all right, Mark, we're all here. Everything is going to be fine now." I felt my hand being squeezed comfortingly and became aware that I was holding on to someone very hard. It wasn't Simon's voice or Simon's hand. It was Gary Jackson.

"And Mark?" Asking about my namesake.

"Mark's just fine. Don't worry about it." I felt tears of joy running down my face. My eyes were still closed. I was afraid opening them might wreck the magic of the moment. The danger was past, the nightmare over. That Gary was supposed to be in Morocco didn't bother me much. Stranger things had happened in the past few days.

"Boy, it sure got tense there toward the end," I sighed, loosening up a little. "I really got pretty worried.

"And Jessie? Joe? Genie? Tom? Bets? Bea . . . ?" Asking about people from various periods of life.

"Yes, we're all here. Everybody's fine. Don't worry about it, just take it easy, Mark. Everything's going to be fine."

"And Virginia? I want to see Virge. Where's Virginia?" My eyes were still closed. I loved the idea of being in this warm comfy womb with all my friends, everyone I had ever loved. I was going to get to hold and touch and talk to them all in this new wonderful world. I wanted to start with Virginia. We had a lot to say to each other. We had been through so much shit together. And now in this big happy womb we could probably say things to each other we had never been able to say before.

"We don't know where Virginia is, Mark. Don't think about her now." This soured things some. Everyone else seemed to be here, where was she? Had she not made it through the shit-storm apocalypse? Was she a casualty? Were there others?

"What happened to Virginia?" I pleaded.

"We don't know, Mark. It would probably be best if you didn't think about Virginia right now."

"There was so much I wanted to tell her." I was crying.

"There's nothing you can do about it, Mark. Try not to think about her."

"And the war in Vietnam?" I asked, trying valiantly to change the subject and also out of genuine curiosity. I wanted to know how everything had turned out. "And the whole race thing, and pollution, the ecology?"

"Don't worry about it, Mark. None of that stuff really matters now." So all that is done and gone with, I reflected.

"Gee, you know I really took all that stuff seriously."

"I know you did, Mark, but don't worry about it, just relax and get some rest."

I lay back and tried to figure out how to make the best of my situation. The first problem was that I didn't really have a very clear idea of what my situation was, and since no one seemed to want to talk about it I didn't see how I was going to figure it out.

"Mark, this is Stan." I felt someone take my hand.

"Hi, Stan," I said, still not opening my eyes.

"He's been there too. Maybe he can help you," someone said.

"Sure hope so," I said. "I seem to be having trouble adjusting. Can I open my eyes?" Stan, Stan, I thought. Who the hell can Stan be? Stan Getz? If I was in some sort of eternity situation with Getz I might be able to adjust, but I would so much rather have had Coltrane around. But if Stan wanted to talk to me it was better than nothing.

"You can open your eyes if you want," said Stan.

"Sure," I said, trying to believe it as I opened my eyes slowly. I was ready to see almost anything. Angels and pearly gates wouldn't have surprised me, but I was sort of half hoping to find myself in my bedroom in Barnstable. I looked around very cautiously, taking in as much as I could, like a little kid on Christmas morning. Everything was aglow with a soft light, but there was no new bicycle, no mommy, no daddy, not even Gary. Someone had lit a kerosene lamp and a few people were stirring around.

Stan I had never seen before. He had long reddish hair and a beard and was sitting on his haunches holding my hand, completely naked. "Stan understands," I said to myself over and over again.

"What happened?" I asked, putting it as directly as possible.

"We don't know what happened, Mark. All we know is that for a time at least we must try to use less energy, so just try to relax."

I looked at Simon, who was beside me. He was dead. I had killed him. I had drained away all his energy.

"Don't cry," Stan said gently.

Crying was using up energy and if I wasn't careful I would drain away all the energy. Everyone else was perfectly quiet. I looked at Stan pleadingly, sorry for what I had done and not being able to make it right. He quickly looked away from my eyes and I felt even worse, knowing that had our eyes met he might have been killed instantly.

"Don't worry, everything's going to be all right. Is there anything you want?"

"A cup of coffee?" I had no idea of what was possible or impossible, but a cup of hot coffee would sure taste good.

Coffee was something that wasn't grown within several thousand miles of us. It would never be a "natural" part of our lives. Coffee was a product of our exploitive imperialist system. At least I hadn't asked for Coke. It would have been more cool, more peaceful, more soulful to ask for mint tea but I wasn't really interested in mint tea. It was coffee I wanted.

I watched another caveman violently and angrily smashing and splintering wood. I wondered what he was so pissed-off about. That I wanted coffee? That I had woken him up? That I was wasting so much of our limited energy, and all for a cup of coffee?

"It's all right, Stan. I really don't need a cup of coffee."

"If you want a cup of coffee you can have some." I was deeply touched by how much they were willing to sacrifice for me.

"It's really OK, I'll be fine." The woodcutter stopped. Peace came to the room again. "Thanks for everything, Stan." I let go of his hand and closed my eyes again and pulled the sleeping bag over my head.

I would draw deep into myself until I could talk, move around, without hurting anyone. I wasn't going to drain any more precious energy.

It wouldn't have been very hard for me to do without coffee or cars or any of the other things in my life that were the product of so much pain for others. Sure, I had moved out to the farm to grow my own food, make my own house, do without cars, do without so much that was tied up with pain. But maybe if I had done more sooner, maybe if I had trusted and followed more what I knew was right, maybe energy wouldn't be so desperately critical now, maybe Virginia would be here. Maybe.

Like the Jews in concentration camps as the Nazis took out their gold teeth, we all stopped, froze, didn't move a muscle, and were passed over for dead. We all became cells of a larger organism. There were billions of us. One of us would breathe and then another, each holding the spark of life for an instant and then passing it on. Playing a shell game with our precious ember that would bring us all back to full being as soon as the danger had passed. What a brilliant strategy.

But then it dawned on me who I was. I was Curiosity. What a terrible thing to be; Curiosity at the dawn of time. I couldn't help myself, I knew I was going to fuck everything up.

No one else was interested in talking about things. They didn't even know what talking was yet. First I'd get them into language and from there build back all the old shit, just to see if I could do it, just because I was curious. As soon as I showed them about fire, the next thing you know I'd be trying to put a telephone together and fucking around with steam engines. If they had any sense at all they'd kill me now, before I go and wreck everything. But they probably wouldn't have the faintest idea what I was talking about. I'd have to show them how to kill and then it would be too late. They'd be hooked.

I remember things I'd read about Mu—Atlantis. They must have reached this point and then things started all over again in little caves just like this one, where someone screamed in time. How often had things started from scratch again? Was it different every time or always the same? How many ends had I been through? Was I making the same dumb mistakes time after time or was I making some sort of progress?

I couldn't help thinking things that made me want to laugh. Maybe if I had voted in the '68 elections things would have turned out differently. Old rock-and-roll songs drifted through my head.

After what seemed like years if not millennia, people started moving around some. I heard the sounds of someone building a fire and opened my eyes slowly. The sun was up and people were getting dressed. I breathed a huge sigh of relief. The sun had come up and life seemed to have survived. I felt a special warmth flowing through my body. Not because it was that important to save energy any more but just to savor life, I closed my eyes and reveled in it. We had made it.

After a while I felt a hand gently shaking my shoulder. "It's time to get up, Mark." It was Simon's voice. He was all right.

If he had come back to life maybe everybody had come back. Maybe even Virginia was all right. I opened my eyes again and smiled at Simon.

"Everything's OK," I said. Simon smiled. "Thank God that shit is over," I said. Simon nodded and we embraced. It was sure good to be back. Good old Simon. Good old people. Good old sun. Good old planet.

Just about everyone who had spent the night there had already left. One guy came back up to the house and said that our car was blocking his way. "You really from Massachusetts?" he asked. "Yup." "Far out," he said, and Simon and I gathered up our sleeping bags and headed out to the car.

A Cup of Mu Tea. We went to the Marine Inn coffee shop to get a little breakfast. I'll never forget Simon's groan and horrified look when I ordered. "A cup of Mu tea, please." It was exactly the right thing to do.

"Mu tea? I'm not sure we have any of that," the waitress replied. Another customer helped out. "Ain't that just some sort of Chinese tea?" And she brought me a cup of Mu tea. It was probably just some magically transformed Tetley or Lipton.

"Is the tea in the leaves or in the tongue?"

I was trying out the new world and my new self. If I could get a cup of Mu tea in the Marine Inn, that was quite something. I mean, what do you have to have before you say "Miracle"?

How could it be that everything made such perfect sense, that I was thinking so much, so well, feeling so much, so well, seeing so well, hearing so well, knowing so much, so well.

That everything strange that had happened to me in the past few days was all in my head was a possibility but it didn't seem to be very likely. Something very big was happening, and I was figuring it out as I went along.

Part of the confirmation that something really had happened was the price of tobacco. The last time I had been in town a tin of tobacco had cost $1.20 and now it was $1.80. The supermarket was very strange. There were no other customers in there. There didn't seem to be very much left on the shelves. Did money mean anything any more? Did I have to pay for anything or could I just take whatever it was I wanted?

It was very important not to run out of tobacco. I picked up as many tins as I could carry. Smoking was an important reminder of who I was. It was my clock. Cigarettes seemed to keep time. They had a continuity with the real world that I seemed to be losing. As long as I smoked cigarettes I was alive. As far as I knew, dead people didn't smoke cigarettes.

I was walking out of the store with seven or eight big cans of tobacco just as Simon walked in from the bank. He looked upset with me. "Mark, do you really need all that tobacco?"

I felt slightly ashamed and defensive. Simon wasn't a

smoker, how could I expect him to understand? The manager of the supermarket was looking on with disbelief and maybe a little fear.

"Mark, did you pay for these?"

"No, Simon. I figured that if I was supposed to pay for them he would say something," pointing to the manager. He was just staring, not about to interfere. I could have picked up a cash register and he would have just watched. The idea that this wild-eyed kid would just stroll into his store, pick up over ten dollars' worth of tobacco, and walk out without the slightest pretense of hiding the stuff was too much.

Simon talked me into putting most of the tobacco back. I kept one can and some papers and Simon paid for them.

Imil riggle ugle roo. What I would like to know is why no one ever told me there was something like this. What I would like to know is what the fuck is going on.

Skimmy zoo a loop de roo—the problem is what to do? What to do ought to do. I've always thought 'bout what to do and why to do what to do and not to do.

There's naught to do. I always knew there's naught to do—but what to do, ought to do, once you know there's naught to do.

I had hoped that if we could just get to the bank where we had all that money—lubrication to throw at obstacles—it would compensate for my growing inability to deal with things. But money seemed to be cracking up as badly as I was. Prices all screwy. Where is the fucking bankbook? How do I sign my name?

We had always felt vaguely shitty about that money anyway. Capitalism, parents, etc. And to use it now when things were breaking down was obscene.

Simon decided we should switch over to his theoretically more reliable vehicle. He didn't want to drive Car Car and was probably losing faith in my driving. But his car needed some work, so Car Car and I trailed him to the gas station where we said loving good-bys while Simon got his car fixed.

The last day on earth and here we were using blood money
to make some poor slob fix our carburetor instead of spending
his last day with people he loved.

But there were signs that it was all right. It even seemed at
times that people were dying gladly to be able to make some
contribution to our progress. Knowing winks. Light rays
through the clouds. An old guy in a gas station cashed an old
crumpled-up traveler's check I found in my wallet without
asking for any identification or even checking my feeble attempt to remember my signature.

"Simon, let's go back to the farm." I was in tears about
what people were doing for us. I could do without using the
precious last bit of gasoline. I could do without getting a place
on the last ferry. I could die without seeing Virginia or my
family.

But somehow my willingness to turn back was part of what
made me such a good carrier of everyone's hopes and fears. It
seemed they all wanted me to be them. I did the best I could,
packing up all their hopes and fears, bruising and pushing
them out of shape as little as possible, expecting that somewhere up the line I would run into a better messenger, for
whom I would die and pass on all my gathered hopes and
fears.

So we kept moving toward Vancouver. I think the basic
idea in both our minds was still to find Virginia and hope that
that would somehow straighten everything out. I also thought
that I had become a hydrogen bomb and that someone in
Vancouver could defuse me or fly me to New York or that
Simon and I had somehow become capable of traveling backward in time and were going to go back and straighten out
the things that were about to result in the end of everything
or . . . or . . . Simon was also thinking that in Vancouver
he'd have a lot more help managing me, and that from there
we could get hold of my parents. Neither of us had had any
practice with what was going on and were just stumbling
along. Vancouver seemed the best direction to stumble toward.

On the way to the ferry, "Mark, you know there's been an earthquake in California?"

"Yes, I know that, Simon."

Did I know that? I probably would have answered yes to almost anything anybody asked me if I knew. Almost everything seemed like something I knew. That it was somehow connected to my scream the night before was obvious. That Virginia had been killed in it was also obvious. Simon apparently didn't know that yet or was trying to keep it from me.

How did Simon know about the earthquake? Was he beginning to be able to know things in my way too?

I was in the land of light without shadows and Simon was in some sort of twilight. He was the link between me and the darkness. I couldn't deal with the darkness so Simon was in charge of all that. I was afraid that if he caught on to too much then he wouldn't be able to deal with the darkness either and then someone from the darkness might do something bad to both of us. Simon had to find someone else and bring him into the twilight before he could come into the light. I hoped he understood that.

There were lots of people back there whom I loved, lots of people I wanted to have with me in the land of light, and if I lost Simon there would be no way for me to get back to them or for them to get to me.

We got to the ferry landing in plenty of time. There was only one car ahead of us, a beat-up station wagon with a middle-aged man and a little girl. I wondered if they were traveling backward in time too, but most of the time I spent clutching my knees to my chest, trying to keep my body from turning into light and trying to make the ferry come and trying trying trying.

Things were happening faster and heavier than ever. Every moment an odyssey. I was beating off wave after wave of screaming flesh-tearing and constantly trying to make Simon feel that everything was OK.

I'd feel unbearably hot and sweaty and Simon would say he

felt cold. Ten minutes later the situation would reverse. After fighting off the most powerful rush yet and just lying back, completely exhausted, trying to get my breath, I glanced over at Simon. He was looking at me with utter bewilderment.

"You know, Mark, this is certainly turning into a strange trip."

"You ought to see it from here, Simon. You ought to see it from here."

I hoped that all the terrors were simply a matter of earning a place on the ferry, that God or whoever simply didn't want me in the Powell River area. But once we were on, the shit didn't stop, it just got worse. Maybe the next ferry or getting to Vancouver would do the trick, but I was fast losing hope that whatever was going on was going to have a nice simple answer.

"You know, Mark, this whole thing is really giving me a whole new outlook on mental illness."

"Yes, I expect it would." If Simon wanted to think that that was the explanation for what was going on, it was fine with me. Whatever model he wanted to use was fine.

"You know, I don't think I ever really understood it very well before. This puts a whole new light on it."

"Doesn't it? Even though I worked in the hospital and have dealt with it and thought about it a lot, I never really caught on before."

"It's giving me a whole new respect."

"It's been a very well-kept secret. No one talks about it at all. It makes sex and drugs look like apple pie."

That crazy people were into something very real, some sort of truth, was not a very original thought. The only thing that had kept me out of the nut house till now was a certain form of denseness and/or cowardice. That the truth was what was driving me nuts, followed.

In my more lucid moments I realized that insanity was a fairly reasonable explanation for what was happening to me. The problem was that it wasn't useful information. Realizing

I was crazy didn't make the crazy stuff stop happening. Nor did it give me any clues about what I should do next.

For me to have sat around calling the crazy stuff "crazy" would have been the most wasteful, unimaginative thing I could have done. There were so many much better things to do with it. Like acid revelations, some of it now looks trivial or meaningless, but much of it remains as valuable to me now as it was then.

The trouble was that there was much too much, much too fast. A lifetime course in sexuality crammed into five minutes, followed immediately by all of Russian literature and a career as a prizefighter, playing in stereo with an exhaustive study of medieval imagery related to theories of higher math. No five minutes to get from class to class, let alone evenings to think it over. What I suspect about most of the stuff I've thrown out as nonsense is that if things had gone a little slower, if I had had time to copy over my notes and get the right perspective on it, those things too would have been important.

I was thrilled to be picking up so much so fast, but always in the back of my mind was the ominous: Something's trying to fill me in on everything at once. There must not be much time.

The Voices. Testing one, two, testing one. Checking out the circuits: "What hath God wrought. Yip di mina di zonda za da boom di yaidi yoohoo."

By this time the voices had gotten very clear.

At first I'd had to strain to hear or understand them. They were soft and working with some pretty tricky codes. Snap-crackle-pops, the sound of the wind with blinking lights and horns for punctuation. I broke the code and somehow was able to internalize it to the point where it was just like hearing words. In the beginning it seemed mostly nonsense, but as things went along they made more and more sense. Once you hear the voices, you realize they've always been there. It's just a matter of being tuned to them.

The voices weren't much fun in the beginning. Part of it

was simply my being uncomfortable about hearing voices no matter what they had to say, but the early voices were mostly bearers of bad news. Besides, they didn't seem to like me much and there was no way I could talk back to them. Those were very one-sided conversations.

But later the voices could be very pleasant. They'd often be the voice of someone I loved, and even if they weren't, I could talk too, asking questions about this or that and getting reasonable answers. There were very important messages that had to get through somehow. More orthodox channels like phone and mail had broken down.

The blanks were a lot like the voices: it's hard to say exactly when they started. At first there'd be only an instant or two I couldn't account for. Later I'd be missing whole days. I'd feel myself going away and then I'd feel myself coming back. I had no way to gauge how much time passed during the blanks. When I came out of them anybody could have told me anything. I wouldn't necessarily have believed it but there was no way I could count it out either.

Sometimes when I got back from my little cosmic jaunts it looked like no time at all had passed in my absence, but so much had happened to me that I felt I must have managed to cram a year or more into an instant of everyone else's time. Other times when I came back it was as if I had been in some sort of suspended animation. Years had passed for everyone but me. One way or the other I was out of step. That much was clear.

I don't understand. I don't understand what it is that I don't understand. Whatever it is, it's something I have never understood. I don't understand why it's all of a sudden so important that I don't understand.

I didn't exactly lose contact with objective reality. There was just so much more going on.

Had someone asked me about what was going on, I would have had quite a bit of trouble taking the questions seriously and even more trouble getting my voice and words to work right. I would have been much more interested in their clothes or face than the questions, and would have thought they were really asking something much deeper. I was on my way to Vancouver, and knew it most of the time, but if asked where I was, that would have been a long way down the line of answers that came to mind.

I can probably tell you as much or more about what really went on those days than lots of people who were sane: the comings and goings of people, the weather, what was on the news, what we ate, what records were played, what was said. My focus was a bit bizarre. I could do portraits of people who were walking down the street. I remembered license numbers of cars we were following coming into Vancouver. We paid $3.57 for gas. The air machine made eighteen dings while we were there.

We arrived in Vancouver in the late afternoon. At that point I knew very clearly that the world was ending and that it was my fault. The only hope was for me to get out of the car and drown myself in the harbor. But somehow in downtown rush-hour traffic Simon managed to stop me and the voices seemed very disappointed with me for not trying harder. I had really really really fucked up big big big. I was sure that the next stop was hell and even more sure that I deserved it.

The next stop was really the Stevens Street apartment, where I had said good-by to Virginia only two weeks before though it seemed very much like lifetimes. Everyone but Sankara was out. Sankara seemed to be looking at us like we were ghosts, but he was trying to be cool about it. I muttered something about having to lie down and went into one of the bedrooms and lay down, trying very hard to get some sort of grip on myself.

I spent the next few hours desperately trying to figure out what was happening to me and how to clue Sankara in on it. I'd come up with something that seemed right, get up and go into the living room, where Simon and Sankara were talking, and try to explain everything. Sankara would just say, "Sure, far out, that's cool." I obviously wasn't putting it right, so I'd go back to the bedroom and try again.

Somewhere in there Sy and André came home and I tried to explain it to them too. They had similar reactions. I became more and more alarmed at how these people could go on like nothing out of the ordinary was happening.

"You know you're in hell, don't you?" The voices said that a lot.

"All I know is that I don't like it much."

"You know Virginia's dead. You know your father's dead. You know the world is ending. You know you're dead. You know you've killed a lot of people. You know you're responsible for the California earthquake, the death of the planet. You know you have a mission. You know you're the messiah."

"I know I feel that way. I know I think that might be so. But I'll be damned if I'll take my word for it. People think a lot of screwy things."

Astral Sex. What can I tell you about astral sex? There was a lot of it and a little goes a long way. I remember thinking at the time that if nothing remotely sexual ever happened to me again I'd have no grounds for complaint.

Like lots of what I ran into in my strange journey, it seemed like compensation. For one reason or another sex as I had known it was no longer possible. For the best for all concerned, men and women weren't going to be allowed to see each other any more. I had some cosmic clap that had to be quarantined. I was going backward in time and didn't have a body any more. I couldn't be unfaithful to Virginia or she'd kill herself. I couldn't make love to Virginia or the world would end. So for compensation, severance pay, or whatever, I got astral sex.

Like all the other compensations for the various disabilities I suffered, it was more than a fair deal. I wondered how I had ever worked up much enthusiasm about regular sex.

I was electric with sexuality. Breathing gave me orgasm

upon orgasm. I can't begin to describe what dancing with angels was like. Occasionally the puritan in me would try to worry about having to pay for this some day, but the pleasure was so all-engulfing there was very little room for second thoughts.

I had earthly sexuality too, but like the rest of my earthly life it had become twisted, disjointed, and horrifying. My penis would seem monstrously huge. I'd get hard-ons that wouldn't go away. I'd try to masturbate to defuse my earthly sexuality but couldn't come. I feared that something was trying to turn me into a homosexual. I feared that I was turning Simon into a homosexual and teasing him horribly. There were no nice warm sex feelings, just fear and exploitation.

It's possible that these feeling represented the breakthrough of repressed homosexuality that's terribly clinically significant, but I have my doubts. Heterosexuality was no less threatening to me than homosexuality. I remember telling a voice that seemed to be Virginia, "Sure I can see how it would be frightening being a woman. Penetration, violation, invasion. It would terrify the hell out of me. But to tell you the truth, every time I put it in I was never all that sure I'd get it back. That was scary as hell too."

While I had never had homosexual relations, I had felt physical attraction to men and recognized as much without getting upset about it. I was also attracted to a lot of women I never slept with. My sex life with Virginia was hardly the greatest and represented a general sexual repression, but I can't help thinking that those who blame sexual problems for mental illness are putting the cart before the horse. It would be foolish to deny that sex affects frame of mind but even more foolish to overlook that one's sex life is also, if not more, a consequence of one's frame of mind. Food was horrible to me too, but I have yet to hear anyone say that schizophrenia is a repressed fear of food.

Headlines. "California Earthquake."
The voices. "It's all right, Mark. Just don't do it again."

"I don't know if I can help it!" I cried. "It's such a bitch."
"It's the only way. Only someone like you could do it. Only someone who wanted so badly to never hurt anyone would ever find the key. It's poetry. If you don't understand it now, maybe you will later. Maybe it's the way to hurt the least number of people."

"Sometimes you voices sound a lot like Nixon. I promised I'd never hurt anyone. Please put me somewhere where I can't hurt anyone. Please."

Simon was perfect. The farm was perfect. Virginia was perfect. My mother was perfect. My father was perfect. I was perfect. Lucky Strikes were perfect. The switch to MacDonald's Export and then settling in on Sunkist and Sportsman tobacco was perfect. All the things that were green couldn't have been otherwise. The radio was playing perfect songs. Everything everyone said was perfect. Everything came together just right.

Perfectly awful. Perfectly wonderful. Heaven. Hell. The intention changed, the next effect changed, but never the awesome symmetry, the dazzling perfection of it.

The further down the road I went, the more dazzling the perfection and symmetry. I was riding an exponential curve. I reached critical mass.

It started when I was a little kid. The all-absorbing rush of seeing something just right. Just-right Mommy things, just-right Daddy things, round things, red things, tree things, food things. And they acted like seed crystals. One just-right red thing led to more and more and the crystals grew and grew. And the bigger they were, the more things fit and the faster they grew. These ever growing crystalline perfections were every bit as much a part of me as my arms and legs and infinitely more precious.

Now the crystals were growing at a fantastic rate and all piling into each other. The Bible, concrete poets, and nuclear physics crystals collided, made perfect sense, and became one. The Simon crystal piled into the Virginia crystal into the Zeke crystal ad infinitum. It was like a monster seventy-five-car accident on the New Jersey Turnpike in heavy fog. And they all made such dazzling beautiful sense together. No more dry spells. No missing links. Punctuation became more and more difficult and then just plain silly.

When we got to the Stevens Street apartment raw materials still mattered some. Toward the end a Donald Duck comic book, *War and Peace,* a Ravi Shankar album, the weather, my father, a hockey game on TV, all became interchangeable parts.

There was an international cast. André from France, Sankara from India. Being the only nonwhite, he had to fill in for Puerto Ricans, blacks, Chicanos, American Indians, etc. It was a heavy load but he did pretty well with it.

There were two Jews, which was useful. "Sunshine Movers" came in handy. There was a pretty good collection of records and a fair-to-middling library. Unfortunately, all they had for musical instruments was a second-rate guitar and a couple of handmade bamboo flutes that, while being very groovy, didn't play for shit.

No non-Swarthmore people and no women, which made things a bit tricky, but like I said, the raw materials mattered less and less.

What Was Really Going On. All I was catching was itty-bitty snatches. A word here, a sentence there. A funny smell, a funny face. Now and then a whole vignette. Putting it together was like trying to make a movie from a bunch of slides that had nothing to do with each other.

Why is Simon turning green? Why is Sy beating me up? What's that awful smell? Why is André winking at me? Why won't they let me go outside? What the fuck is going on?

What was going on was several people dealing as best they could with a very difficult, unfamiliar situation: a friend gone psychotic.

Apparently suffering a great deal. Incoherent most of the time. Incapable of understanding anything said to him. Moaning, screaming, smashing things. Completely unpredictable. And the cherry on the whole show—he doesn't sleep. Some six-day house guest.

What was really going on was Simon's job. I had other things to do. But when I did manage to check in, that I was very different from other people and being treated very strangely, and in a great deal of physical pain and not hearing, seeing, smelling, tasting, walking, or talking right, was hardly delusional.

What could they do? Putting someone in a nut house isn't a nice thing to do to someone. There are lots of pressures in the hip community that make that sort of decision even harder to come to than normally. Doctors don't know anything, mental hospitals are repressive, fascist, etc. Hippies are supposed to be able to take care of their own. "Schizophrenia is a sane response to an insane society." "Mental illness is a myth." The Sanskrit word for crazy means touched by the gods.

I vaguely remember Sy's threatening me. "If you don't shut up we'll have to put you in a nut house. You've been yelling all night." I laughed. "Fine hippie, fine revolutionary, fine peace-love brother you turned out to be."

It was a cosmic barroom brawl. Like most it had something to do with religion. My team was fighting for minority plank No. 234: Everyone gets saved. Fighting against notions of chosen people. Trying to convince everyone that no one really knew much. For sure no one had come even close to putting it all together. So the best we could do was present a united front of ignorance rather than our pathetic fragmented pretensions.

I was the clock. As long as I could keep breathing, there was still time. We were badly behind and needed all the time we could get. One of our key strategies was to find out what everyone knew or thought they knew and then publish-broadcast-ESP it to everyone. And all the time thinking that what I was thinking was absurd and very unlikely but a bet that had to be covered.

Suddenly Sy was shaking me by the shoulders, looking very

unfriendly. He must have been frustrated to the point of tears.

Fuck shit if my crazy hunch didn't turn out to be right. Here's a Jew who wants to stop the clock. Well, if it comes down to one on one, me vs. Sy, no sweat. I'm not in the greatest shape but he couldn't do much damage. Besides, wasn't he into pacifism, peace-love, etc. ?

Boomzapplewomp! Wow! Where the hell did he learn how to throw a punch? I never saw it coming, which didn't mean that much. There was lots of stuff I wasn't seeing. He was slugging my chest. It was hard to tell the heartbeats from the punches. It all just rolled together. I was having a heart attack. Sy hit me a few more times. I went down hard.

Sy was making me get up. Someone had slashed my temples with razors. There was blood. Something had something to do with Maharishi, with my old girl friend, Betsy, in Houston with Harry Reasoner and mission control and gay bars, and watching on TV something called Operation Jack-in-the-Box battling against some acid-freak mutant from the year two thousand, into time travel, trying to have things his way. I wasn't sure which side he was on, but he had a thing about black people and electroshock and Thomas Edison and heroin and being wired to the fact that my father, besides being wanted by Israeli zealots, wasn't able to give up smoking. And someone making me hold on to the refrigerator door handle and not being able to move a muscle. And André, where the hell were those French when you needed them, came in saying something about Paris burning and telling Sy to let up on me and that he'd be in pretty rough shape too if he'd had my dose of bad news. And I cried and cried and cried, begging Sy to just give me a little time. Maybe if I had paid more attention to Bucky Fuller. "I'll adjust better. Please, another chance. I'll pay better attention. Please, another chance."

After a while a reasonable routine for dealing with me was worked out. A twenty-four-hour watch was set, sharp and dangerous objects were put away, and things calmed down a little. There was some talk about hospitals but Simon held fast to his promise to me. There was a lot of telephoning. The Barnstable house, which was the only number I could remember, still never answered. Simon somehow managed to get my sister Edie in N.Y.C. on the line.

"Mark?"

"Don't worry, Edie, I won't tell them a thing," and I slammed the receiver down.

Many hours were taken up trying to decode my ravings, in hopes that if they knew more about what was going on in my mind they could snap me out of it. Most of the time I was honestly trying to be as informative and straightforward as possible, but there was so much to tell and things kept getting more and more confusing and it was so hard to understand what they were saying or make my own voice and words act right. But things seemed to be working out all right.

Hello. I am here. I am Mark Vonnegut and all that that entails. That's Simon there and Sy there and André there and Sankara there. We all went to Swarthmore. We are in Vancouver, British Columbia, Canada. I can remember lots of things. I can think about things. I can understand what people are saying and they can understand what I am saying.

It never lasts very long. It's lasting less and less. I keep going away. It keeps getting harder and harder to come back. I stop being Mark Vonnegut. Simon stops being Simon and so on. I stop being able to remember things, think about things, or understand what people say. It stops being Vancouver, British Columbia, Canada. I get swept away. I keep making it back, but it's getting tougher and tougher.

In a funny way it's almost fun, having everything be so fucked up and managing to adjust. I guess you might say I'm proud. Proud of me, proud of my friends for managing to deal with this thing so well. For most people this would be the end of the world. They'd panic, their friends would panic. Things would get trampled in the stampede. But we've kept our heads, made the necessary allowances, and can just ride this thing out.

I'm pretty much just putting in time waiting for this cloud to blow over. Waiting for something to come along to make some sense out of all this. Killing time, waiting for some sort of cavalry to come over the hill. There's really not an awful lot I can do but wait. As long as there's no panic, we can hold out damn near forever.

And Then Along Came Warren. Actually we went to see him. Warren was a holy man of sorts who was supposed to drive the evil demons out of me or maybe just talk me down or at least come up with some explanation for what was wrong with me. The Stevens Street folk and Simon were getting desperate.

We first heard about Warren from Luke. Luke was wandering around the Kootenays feeling very untogether. One day he came across this old man who, as Luke put it, was living the most together, organic, spiritual life he had ever seen. It was Warren. Vibes happened and something like a guru-disciple relationship went on for a few weeks. Luke credited Warren with having helped him a great deal. All this had taken place a year or so ago.

Then we heard from Sankara, André, and Sy that they had run into a really far-out old man, long white hair, flowing white beard. He did Ching reading, numerology, and other things and had spiritual powers of some sort. They were getting more and more into him.

Sure enough, it was Warren. I had had lots of opportunities to go see Warren but always managed to pass them up. Maybe if I had met him earlier it would have helped lessen the shock of our first encounter.

Now there was lots of talk about Warren and all his spiritual gifts, wisdom, and powers, and that he probably knew all about whatever had gone wrong with me. I dreaded going to see him or having him come to see me. I'd never gotten on very well with guru types and was perfectly happy with the adjustments that had been made for my disabilities. Killing time till the cloud blew over. But maybe the cloud wasn't going to blow over until I faced Warren. Maybe Warren was in charge of the cloud.

I don't know how many of us went. I don't remember how we got there. I don't even remember whether I knew we were going to see Warren.

The door was opened by this white-haired, white-bearded man, skinny as a rail, with sunken raving eyes and a huge hook nose, in a white-robe, holy-man outfit.

"Welcome to my temple."

Lots of white, incense, burning candles, little altars here and there, a mishmash of religious symbols and objects. We were supposed to sit on cushions on the floor. He had a chair.

I can't believe that I and these other people here are really sitting on cushions in front of this guy doing a white-robe bit in such a rinkydink put-up job of a temple.

Gurus as a group are generally a kindly lot. But there was noting gentle or kindly about Warren in his appearance or manner. His face and the face that had engulfed me some weeks earlier had a lot in common.

I don't remember much of what was said. I blocked it out at the time: Whatever else happens here, don't let the joker trick you into saying the Lord's prayer backward. A limited objective, you might say, but it seemed the most I could handle at the time and when I left I wasn't even sure I had managed to achieve that.

"Look, sweetheart, I don't give a shit what you say."

"OK, pops, snap-fizzle-crack-pop. Sure, War."

Nothing pissed Warren off more than my calling him War, but I didn't dig his calling me sweetheart much so I figured we were even, at least on that score.

Disbelief, naked terror, frustration, towering rage. This can't be happening. I have to sit here and take this shit? I was furious at Simon. I had put him in charge of reality and he had really botched it. Judas? Was this what he had been up to all along? To deliver me into the hands of War? All that feigned fuzziness, leading me along? What was in it for him?

Could I come up with a counteroffer? He wouldn't look at me. He had the look of a guilty child.

From not eating for quite a while I had developed a facial tic to go along with the general shakiness of my whole body. I was confused, upset, scared. Warren did everything he could to amplify all this. He challenged me to try to stop the tic in my face. He seemed to be trying to impress upon me the fact that he and not I was in control of my body.

"You are dust dust dust. You will die and nothing will remain." True enough, but not really what I needed to hear at the time.

Someone from the Stevens Street apartment had briefed him about me. He used the information as if he had just divined it clairvoyantly.

"You had a girl. She is not with you now."

War was hooked on notions of spiritual power, satanic or angelic didn't make much difference to him. If I had had an inclination to believe that maybe he was somehow hypnotizing me or in control of my heartbeat or an important part of some cosmic plot—candy to a baby, dope to an addict. He did everything to expand and amplify such notions.

He talked about earthquakes and other cataclysmic events. "All this will pass away. There will be nothing left. Nothing."

He kept changing subjects so often or jumbling them all together that it was hard to keep anything straight.

"Do you see the way the light comes through the curtains? Mountains will crumble into the sea. You had a girl but you didn't love her, all you wanted to do was fuck her. I have the mayor in my pocket. I know the Koran backwards and forwards. The forests are burning out of control. The Kennedys will all be dust . . ."

There was a long, long recital of my sins and transgressions. Lust was the biggie. Maybe he was going to straighten everything out by slipping me a whomping dose of acid. There was a direct link between my fuck-ups and mountains crumbling, forests burning, and all of human suffering.

Everything was dying outside. The earth was passing away.

Like the tic in my face, it was something I could do nothing about. The only safe place was in Warren's rinkydink temple. It was like what happened when Atlantis sank, the end of the land of Mu. I had a feeling Warren and I had both been there and had more or less the same conversation. It would probably happen again at the next apocalypse. What a bore.

I looked around the room. No women and no blacks. A petty point, I suppose.

Warren was real. I wasn't hallucinating him. The other people were acknowledging him as real. If Warren was real, anything was possible. His antics made my hallucinations pretty pale. The voices were the soul of rationality, salt-of-the-earth common sense, next to what he was saying. My wildest thoughts suddenly seemed much too conservative to deal with what was really happening.

If I had been difficult to deal with before Warren, it was nothing compared to what I became afterward. A nuisance turned menace. There was indeed something very heavy and of vast proportions going on. All those thoughts, the voices and the visions, weren't just ways to while away the time, things that I might some day turn into short stories. There was, in fact, a danger, and I was an important player in whatever was being played out.

A clinical psychologist's view of the situation might be that before Warren got into the act I was not actively suicidal or combative. Afterward I was. My paranoia, previously vague and intermittent, almost playful, became full-time focused and anything but playful.

Paranoia was the best way to deal with my situation, the most hopeful way to make any sense of the things that were happening to me. If there was no sense to what was happening, no intention, malignant or benign, then there was no hope. Would you rather be chased by a pack of wild dogs that were hungry or a pack of dogs that had a master who could, if he wanted to, call them off?

* * *

Warren himself was hauled off to the nut house a few weeks after I was. As I found out later, it wasn't his first such trip. An interesting footnote to the whole thing is that he was picked up by the cops from the lawn in front of the Stevens Street apartment. The diagnosis: paranoid schizophrenic. A couple of weeks after that, a freak wandered in off the street claiming that God had led him there. He wrote poetry all over the wall and had busted out of a nut house somewhere in Ontario. I don't know what it was about the Stevens Street apartment, but the odds of such a chain of events says something.

Suicide. The twenty-four-hour watch system broke down from time to time. I remember coming out of a long blank during which I had made love to every living thing, ingested gallons of every poison known to man, and called the devil's bluff in a game a lot like seven-card stud in an end-of-the-world bacchanal. I was still moving but Simon and everyone else was out cold. I had relived the history of man and it was mostly ugly, brutal, and macho. My dead grandfather was congratulating me on winning. I was the toughest bastard who had ever lived and my forefathers were very proud of me.

I got up and went into the bathroom. The mirror in there was the best way to broadcast back to planet earth.

"First I'd like to thank all the billions of people, animals, and plants who made this possible."

Looking in the mirror I could see that my body had become a composite of all bodies. Half my face was Asian, an arm and a leg were black. But it was more subtle than that. Everything that had ever lived had contributed their best cell to make what I now called me.

I tried to open the bathroom door but it wouldn't budge, and I finally understood what I had to do. My life had been spiraling toward this place and moment, pulled closer and closer to the vortex, and now I was there. I cheerfully drew myself a nice hot tub, found the razor blades they hadn't hidden very well and a gallon jug of Clorox. I wasn't unhappy or bitter, I was humming tunes from "My Fair Lady." I thought it would be lots of fun to see if I really could kill myself, but Simon interrupted my little party before I could decide whether it would be better to slash my wrists and then drink the Clorox or vice versa.

At other times suicidal longings came from desperate unhappiness, but everything was so confused I couldn't do a decent job of it. I'd become convinced that something like sitting in a certain chair, looking crosseyed at a psychedelic poster while I chanted Om and clicked my heels together, would do the trick. It became very hard for me to tell when I was committing suicide and when I wasn't.

I had thought a fair amount about suicide before I went nuts. It was often in connection with thinking about what sort of positive move I could make toward solving the problems of the world. The only way out of the mess the world was in that I could see was to have fewer people. Maybe killing myself and thereby making one less mouth to feed, one less body to clothe, one less excuse for the *New York Times* to kill trees, would do more good than anything else.

I believe now that if I placed a twelve-gauge shotgun in my mouth and pulled the trigger, I would cease to have consciousness. I find it a comforting belief. Much of the terror of then was that I had done that or the equivalent and it hadn't worked.

Before the crackup, suicidal impulses had been prodded by my mortality: Since some day, why not now? But suicide now sprang from desperate fear of immortality. I kept dying and maintaining some form of consciousness.

Down from one fifty-five to about one twenty-five pounds, deaf, dumb, and blind, convulsing in my own puke, shit, and piss. If something wanted me to suffer, how much more could they want? If there was a finite amount of suffering in the world, I was sparing someone somewhere something. I was a first-rate safety valve.

I don't pretend to know any more than anyone else about what happens after death, but if there is such a thing as hell and it's anything like some of the things I went through when I was nuts, and you can avoid it by doing things as pretty as not coveting your neighbor's ass, by all means, DO NOT COVET YOUR NEIGHBOR'S ASS.

At some point I gave up clothing. It was just too sticky and confining, almost like drowning. No clothes would have maybe been OK if I hadn't taken it into my head to make a break for it. André and Simon tackled me before I got very far, but a neighbor saw me and told them if he saw me anywhere near his kids, he'd shoot me. Other neighbors were going to call the cops about all the noise I was making, but the Sunshine Boys always managed to calm them down. Somewhere in there I threw a huge rock through the living-room picture window.

Gradually it became clear even to Simon that they might have to put me in a hospital, if only to save their own sanity.

Tea Party. Twelve days without food or sleep, twelve very active days, hadn't done wonders for my physique. Even when my eyes were seeing fairly straight, I had a hard time recognizing myself in the mirror. I looked a lot like pictures of refugees from Hitler's concentration camps. I wasn't as alarmed by the weight loss as amazed and curious. But there were so many amazing curious things happening that I didn't spend much time on it.

My friends were alarmed. Mental illness being a myth and schiz a sane response to an insane world was all well and good, but this kid's about to starve to death.

As we found out later, death by starvation wasn't a far-fetched possibility. According to doctors at the hospital, another week or two would have done the trick. In the good old pretranquilizer days a fair number of schizies went that way. A few still do. Your brain, only about 2 percent of your body weight, consumes 20 percent of your energy. No one's brain is moving like a schizophrenic's, not to mention the calories burned running amuck. Stop eating, make it a twenty-four-hour, no-time-out day, and you've got one hell of a quick weight-loss program.

How to get some food into Mark? Their opening ploys were simple enough. Cook food for everyone, give me a plate too, and make like it was a normal meal. The funny thing was how uninterested they were in their own food. All I had to do was shift my weight slightly or lean forward, all eyes would rivet on me and my plate. I teased them some. Pick up the fork, get a little rice on it, start bringing it toward my mouth (you could have heard a pin drop), drop the fork back on my plate, and roll on the floor laughing. It was just too damn funny. Besides, I knew full well that thousands of Bengalis bit the dust for every bite I took. Besides, there wasn't much point in eating when I wasn't really hungry.

Having everyone so eager to have me eat might have very logically led to thoughts of poison, but it didn't. Even though it smelled a little strange, I knew it was real food. To have eaten it would have proved I was just another jerk raving his brains out, that the world was unsavable, that humanity had no class. Explaining how would take a lot more space than it's worth. Take my word, it was crystal clear.

Later, when I did feel sure they were poisoning me, I hummed down my tea without a second thought. Refusing the poison would have been exactly like accepting the food.

Since the communal dinners were such a flop, they tried a few more things and eventually arrived at the tea party. The tea parties were anything but casual. They were ceremonial rituals. Everyone had his assigned place. The furniture was arranged just so. Seven yellow candles, no electric lights. I sat dead center on the big couch in my sheet, which was the most they had been able to get me to go along with by way of clothing for some time, Simon on my right, Sankara on my left. Sy and André had the seats on either side of the couch. The tea consisted of one huge mug placed in front of me. After a bit of ceremonial rambling I'd gulp down the tea and spit back the last swallow, which was then passed around and theoretically drunk by the others.

That the tea tasted a bit strange wasn't wholly attributable to my disordered perceptions. It was loaded with vitamins, protein concentrate, brewer's yeast, and anything else they could think of. My sense of taste was as badly screwed up as all my other senses, which had a lot to do with my giving up food in the first place and is also why so many schizies think they're being poisoned. I don't care how much you trust the people around you, you trust your own senses more. It sure don't taste like tomato juice.

I was very grateful that they were poisoning me. As usual, I was looking at things in more than one way, but I couldn't see anything but good coming from it. First, I had reached the point where whenever I could think straight enough to want anything, I wanted to die. They were putting me out of my misery.

Second (a bit more complicated), at each tea party they concocted a new and yet more deadly poison. Each segment of humanity mixed up what to them was "poison" and flew it into Vancouver. If I drank it and survived they'd come over to our side, they'd believe that pain and fear were unnecessary, that nothing was poisonous. Some of the poisons were of the pedestrian sort, like cyanide and arsenic, but more often I was drinking distilled hatred and guilt, racism, greed, and the like. My body might be useless in terms of the things I wanted to do with it, but it had been transformed into a filter through which all the poisons of the Earth could pass and come out sweet and pure as spring water.

This of course was all beside the point to my friends. They were just grateful to have stumbled on a way to get some nutrients into a starving friend.

Father. "Good night, sweet prince, whoever you were or thought you were. Please let me go, Mark." Dad.

Of all the awful news I was dealing with, Virge's death in the earthquake, impending nuclear holocaust, my father's suicide hit me hardest. None of my friends came right out and told me. Things hadn't exactly been going my way and it looked like I'd pretty much had my quota of news. But I knew.

From as early as I was old enough to worry about such things I had worried about his either drinking himself to death or blowing his brains out. He had hinted at it fairly broadly from time to time. Sometimes I thought the only thing holding him back was fear of how it would affect me. "Sons of suicides find life lacking . . ."—Rosewater.

Being still able to talk with him took some of the sting away. He actually seemed pretty cheerful. Maybe he had somehow driven me nuts just so he could say good-by and explain a lot of things he hadn't been able to before.

"I'm sorry about this, Mark, but think how hard it would be for me to resist this sort of thing. I just wanted to dance with you once before I left."

> How can it be true
> That I'm talking to you
> In a way so like never before
>
> It's a trick
> It's a snap
> Someone saw through the crap
> We're in a whole nother ball game
>
> I'm calling on you
> With a Jewish Hindu
> I forgot to use the phone
>
> There's nothing to do
> The shit's hit the fan
> Would you rather waltz or cancan?
>
> I don't understand
> How I'm holding your hand
> But it sure beats being alone

I cheated I lied
Found what's inside
I broke all the rules
Used illegal tools
It should have been done long before

I was always convinced
That my words should be minced
But now it seems things have changed
The thought that it matters
Gives my heart patters
Who's trying to tell me it's so?
That there's something to gain?

From this ass-busting pain
Is a thought I'd rather not think
That the world could be saved
By the terrors I've braved
Is worse than the terrors I've braved

I finally said fuck it
I don't want to buck it
I'm tired of being alone

We had some more substantive talks, mostly about World
War II for some reason, but most of it was dancing and giggling. It was lots of fun.

Even then, a few days away from death by starvation, having zilch earthly control and quite a bit of earthly pain, lots of
very nice things were happening. I could hallucinate my saxophone and any side men I wanted. Coltrane, Philly Joe, Can-
nonball, Paul Chambers, Bill Evans, and I whiled away many
an hour with the most nectar-sweet, hard-ass-funky music
ever. I did some solo stuff so beautiful I couldn't stop crying.
Monk and I funked out some lovely duets. Dylan dropped in
one day, Mose Allison the next. With them I just lay back and
listened.

And it wasn't just music and musicians. Poets, painters, writers, historical figures, movie stars, old friends. Some I invited, some showed up all on their own.

Pain and anguish was all that came from trying to maintain contact with the world as I had known it, a world I was no longer able to do anything or be anything in, a world where Virginia and my father were dead and all sorts of other awful things were happening. The nice thing happened when I just gave up on all that.

Time to Go. My father and others had wanted to tell me but things moved too fast. There was no way to get word to me through normal channels, but somehow I had caught on. Not fully maybe, but enough.

One big clue was a line in my father's last letter to me. He was talking about his teaching at Harvard and how he was giving it up. "At least it gave me a chance to get to know people who are at home on Earth." If he wasn't at home on Earth, then where was he at home? Was I too not really of the Earth? Did he owe allegiance to some other place? In the crunch, would he sell Earth down the river? Was I going to have to choose between Earth and my father?

The overall tone of the letter was apologetic. His overall tone for the past couple of years had been apologetic. What was he apologizing for? He knew I didn't dig his New York City fame and fortune bit and the shit he was putting Mother through. He was always saying he had been a not so hot father, which was absurd. But there seemed to be something else he was apologizing for. Something much bigger.

He and some of the other voices kept trying to get me to curse him. There were numerous indications that that would make things a lot easier for me, but I couldn't get into it. There's a Thoreau quote I like: "No man ever profited by cursing his father, no matter how much a curse his father was to him." And my father has been anything but a curse to me.

It was time for everyone who wasn't really at home on Earth to split. If only we could get the hell out of the way and let things take their course. We were nuns milling about in between two opposing armies, keeping both sides from seeing each other except through our eyes. Between man and God, between the living and the dead, the past and the future, between blacks and whites, young and old, men and women.

Maybe a good battle would clear the air. After the dust settled something better could be built. But no matter what side I chose, no matter how the lines were drawn, I was pretty sure that I'd be purged afterward. My interests were in the ambiguity. I had nothing to gain by things becoming clear and everything to lose. That's why I was milling around unarmed in the middle of all those battlefields.

But the time when ambiguity could stay was past. I either had to be as big a jerk as everyone else or get the fuck out of the way.

February 14: Valentine's Day. Oh, God, it was awful. The end. So fucking hopeless, so fucking lonely. And getting more and more so and worse and worse. And harder and harder to hang on. And oh, Mother, how did your poor son end up in such a depressing hopeless meaningless mess? And oh, Father, what's gone so terribly wrong?

No more chances. No more people, trees, music, dogs. No more anything.

But then suddenly I had allies. "I thought you guys would never get here." Simon and my father, or damn convincing hallucinations, were holding me up and talking about getting me the hell out of that apartment. I hadn't been allowed outside since my nude sprint around the block.

We were in a car going somewhere. The fuckers didn't have me yet. My waiting game had paid off. I had allies.

I'd give almost anything for a tape of my ride to the hospital. My father had a lot on his mind, but still, not to have brought along a recorder verges on criminal neglect. My finest rave is lost forever unless you believe in that big cassette in the sky.

I didn't think my rave was being lost at the time. I didn't

know it was just a normal day with a normal father and a normal friend of his son taking his son who had gone crazy to the sort of place you normally take someone who's gone crazy.

It was bop talk. Like a '50s DJ. I wasn't thinking, it was just all there. Words a mile a minute. No second thoughts. No need or time for them. Music.

Wazzzzzzzzzzzz Wassa what I thought my rave-a-rap a' doin'. Passwords. Getting through to different teams and getting them to climb aboard. Start a bandwagon. For what to start a bandwagon? For to show those fuckers for to keep life going. I had something that made H-bombs look like ladyfingers. I had rhythm. And ain't no mother fucker nowhere nohow gonna take it away.

"Hey Giuseppe, how good you think that joker swim with some nice new cement booties?"

"Get the fuck out of the way. The team is coming together, coming through. Anybody I ain't talkin' to ain't gonna get talked to by nobody. Climb aboard or get run the fuck over, Jack. Get with it, Jack, or get off it."

I had some modest goals. Like letting a few people know I wasn't dead, that I was still in there somewhere. That I was salvageable. I had some immodest goals, like saving the world.

One thing a tape of my ride to the hospital would show was how I was responding to outside events. It was a dialogue. I'd give some sort of a blues rap and then there'd be some horn or something which was a "yes" or "amen" from all blues freaks. I'd do a Mafia thing and they'd answer a woman's thing and they'd say yes yes. A video tape would be even better. Flashing neon signs and I had some very good raps. Jackhammers had some very encouraging things to say. And big diesel trucks and fire sirens. Who would be dumb enough to try to mess with me and Mack trucks, sirens, electricity, jackhammers, and traffic lights all on my side?

Hospital. Back at the apartment Simon had asked me if I was ready to go to the hospital. Sure I'm ready to go to the hospital. I'll go anywhere. Father seems very worried, very nervous. I guess there's no time to ask questions. Maybe everything will be explained at the hospital.

Remember Lot's wife. Full speed ahead. This train is bound for glory. Simon's driving beautifully, the car's running perfectly. Who's against us? How can we lose? We're on our way, great God, we're on our way.

The shifting is music to my ears and the lights are all turning green. Hold on tight, we're goin' to make it. We're passing everything on the road, and I hear myself rapping, cursing nonstop, hitting every password just right.

And Simon gives a "Wa hoo," double-clutches down to third, and passes another car. What a ride!

Why are they taking me to a hospital? Why is everything whizzing by faster and faster? Why am I holding my breath? Why do I feel so strange? Whatever is wrong is very strange. This will doubtless be a very strange hospital.

When the car finally came to a stop, the place looked like the Hyannisport Kennedy compound. I complimented Simon on his driving. My father and Simon turned and looked at me somberly.

When they left me, when three guys dressed in white started walking me down that long hall, half holding me up, half holding me down, I understood. I had gone too far. I was putting too much on the line. Simon and my father couldn't go the whole way with me.

In a way, it was a relief not having any allies any more. Now if I fucked up, I fucked up on my own. I wouldn't drag a lot of people through the shit with me. But maybe it was just a holding action. They were putting me in cold storage and going out to get more allies.

Clunk, into that little room. Cuzzzunk, a huge mother bolt ran the whole width of the door. A separation chamber? No one could breathe the sort of stuff I had to breathe to keep alive.

A soft voice through the door: "Mr. Vonnegut, would you like something to eat?"

"If you can cook it, honey, I can fuck it."

* * *

One of the many worst things about being nuts was being so goddamned important. Who was I that such powerful mysterious forces were buggering around with my life? One team would come through cramming my head full of new knowledge, the next would sneak in and erase all the new stuff plus a lot of the old. I'd be crucified and resurrected several times a day.

If I died lots of wonderful things would happen. If I died lots of awful things would happen. I was a rag doll between two bull mastiffs with very little way to know which one I wanted to get me, let alone have any say in the matter.

NOW IS THE TIME FOR GODS TO STAND UP FOR BASTARDS. The voice didn't even have the courtesy to tell me it was Shakespeare.

As usual, it seemed like the voices were trying to help, trying to give me some clue about what was going on. As usual, it didn't help much. Who was and who wasn't a bastard? What sort of things are gods and bastards going to do? When is now?

"Now is the time for gods to stand up for bastards." Hmmmm. Is this good news or bad news? Am I a bastard or am I one of the guys the bastards and gods are going to kick the shit out of? How do you tell? Even biologically it's hard to be absolutely sure, and I doubt that that's what's the issue. It seems too petty for the gods to get caught up in.

If bastard just means mean nasty people, I don't see why the gods would feel the need to stand up for them. Mean nasty people seem to be doing just fine without any help. After a certain amount of time of the gods standing up for a bastard, wouldn't he stop being a bastard and become more and more legitimate? And then wouldn't the people the gods had not stood up for become bastards? Is a bastard's legitimate issue a bastard or legitimate? A bastard's bastard?

Some sort of social upheaval? It's only fair but it will probably be pretty violent and ugly. Bastards aren't called bastards for nothing. But all in all I'm more or less inclined to go along with the idea. It'll give everyone a chance to walk around in the other guy's shoes.

Philosophical sympathies for and against gods standing up for bastards aside for the moment, just where does this leave me? Inasmuch as I am a white middle-class American hetero-sexual male, I guess I'll get my ass kicked in. Inasmuch as I'm a down-under hippie revolutionary, alienated from the reins of power and persecuted by cops, I imagine I'm eligible for some sort of aid under the gods-for-bastards program. I guess what it boils down to is whether or not I've shat on more people than have shat on me.

If there's going to be any fairness to this thing at all, it will have to be on a situational basis. Though I suppose bringing fairness into it will probably be considered whining and not very wise, as most notions of fairness and morality are used against bastards to support the status quo.

My best bet is probably to rid myself of any notions of entitlement I might have hanging around. Just a little added incentive to carry out the sort of overhaul I've always had in mind. What I'll really get my ass kicked in for is any notion that I'm Virginia's legitimate lover. That makes Vincent eligible for support under this gods-for-bastards program. The same probably holds true for poor Ma in the Pops-and-new-woman situation. I should just forget Virginia and go bust up someone else's thing.

I was sorry I inherited money, but glad my bundle wasn't a super-whopper. Sorry I owned a car, but glad it was just a VW.

Hollywood Hospital. What's in a Name? If you were terribly confused, desperately trying to get your bearings without the faintest idea of where you were or what was happening, if you finally got your mouth and tongue to work right and finally managed to ask "Where am I?" what would be the worst possible thing someone could tell you?

I suppose that, my mind being in the shape it was, I would have managed to get something strange out of whatever any-

one said. I would have anagrammed almost any name into
something perfectly wonderful or perfectly terrible. But Hollywood?

That one didn't need much work. It didn't call on my
knowledge of medieval mysticism or Russian lit.

After chewing on that awhile and getting my words to
work right again: "Hollywood where?"

"Fifth Avenue."

I was too dazed to manage another question but the orderly volunteered some additional information. "New Westminster."

"Tower of London, man for all season." At last, a use for
my liberal arts education.

If being in Hollywood on Fifth Avenue in New Westminster isn't being caught in a time-space warp, what is?

"It all fits except where is Iowa City?" But the orderly was
gone and the door was locked.

Well, so here I am in a mental hospital. It took a while for
it to sink in. In a way, I knew it all along. Simon and my
father had talked about it and I had been able to pick up on
some of what they were saying. The nurses and orderlies, the
little room, the needles in the ass, it all added up: mental
hospital.

It took a while before I was able to pay much attention to
the fact. I was all taken up with voices, visions and all. I
vaguely knew I was in a mental hospital but it wasn't any
different from being anywhere else. Where I was was beside
the point.

Little by little, with the help of massive doses of Thorazine
in the ass and in my milkshakes (which was all they could get
me to eat), little by little it started mattering to me where I
was and what was going on.

For a while I was convinced that the whole thing I was
going through was my father's way to help me give up cigarettes. Here I was, thinking the end of the world or worse
was happening and what was really going on was all about

cigarettes. It was like the Trafalmadorians getting the earth-
lings to build the Great Wall of China to send a little message
to a second-string messenger carrying a message that just said
hello.

Some lesson. "Cigarettes, Dad?" "Cigarettes, Mark." "Shit,
Pa, who would have guessed?" "Well, it took you quite a
while, Mark." But then when I said I wouldn't smoke any
more and they still wouldn't let me out of my little room, I got
suspicious that cigarettes weren't the whole story.

Little by little it sank in. It was all on the level. This was a
real mental hospital with real doctors and nurses. It wasn't
some weird put-up job designed by my father or anyone else.

The only weird thing about this hospital was that I was a
patient here. Everything else made sense. All the other patients fit nicely into my idea of what mental hospitals were
about. They were all victims one way or another. They had
been dealt lousy parents, lousy jobs, lousy marriages, lousy
friends, lousy educations. They hadn't had breaks. No one
really loved them. I just picked up bits and pieces, but it all
kept adding up the same. I'd see a husband or wife or mother
come in to visit them and I'd wince in pain as the various
pictures of what their lives had been came together. Their
craziness, their being in a mental hospital, was so understandable. Good, brave people who had done the best they
could until it was just all too much.

What was my excuse? What more could I have possibly
asked from life? For them there was some hope. Call it therapy. A change of job, some understanding of themselves and
the people around them: given half a break, these people
could make it. Maybe if they got eighty acres back in the
mountains or something.

Most of the patients were older. I was the only one there
with long hair or a beard. Some discarded old people, a lot of
middle-aged people who had gotten messed up with alcohol,
a few junkies, plus a few other misfits. I worried some that
my being so different from the others meant they didn't really know how to deal with whatever my problem was. I had

been put in the wrong bin. In a way it was the same for me, but the only way I could get to feel the sameness was by stretching definitions quite a bit. It felt lonely.

Three days after my commitment, Virginia showed up at the Stevens Street place, all refreshed, full of adventures, new insights and hopes.

"We've got some bad news, Virge. Mark's in the hospital."

She didn't think even for a minute that maybe I had had an accident. She knew immediately what kind of hospital I was in. My parents and lots of my friends showed a similar lack of surprise. It seems that they all felt I was crazy, but also felt that I had worked out such good ways of dealing with it that I had effectively turned a sow's ear into a purse. They all hoped I'd be able to keep it up, but feared it just wasn't possible. It also seems that these feelings depressed the hell out of everyone who cared about me because no one could think of any way to intervene.

I found all this out later and it was very much news to me. I thought that everyone thought I was strong as an ox. I myself didn't think I'd ever really crack, especially after finding the farm. But as it turned out the only one who was surprised about my going nuts was myself.

"You're in a mental hospital, Mr. Vonnegut."

"That's ridiculous. I've already beat the draft."

Simon and Virginia came to visit me every day, but they weren't allowed to stay very long. I remember the first time I saw them coming down that long, long corridor and the doors were opening like magic and they seemed to be gliding on clouds more than walking. They were gods. All I had for clothes was a sheet draped around me as best I could. The three of us would sit holding hands, creating a conspiracy of warmth and sense against the cold senselessness all around us. They'd very patiently answer my questions. I wanted to know what the hell had happened and was everyone all right, and why couldn't they take me home with them, and where was I really, and could I see Luke again, and how was Zeke, and and . . .

It was all very fuzzy, a little more solid than my hallucinations but not much. Little by little it sank in that I had gone crazy, but especially during their early visits I was pretty sure that the mental hospital bit was just a cover for something much bigger. I felt very much like a hero. I was in pretty wretched shape but it wasn't for nothing. Because of my efforts countless lives had been saved or ecological disaster averted or a new consciousness had come into the world or or . . .

My father visited me two days after committing me, but they wouldn't let me out of the seclusion room. I remember vaguely realizing he was there and trying to get to the door to talk with him through the little hole, but I kept fainting every time I tried to stand up. He pushed Bruno Bettelheim's *Children of the Dream* through the hole.

I spent seven days in that windowless everythingless room, and then they left the door unlocked some, let Simon and Virginia stay longer, gave me some pajamas, and moved me into an unlocked room in a locked ward.

The Doc. Virginia and Simon had told me that Dr. Dale was my doctor. I have a fuzzy recollection of walking up to some doctor-looking person and being totally absorbed by his gold tie clip. I suspected it was the button to end the world so I didn't touch it. I'm pretty sure it was Dr. Dale. I don't know who else could be so tasteless as to walk around a mental hospital wearing the button to end the world.

The first meeting I really remember with the good doctor was when I was starting to be able to speak English again and making a brave attempt to regain some of my dignity. Trying to be very sane, I went up to him and asked if he was my doctor. He said he didn't think so.

"You're Dr. Dale, aren't you?"

"Why, Mark, of course. I didn't recognize you with clothes on." He had a talent for saying the right thing.

I often look on him as one of God's little jokes on me. When I was in desperate trouble, what saved me from a fate worse than death? To what do I owe my life? Was it love, affection, understanding, friends, wisdom? No no no. It was a man who looks like a poor copy of Walt Disney, drives pink Cadillacs, wears baby-blue alligator shoes, and appears to have the emotional depth of a slightly retarded potato.

I was back to being polite, the well-tempered paranoid. I didn't have much choice. If I wasn't polite, they could stick me with those needles or put me back in that little room or take away my visitor privileges or any number of other things. Besides, there didn't seem to be any urgency or anything to be gained by not being polite, the way there had been before. So I was polite. There was time.

There was a fair amount to be polite about. There were silly rules about where I could and couldn't be. I had exhibited some fairly alarming behavior, but still the lag between my being trustable and their trusting me was a bit long at times. It seemed to take them forever to believe that I was capable of keeping clothes on or not being combative or able to go anywhere without an orderly watching over me. At several points I was on the verge of saying, "Come on. That's really not necessary any more." But I never did, mostly because they always seemed to catch on sooner or later, but also because I didn't particularly want to be reminded of what a problem I had been.

The big thing I was polite about was what a bunch of fascist no-goodnik stupid creeps they were. Spiritual mud puddles. Tight-asses. Their straightness made a laser beam look like an indecisive snake with a broken back. They utterly lacked poetry or even slight sympathy for anything vaguely poetic. Not so much as a glimmer of anything you could call curiosity about anything. Insight? Forget it. These were beyond a doubt the dullest, least inspired people I had ever run into.

Why on earth had my father and Simon signed me over to their care? What on earth did they think these people could do for me? How on earth could they have signed me over to a man who drove pink Cadillacs, whose clothes and taste and whole being virtually screamed fascist spiritual mud puddle? How could they have been so dull, so unimaginative? I felt more embarrassed for them than betrayed by them.

Doctors and mental hospitals were a mainstay of the corrupt establishment. Mental illness was just a tag used mainly for purposes of oppression. If the staffs of these places weren't out-and-out evil themselves, they were at least pawns manipulated directly or indirectly by people who were. I had never given my unqualified endorsement to such statements, but they were very much a part of the air I had been breathing for the past few years. Many of my friends accepted such things as unquestionable fact. Just about everyone I knew would feel some sympathy for such views or maybe just guilt for not being able to go along with such noble sentiments.

They were and are noble sentiments. Their happening to be untrue doesn't affect their nobility, only their usefulness. Maybe hopeful is a better word. It all got twisted into calling some people evil but that's not how it started. It started as a hope that the pain suffered in mental hospitals was avoidable.

So there I was, subject to the whims of fascists. I didn't find much to challenge the idea that these people were indeed a part of a no-goodnik oppressive machine of some sort. My only hope was to be polite. As soon as I wasn't a patient any more, I could be as stupid as they were and get away with it. For the time being, however, I had to be supergood.

Dear Everybody: Well, fuckers, I did everything just like you wanted and now I've ended up in a padded cell. What do you say about that? I can't think of anything I really regret, anything I'd do differently given another shot. The whole idea people are trying to ram into me from a million different angles is that since I'm crazy I must have made a mistake somewhere, but I can't buy it. The idea is, as soon as I recognize my mistake and decide to do things differently, everything will be fine and I can get out of here. Well, shit if I can figure out where I went wrong.

One thing that makes me suspicious is that everyone seems to have a different idea about what sort of mistake it was I made. Maharishi probably thinks my mistake was not doing my meditation faithfully. Lots of the nurses and orderlies seem to think my beard and my long hair were my real mistake. The other day they helped me out with that by holding me down and cutting it all off. I guess Freud would say I've repressed something. Some of my friends seem to think it's that I wasn't open and sharing enough. Others think I wasn't eating the right kind of food. Lots of people are pretty sure it has something to do with drugs. One doctor here has it all figured out that I went crazy because I didn't try to get a good job and make some sort of contribution to society. The whole reason I got into this mess is that I was throwing away my college education by trying to be a farmer out in the bush. The other morning someone came to the little hole in the door in my seclusion room and told me that if I could just accept Jesus Christ as my savior, everything would be fine. That Jew faggot, Jesus, I wonder where he thinks I blew it.

Well, I'm sorry, people. I must be the most perverse bastard going but I can't think of anything I did that I can see as my big mistake. I was trying my damnedest to do the best I could and I don't feel like reneging on any part of it. Love and kisses, Mark.

There wasn't much to do in the hospital. Most of the time I just sat around and tried to figure out what had gone wrong. Oh, what rotten luck, a shitty break. There I was, going along doing the best I could, and then this happened. Such an impertinence. It's like I was walking through the woods and a tree fell on me and broke my leg. Well, so much for whatever I happened to be doing in the woods. Now I got to deal with the fact that my leg is broken. Unforeseen, unplanned, a detour.

But it wasn't like that. It had a whole other flavor. It fit in so well. My craziness had everything to do with what I was doing. When it happened, it was more like I was stumbling along a dark, deserted road trying to get somewhere and a huge mother limousine picked me up and took me where I was going at a hundred miles an hour, using short cuts I didn't dream existed. In the end I decided I didn't want to be there, but if it weren't for the limousine I'd probably still be on that road, still trying to get there.

Had farming been what I was doing, things might have been different. Had clearing land or building a house or getting a place set up for goats and chickens, carving a home out of the wilderness, getting gardens ready to plant, been what I was up to, things might have turned out differently.

There was no way I could have been up to those things, much as I wished I were and tried to make myself be. Let's face it, someone with a B.A. in religion from Swarthmore, raised upper-middle-class intellectual, living in British Columbia, twelve miles by boat from the nearest electric light, has got to be up to something weird.

Clearing land, gardening, building the house was all just a front. I was into being good, being right. Truth, beauty, and saving the world, liberation, enlightenment, and salvation. I was playing for the highest stakes I could find. I had been given all the breaks anyone could ask for and more. Generations had spent their lives worrying about money so that I wouldn't have to. I didn't have to do anything. So the only way I could do anything was to do something very, very much worth doing.

Worth doing. I was into something worth doing.

Faith. If there had been less faith maybe I never would have gone nuts.

"I believe in you. Yes, I believe in you." A chorus sometimes comforting, sometimes cruel. It was nice to be believed in but it also meant that all the awful things I thought might be going on were going on. People were saying "yes" to my worst nightmares.

"I believe in you. Yes, I believe in you." Sometimes it was my father, sometimes it was Simon. Sometimes it was Virginia. Sometimes it was God, sometimes it was Jesus. Sometimes the whole world seemed to be singing to me in chorus, "I believe in you. Yes, I believe in you." Sometimes people really said it.

"I believe in you."

Well, that's just fine, mighty nice, but what, just what is it about me you believe in? Is it that I'm some sort of messiah or simply that I shouldn't be shot or simply that I'm still alive? That I'm very special or just one of the guys? That I can perform miracles, that I've got a direct line with God, that what I'm saying and doing is right, or simply that everything will come out right in the end? That I'm not acting this way just because my parents broke up or Virginia balled Vincent or I've sinned somehow and am being punished? That I'm a racist sexist fascist chauvinist pig? Or that even if I am it's OK and you still like me? That I shouldn't be committed to a nut house? I mean, believing in me is swell but could you be a little more specific?

"We believe in you. Yes, we believe in you."

That's real nice, but just what does this belief entail by way of implication for action? Are you going to just sit there believing in me or are you going to do anything about it? Does it just mean that you won't sell me down the river or that you would sell your mother down the river for my sake? Would you sacrifice an arm or maybe just a little finger?

"We believe in you. Yes, we believe in you."

I'm not sure believing in me is such a hot idea. I think maybe you ought to consider the possibility that anyone who really believes in me might end up having to go through what I'm going through.

"We believe in you. Yes, we believe in you."

I think maybe you ought to look into the possibility that I'm being used as some sort of Judas goat. Something built me up as believable in and has now taken over my body. I'm not really in charge any more. I think maybe you ought to consider that maybe killing me would be the best thing.

"We believe in you. Yes, we believe in you."

Hope. If there hadn't been so much hope I might never have gone nuts. If we hadn't all believed and hoped that the world could be a much better place. That pain and suffering was unnecessary. That there really was a way.

And Charity. Maybe if everyone hadn't been so polite, so reluctant to make any sort of judgment.

Mickey Mouse. One thing I noticed about the lag between being trustable and being trusted is that the doctors are always the last to catch on. The first to realize you've gotten better and start to treat you accordingly are the other patients. The realization flows up the hierarchy rather than down. After the patients catch on, then the maintenance staff and the lower orderlies realize you're OK, and so on through the various orders of nurses until the news reaches the doctors.

It works the same for relapses. Doctors and nurses continue to treat a briefly recovered patient as well days after the other patients realize the poor joker's completely out of his mind again.

The doctors and nurses seem to realize some of this more or less consciously. They take their cues from other patients and the less professional staff. As soon as they see patients willing to talk to and treat another patient as improved, they check it out.

Most of how you're treated in Hollywood Hospital, and I suspect most others, is determined by how you are dressed. If you have on a suit and tie, there's no such thing as a locked door. With nothing but a sheet, there's no such thing as an open one. I started at ground zero. I didn't even have a sheet. Moving up the ladder was painfully slow. Slippers are the first goodie after the sheet. If you continue to be good, you get the most ridiculous, ill-fitting pajamas you can imagine. If all goes well after that, you get better-looking pajamas and more mobility. Then come ridiculous pants, and so on and so on till you start getting some of your own clothing back, and then the big day when you get shoes. Shoes are the biggest day in the career of a patient.

All this saves the staff a lot of time. They can just look at a patient and know they're dealing with a "pajama, stage 3" and act accordingly.

It's possible to cheat, which I did every chance I got. You go to the bathroom ostensibly to wash your hands when someone a few levels above you is taking a shower and borrow his clothes—instant promotion. You get visitors to smuggle in a decent pair of pants—suddenly a whole new wing of the hospital opens up to you. Clothes alone don't always do the trick. You've got to stand next to a locked door with just the right sort of aloof impatience and walk with just the right stride or a whole week's progress can be wiped out in nothing flat.

You play mommy-daddy games for all they're worth: But Dr. . . .said . . . or Nurse . . . has been letting me . . . again with the right impatience, the right tone of voice.

It seemed awfully Mickey Mouse. I complained a lot about it, but at the time I appreciated it as a nice change of pace, a game whose rules and objectives were transparent and trivial. Trying to get out of the mental hospital was a nice vacation from being a good hippie, battling the forces of darkness, trying to figure out if an apocalypse would be a good thing or a bad thing.

I had blown my cool. I had done a lot of silly things, things that would have made sense if what I thought was going on had been right, but I had been wrong. The world wasn't ending. There was plenty of oxygen to go around. Virginia hadn't died. My father hadn't died. Extraordinary measures weren't called for. I'm OK.

There was nothing to do at the hospital. As soon as I was OK, I was bored. I wrote some, played the broken-down pi-

ano in the day room, read some, talked to some of the patients and staff some, but mostly I just wanted to get out.
    What were they doing for me? Pills three times a day. No
doctor saw fit to try to explain what had happened to me or
what if anything I should do to avoid its happening again. A
doctor named McNice and I had some very pleasant, urbane,
sophisticated chats about Russian literature, religion, and a
lot of other stuff. We sat around making sense out of all the
apparently senseless things I had done. I knew that the things
I had done made sense. It was nice that he didn't just throw
it all out as crazy. He had a certain respect for it, the sort of
respect it deserved. I didn't learn anything I didn't know
already but we had pleasant enough conversations.

    If you had broken your leg, would you be trying to "deal
with it"? Forget about it. You were sick and now you're well.
Me thinking, talking to myself. At the hospital they gave me
no such advice or any sort of advice at all. By intention or
default I was left pretty much in a vacuum to figure things
out on my own.
    "What happened?"
    "You've been a very sick boy. We don't have all the an-
swers."
    Treating it like a broken leg was probably good advice. I
tried to stick to it but it went very hard against my grain. I
had had a long career and a lot of fun making mountains out
of molehills, milking experiences for all they were worth. A
life in prison out of eighteen hours, a marriage with lots of
kids from a casual affair, genocide from stepping on an ant,
and on and on. And here I had a real live mountain to try to
turn into a molehill.
    No one else seemed inclined to treat it like a broken leg.
Everyone had their own little theories, but there was a consensus of sorts. The consensus was that whatever else it
might be, it was definitely "heavy." It wasn't like a broken leg.
There's nothing heavy about a broken leg.
    Heavy heavy heavy. It wasn't just my comrades in arms,

fellow hippie freaks. When the doctors told me they didn't have all the answers, the nurses, the orderlies, fellow patients, my parents, everyone, all their faces seemed to be saying, "Heavy, heavy." If I had broken my leg, would the doctors have bothered to tell me they didn't have all the answers?

My father flew up from the "real" Hollywood, where they were making a movie of *Slaughterhouse Five,* and spent a day visiting and taking me out to lunch. He, like everyone else, seemed to think the whole thing was very heavy. I was feeling OK and just wished everyone would just forget about it or treat it like a broken leg.

Mark went bonkers. What does it mean?

I just couldn't get into thinking about it much. So much had happened, I had so much more raw material than anyone imagined, that I could spend the rest of my life sorting it out and just barely scratch the surface of "What does it mean?"

Maybe I didn't think much about it because of all the Thorazine they had pumped into me. Thorazine makes thinking a pretty unprofitable proposition. Or maybe when enough people tell you you're crazy you lose a certain amount of interest in trying to figure things out. Who wants to take a nut's word for something even if that nut happens to be you? Another thing was that being in a nut house was small change compared with most of the things I had been convinced were happening. "Oh, I've been committed to an institution for the mentally disturbed. Well, if that's all it is, why bother me with it? I was worried for a bit there that something bad had happened."

Getting Out. The first time was a funny combination of running away and being discharged.

Dr. Dale, who was in charge of me, had to go to some conference in Hawaii. He was going to be gone only a week and left orders that I was not to be discharged until his return. In the meantime, Dr. McNice was in charge of me.

I had been ready to leave as soon as I got there. I recognized that that might have been foolish. I had been in strange shape and a mental hospital was as good a place as any to put me. But that was then, a whole two and a half weeks ago. I was OK now. I didn't want to spend an extra minute in that place.

If I stayed in that hospital till Dale got back I'd go nuts again. Those stupid rules, those stupid nurses, stupid order-lies, that awful food, all those nuts wandering around doing crazy things. Also, there was no guarantee that I'd be let out as soon as Dale got back. All he had said was that we could talk about it then.

How could I convince a man who drove Cadillacs, wore baby-blue alligator shoes, etc., that I was sane? Why should I have to?

I recognized his brief absence as a golden opportunity that might not come again. Dr. McNice was a soft touch for mysticism and literature and had a bit of sympathy for hippiedom. A liberal. If there was one thing my life had taught me, it was how to manipulate liberals.

I didn't think I was being tricky or devious at the time. I was just trying to have the reasonable thing happen: my getting the fuck out of the nut house.

After a few more urbane chats about medieval mystics, the Dead Sea Scrolls, Jung, and the fallacies in Freud's essays on religion, we decided my brain was in working order.

"I feel fine. I have a place to go with good people who love me and want me back."

What liberal, especially after such a nice chat, could say no? According to Dr. McNice, I had my walking papers. The staff was split. The nurses seemed to run about two to one against my being dischargeable. The orderlies were two to one in favor. I packed up my things and did the best I could to avoid the controversy.

Virginia was going to pick me up in the morning. Back to the farm, back to Zeke, back to where life made sense.

I asked some nurses who were in charge of such things to fill me in about what the pills I had been taking were and if

they would give me some to take along in case I started getting shaky again. I met with no real information, a firm "no"
to taking any pills with me, and thinly veiled threats about
cops. I split during the opposition's coffee break. It was
March 7. Three weeks of Hollywood was plenty.

If disease was a cleansing process I was some clean. My
ideals, hopes, friends, and life style had all come through it
with me. We had been tried and had come forth as gold.

We wasted no time. After a brief visit to Stevens Street, we
were on a ferry an hour or so after my exit. Virginia had
Simon's car.

If misunderstandings between Virge and me had had
something to do with my going nuts, that was all going to end.
I was going to be straight out with everyone about everything,
but especially with Virge about sex.

"Virge, our sex life has been a disaster from the word go.
Part my fault but part yours too. You're all screwed up about
men. Every time I've tried to talk about sex, you get rigid as a
board. Don't you know you're denying yourself and it sure
isn't doing me any favors?

"And other stuff too. Ninety percent of your new-age liberation stuff is full of shit rhetoric masking a scared little girl.
Probably half the things I think are all screwball, but that's
'cause I had to figure them out all by myself with no outside
feedback. Whatever else happens, I'm not going to keep any
of this shit buried inside any more."

She didn't seem terribly interested in responding to any of
this. Maybe there was something that eclipsed this stuff and
made it irrelevant.

"Mark, you're sane, you're very sane," was about all she
could muster. She seemed afraid of me. I had never seen that
before.

There were several things that needed asserting. I was not
crazy. I had not been permanently damaged. I was no goddamned invalid. Being dismissed, coddled, or humored was
not my idea of a good time. I wanted to fight all the screwy

conclusions people might want to draw from my going bonkers. Conclusions about me, the farm, Virge, my parents. Conclusions about the past, about the present, about the future. I've never been much of a conclusion fan anyway, and the ones people seemed most likely to draw were simplistic and insulting to boot.

Energetic and tough as nails as I was, there were several things worrying me. One was what had gone on in all those blanks. I knew about the picture window, running around naked, and a few other antics, but had I seriously hurt anyone, possibly even killed them? Had I unforgivably insulted anyone? Those blanks could have been filled with anything.

Was medical information being withheld from me for my own good? A brain tumor? Something incurable that was going to land me in the bin over and over again and again no matter what I or anyone else did or didn't do?

And what had happened to the rest of the world while I was away? Was there news about my family or friends or the world situation that I'd be told about as soon as they decided I could take it?

Would everybody be afraid of me?

And still in the back of my mind was the suspicion that, crazy as I had been, there were some very real and valuable things back there, and just what did that mean?

It was a lovely day for a ferry ride. So nice to walk around without nurses and ass-busting orderlies everywhere.

Simon and good old Car Car were waiting in the parking lot at the Works. The place had changed ownership, which upset me some. I wondered about the wonderful waitress I was sort of in love with. I wondered if she was unhappy about it, though I figured she'd do just fine wherever she was, whatever happened. The mill stacks were, per usual, spewing forth their poison puke. B.C.'s prime minister called it the smell of money. The world's largest pulp mill, using three times as much water a day as New York City. What kind of neighbor was that for Eden? Just one more thing my going crazy hadn't managed to put much of a dent in. Nixon was going to visit China. That was a step in the right direction, but there were just as many cars on the road as ever. My parents were tentatively getting back together, but I didn't really know whether I wanted that or not. Bengalis were still starving. I don't remember what the Dow Jones was doing. Virginia was treating me with a new respect, a new caring. Maybe something good would come out of all this.

We went out to Prior Road. Virginia and Simon got into his car and I into mine. It was the way I wanted it. Being trusted to drive my car alone was a big step. They drove behind me, which bugged me slightly. I wondered if they had planned it.

Zeke was waiting for us at Prior Road, in exile from the farm because Tanga was in heat. He was suitably excited and thrilled to see me. Did Virge think I was faking it, working at appearing beautiful by loving my dog? Fuck you, Virge. If you can fuck Vincent, I can play with my dog. I'm jealous? I'm competitive? I'm brakes? I'm holding you back? This feeling ain't just in my head. You yourself have admitted how sane I am. I said nothing but resolved not to bury it any more. If this was to be the new age of honesty, etc., I'd be fucked if I was going to play straight man to everybody else's liberation any more. Especially Virginia's.

I was a little wary about Simon. What was in those blanks? I knew he had been with me through most of them. What did he think: Was he afraid of me? Disgusted with me? Could he trust me? What was our new relationship to be like? He seemed pretty free and easy and I was greatly relieved.

We were each other's complement, which was why we had made such a good team going backward in time. No points of friction. If I felt like stomping Vincent it was because he struck me so much as a parody of myself in questionable taste.

Prior Road. What did they know? What did they think? It felt good to be back. Back to a wood stove, back on my turf. Back with my people. When Virginia and I took a little walk she told me she wasn't comfortable there. She was worried that the folks there might consider her responsible for the hell I had been through.

Nick from Colorado. There was this guy Nick. Nick was from Colorado, which he announced like it was important somehow. The first time I looked at him I felt the hair on the back of my neck start to rise. This guy was trouble. He had blue eyes, which didn't help, and long red hair like Columbus, who had fucked this continent in the first place. He was skinny as a rail and didn't smoke cigarettes. I tried my best to treat him like everyone else, but the case against him kept building and building. He wasn't like everyone else. For one thing, he was the one guy there who had just mysteriously showed up. Everyone else I had met before or was well known by someone I knew. They all had good credentials. But who the hell was this cat and what was he doing here?

His body was terrifyingly skinny. When he took his shirt off I had seen more flesh on pictures out of Auschwitz. There was an utter lack of compromise in him, no give. Some set purpose. But here he was in the middle of nowhere. What was this purpose, this resolve all about?

His hair was halfway down his back. His beard hadn't been trimmed for at least a year. He was only eighteen. What caused those lines on his face?

I was sure he didn't eat white bread, was fairly sure he ate no meat. With a body like that, I wasn't sure he ate at all. Lean hungriness. Was he what Virginia had wanted me to be? Was this the revolutionary fervor I lacked, the strength that would have kept me out of the nut house? Was this the young buck come to take on the old, tired, compromised, weakened stag?

I knew there was no way I could talk about these feelings without Simon and Virginia getting scared that Mark was going crazy again, but it wasn't just my head, any more than dreams are nonsense.

* * *

There was a meal and some chatting about spring coming and what sort of future we could expect for our communities. A little shop talk about seeds and fertilizer, etc.; talk about cooperation among the various groups that were in the area. Little by little, people drifted off to various places to sleep. Some to the barn, some to tents, some to different rooms in the main house. There was a double mattress right in the main room, where we had eaten. Virge and I decided that since no one else wanted it, we would sleep there.

It was our first night together in some time, the reunion I had worried about so much just before I cracked. Then it was just wondering about what her having slept with Vincent would do to our relationship. But now so much more had happened.

She started getting menstrual cramps. Transparent and I almost said so, but the old rules were coming back. We just laughed a little about our lousy timing as far as getting back together. All the progress wiped out, all the pluses out the window. Back at ground zero. Any feeling that my craziness was a positive thing, that it was a chance to start fresh, began to sour in my mouth. My sexuality, which I had clung to so desperately, atrophied under the accusing wither of her pains in the gut.

It seemed like cyanide frosting on an arsenic cake.

If I had succeeded at least partly in putting Nick from Colorado out of my mind for just a minute or so, what he proceeded to do took care of that in a hurry. He came into the room with a lantern and started fumbling around. I think he grunted something like "Got to work on my boots."

At this hour of the night? In this room? I looked at Virginia with a funny look on my face, like is this happening or am I nuts again? Is this weird or am I weird? This is our first time alone in more than a month and this joker comes in to work on his boots. As if we didn't have enough shit to deal with.

But how long can it take him to work on his boots? The answer to that: about two hours. After which he blew out the lamp and lay down to sleep, maybe all of three feet away from us, where he groaned and sighed for a while and then got into some heavy snoring. If Nick, as I was trying to believe, was a regular, real person, he sure wasn't starting off on the right foot.

Well, that pretty much shot any chance Virge and I had to talk about much. But we felt a community of having been intruded on. There was good will between us.

I didn't sleep much that night, but it wasn't panicky, I'm threatened, something awful is going to happen, pay attention, no time for sleep, and it wasn't the euphoric breakthrough of having no need for sleep. I dozed off every once in a while but kept waking up again and looking around and thinking some more. It was so nice to wake up somewhere other than the hospital. Not sleeping probably had a lot to do with the fact that I wasn't on all that medication any more. It would probably take my system a while to get used to not having all that Thorazine fog to overcome.

The next morning brought a swell piece of news. Nick was coming up to spend some time with us on the farm, maybe forever. He had asked Simon if he could come up, and Simon had said sure.

Mostly I just couldn't believe it. I couldn't believe that Simon could be so dumb. I was very tired. I didn't want any trouble, any argument, any friction. I just wanted to get back to the farm, where I could relax and let all the shit in my system work itself out. It seemed there was plenty for us all to do without throwing a stranger in the pot. The soup looked plenty thick already.

It was going to be tough enough to try to reestablish my life with people to whom I had been close. People I could explain something to in a few words. Getting to know someone is hard work. With anyone it would have been tough, and Nick from Colorado wasn't just anyone.

Simon, can you really not see what's in that cat's eyes?

Would you please wake up, Simon? Didn't I teach you anything?

Early that day, Simon, Virginia, Nick from Colorado, and I
headed up the lake.

Without Nick it might have been different. Who can say? I
might have been able to relax and live happily ever after at
the farm. But relaxing and feeling at home around him was
about as likely as . . . ? The stream flowing up the mountain? Why not? Had to use some image and the stream did
just that a few days later anyway.

Bea was at the marina. Did she know I had been locked up
in a mental hospital? About the things I had said and done? It
would break my heart to have Bea be afraid of me. She was
my second mother. She had been warm and good to us and
obviously wished us well.

There was no fear in her face, but a deep motherly concern. I must have looked fresh out of the grave.

"Mark, I haven't seen you for a while, you look like you've
been sick."

"Ya, Bea, a little flu and then one thing led to another. I
was pretty sick but I feel a lot better now and everything's
going to be fine. It's nice to be back."

She obviously wanted to take me home and fatten me up
some and didn't think I was ready to go back up to the farm,
but she said nothing more.

Virginia and Simon let me play captain. I was grateful, as I
had been grateful for their letting me drive my car alone.
Nick didn't say much. His face was as clueless, as warmthless
as ever. He seemed to be looking at me contemptuously, wondering what the hell I thought I was proving, waiting for me
to show my weak spot, for me to fuck up.

Just 'cause I've been nuts, just 'cause I weigh a hundred
and thirty pounds, don't get any ideas that I'm not still someone to be reckoned with.

Jumping gracefully to the dock and moving well and or-
ganizing the boat, packing exactly right. If just Simon and

Virginia had been there I might have acted very differently. But here was this new element, this unknown who felt like bad news. I piloted the boat perfectly, docked it without a mistake, sprang ashore and tied it up.

Up the beautiful path to the beautiful farm. Back to life, back to my dreams. Back to home and friends. Back to where I was before I was so rudely interrupted.

Kathy was there alone. Jack was in California and she had held down the farm all by herself for a couple of weeks.

She hadn't been off the farm since before I cracked up. For the first time she really felt that the place was home, that she belonged there. She was radiant. It was good to see her that way. She deserved it.

Brakes. Maybe Nick was there to make me behave. Brakes. The same way Virginia had, the same way I had hoped getting to town with Simon when I had so obviously stopped behaving would. I wasn't supposed to be in Eden. Something didn't want me there and there was obviously nothing in myself that would hold me back, so I needed brakes. I had given up or thrown away my own brakes a few years back. For one thing, Virginia and other things were such good brakes that mine had just sort of atrophied. It was a nice feeling that I could rely on others' brakes. It was a little unfair to them but they didn't seem to mind, or maybe they just didn't notice. So I just set my sights on Eden and put my foot on the floor.

To get to Eden with Virginia and Simon and Kathy, I really didn't have to start from very far away. So much was understood. We were pretty close to the take-off point, where the acceleration gets pretty hairy. But with Nick there it was back to ground zero and lots to be filled in, lots to be established before I got anywhere near take-off again. That many steps away from being an organism, from Eden, from cosmic orgasm. Simon's brakes, Kathy's brakes, Virginia's brakes? I had burned them all to frazzles. They couldn't have stopped a toy truck going uphill.

So it was getting to know you instead of getting to Eden.

How old are you? Where are you from? Did you go to school? What made you drop out? Etc. Very safe stuff.

In a way, I felt like a diabetic who had to explain to those around him what they should do if he went into a coma. It was trickier than that. Much less for sure is known about my thing than diabetes, and I knew just about nothing then. Dale had been planning to fill me in when he got back from Hawaii. I knew that if I could eat three times a day and get to sleep every night it would help. I knew I had been given heavy doses of Vitamin C, Vitamin B3, and other vitamins. I didn't know how they worked if they worked at all, or whether they were just a shot in the dark. I didn't know whether these were things I needed to take just in rough spots or all the time. The tranquilizers were another mystery. I hated Thorazine. I figured it was just a chemical straitjacket to make me less trouble to the staff.

The funniest mistake I made was that I figured grass would help in a pinch. So when I felt myself losing ground I figured I could just do lots of dope and be fine. I remembered hearing that grass had once been used fairly extensively in mental hospitals.

One of the problems was believing that my problem had anything to do with these pedestrian things. There was such poetry in the disease, it felt only right that there be poetry in the cure—which I guess is why so many shrinks go so far afield and have so little clinical success with schizophrenia.

I could think up lots of poetic explanations for why I went nuts: the state of the world, childhood experiences, my parents breaking up, my kinky relationship with Virginia. Any one of a dozen or more explanations made perfect sense, but my relationship with Virginia was the only one within my sphere of influence, and even there understanding why I had gone nuts, if that was indeed it, didn't give me many clues about what I should do next. Merely understanding these things obviously wouldn't help. I had understood them all very clearly for years.

That there were so many reasonable poetic explanations for my cracking up weakened them all. While I was still several months away from a truly reasonable helpful explanation, I began having serious doubts that explanations like the above had much to do with my sanity.

Whatever part Virginia had or hadn't played in driving me crazy, there was no denying that I needed her desperately then. She could have crushed me like a flea. I hated myself for needing the things I needed but there was no way around it. It was all unspoken but she knew that I knew that she knew and so on that we were both walking on eggs.

Please, Virge. I don't want to be this way. I'd rather it was heroin, I swear. What I need I have no right to ask for. I don't love you now. I'm too scared to love anything. Maybe I've never loved anything, but for a while—maybe just a few days will do the trick, I'll try to keep it small—I need your love completely and utterly.

Maybe it's not even love. Maybe it's a lie I need, like how I've lied to you. I know you never asked me to and it was a fucked-up thing to do and it was bad for both of us, but I made you very sure of me and gave you my unconditional commitment. It wasn't for romantic reasons. It was more just a dumb experiment, but it's that sort of half-lie I need now.

Please, Virge, I need a moratorium on reality. Play Doris Day to my Rock Hudson. Maybe we can work out some real love later, but for now the work has got to be curing my addiction. It's the only hope for either of us to get out of this mess at all intact. I need your blessing, Virge. Without it I can neither love you nor let you go. We'll be stuck with my hellish needing forever.

After I had been back at the farm a few days, my resolve to just forget about the whole thing, never terribly strong, crumbled completely. I wanted to fit all the pieces together. It started as a very reasonable attempt to figure out what had happened so that I could avoid its happening again. As I

began to fit things together it became more and more appar-
ent to me that there was very little, if anything, delusional
about the things I had thought or inappropriate about my
behavior. My focus might have been a little off here and
there, but basically I had been right on. There was too much
confirmation from too many different sources that something
very momentous had happened and that I had responded at
least appropriately and very possibly heroically.

The more I thought about it, the more transparent it became. I was slightly embarrassed that they had managed to
fool me as well as they had. What a bunch of transparent,
blundering incompetents.

Hollywood Hospital, Fifth Avenue, New Westminster,
Dale and McNice—now really.

I was convinced that the crisis was over and the good guys
had won, but I wished they had done a better job of fooling
me. I was resolved to live my long, peaceful, healthy, normal
life at the farm no matter what.

I quickly lost all sense of embarrassment about having been
locked up in a nut house. In fact I was rather proud of it.
Even when I stuck to what I and everyone else knew for sure
had happened, the unwritten codes of myself, my friends, all
good radicals and liberals everywhere, gave the bare facts a
certain amount of built-in grandiosity as standard equipment.
That I had somehow saved the world was optional frill.

The humiliations and restrictions I had suffered made
blacks, women, and homosexuals look like fat-cats basking in
the good graces of the powers that be. There was nothing
subtle about what had been done to me. I didn't need any
consciousness-raising meeting to find out that my situation
had not been ideal. Admittedly my oppression and suffering
hadn't been long-term, but if blacks could identify with and
be outraged by what the slaves went through, I could certainly identify with all inmates of mental institutions, past,
present and future.

I was no longer a male wasp heterosexual of upper-middle-
class origin with good intentions. I was a sufferer of the worst

humiliations and degradations afforded by the evil no-good-nik oppressive poison-spewing earth-defiling beauty-raping pigs. I had credentials.

I probably used this angle on my having been nuts more than I really believed it. I was still too confused about the whole thing to really believe anything and too shaky to not use anything that came to hand.

Chess with Nick. I don't know who initiated it. I may have asked him if he played. Maybe he saw my board and pieces and asked if I wanted a game. Anyway, it didn't take long before I was sorry as hell about it.

When we sat down and set up the pieces, there was a look in his eyes like there was something understood between us. I tried to shrug it off.

My chess board was made by my grandfather, Doc. Inscribed in Gothic script were the messages "I do warn you well" on one side and "It is no child's play" on the other. Ominous, ominous, ominous.

The hallucinations and fantasies had had heavy chess content. My father had taught me how to play when I was four. In an informal way I had been chess champ nearly everywhere I had ever been. One or two people I knew could play me about even, but I never ran into anyone who could beat me consistently, though I doubtless would have if I hadn't so conscientiously avoided formal competition.

I lost the first game. I thought I had him a few times, but each time I felt his wrath building and was afraid that if I won something dreadful would happen. I didn't get furious. I didn't cry. I worried that maybe several thousand people were struck down by plague for every pawn I lost, but I didn't let it show.

There was a second game. I felt much looser. I thought I could loosen up and maybe learn something about chess from him. Winning seemed to make him a lot more relaxed. Since he had won one game, there was no way he could feel humiliated or hurt if I won the second. I paid no attention to him.

Just concentrating on the pieces like he wasn't there. Not letting his face influence my moves. I won.

After winning I looked up. Nothing could have prepared me for what I saw. He won one, I won one. How could anybody feel bad about that? But he was furious, glowing red. He was just able to talk—very tersely, as his eyes bored into my brain. "Of course we have to play a third." I tried to beg off but there was no way.

The third game was the worst. My brain was all haywire. The game took forever. I found excuses to go to the fire and get it to tell me what move to make. I didn't trust myself, didn't want the burden of whatever was on this game. He had his helpers too. It didn't take long to see that.

The way he played chess certainly didn't help my impression that he wasn't on the level. That this should be the first person I met outside of the hospital was weird. Chess players like him don't just show up.

I wanted out. Every time I made a good move I thought he was going to throw the board at me. This is no fun, this is no fun, this is no fun. And then to mock me, every once in a while he would look up at me with a cruel smile and say, "Fun, isn't it?"

"Sure," I mumbled. Is he going to kill me if I beat him? Or is he going to get to kill me or win my soul or the souls of those I love if I lose? I wish someone would explain these things to me.

It was something my father had always thought would please me. A chance to play a real master. Somehow he had resurrected Paul Morphy and that was who I was playing. Morphy for morphine, more fiend. Morphy because Morphy ended up in a nut house. Morphy because he was my favorite chess player. "Happy birthday, Mark. Paul Morphy."

"Pretty neat, Pop, but I don't think he likes me much."

I talked to Nick about some of the stuff I knew about Morphy. But Nick's face, per usual, wasn't giving anything away.

How could I tell the others what was going down? This guy

Paul wasn't on the level. This cat was bad news, like the worst, like awful, awful, awful, like please, please, please. Bustle, bustle, smoke dope and giggle while the fate of the world is going down on a chess board in your own kitchen. And you don't even see. Helppppppppppppp!

This was to teach me a lesson. "I do warn you well, it is no child's play." Was I supposed to learn to hate chess because it was a competitive, violent, no-goodnik, ugly thing? Virginia was looking at me oddly from time to time. This might be her idea of just what the doctor ordered for Mark. Teach me to think I'm so fucking smart.

Mostly I just tried to play as if he weren't a ringer, as if it were just a friendly game. Like offering to let him take moves back, playing like there was nothing at stake. He wouldn't take any moves back and his look let me know that if I blew it, there would be no mercy. Mostly I just wanted out, but I have to admit I wanted to show Virginia and Nick and whatever angels happened to be watching that I was no small-time chess player myself. I could almost hear the anti-Mark team gnashing their teeth, amazed again at how they had underestimated little old Mark again.

"Fun, isn't it?" Nick said again. His face twisted. Red bones showing. All he needed was horns.

I could barely see where the pieces were. I kept slipping away and coming back to a game that looked completely different from before. He never stopped looking at me, even when he was moving. Inexorable, inexorable.

"Your game is hopeless. Concede."

"What?" I had been off in a fog. He repeated what he had said.

I looked at the board. It kept blurring and twisting.

"It's a draw," the voices said. "You can keep him in perpetual check."

I summoned all my strength to make my words behave better than the chess pieces.

"It's a draw," I echoed. "I can keep you in perpetual check."

"What?" he said, as if this were a new rule I had just made up. I couldn't argue the point, I just wasn't up to it.

"Check," I said. He moved. "Check." He moved again. "Check." He moved again, bringing about the same position. "Check." I started the interminable round again, hoping he'd get the point.

"You can't do that," he almost whined. "As soon as you stop checking me you're mated, the game is over."

"I have no intention of not checking you," I stammered thickly. His rage was rising. He was going to expose me. He was going to tell about how the voices from the fire and wind had told me my moves.

"So we can both live to play another day," I said incoherently. "A draw. Nice game, Nick. Hope we do it again." I fled upstairs to bed.

Among amateurs, most "touch-move" games are lost on stupid blunders. The game becomes pointless very early: neither player learns anything. I'm capable of playing a good game of touch-move, but I have a hard time enjoying it. I beat players I should lose to and lose to players I should beat. Either way, it leaves a bad taste in my mouth.

Touch-move fans argue with equal fervor that being able to take moves back ruins the game. It's bad preparation for tournament play, encourages sloppiness. Maybe they're right. Maybe we should be made to face the consequences of our blunders. Cold hard world and all.

Life is a lot more like touch-move than friendly chess, but maybe that's because there are so many goddamned touch-move players around.

What I hope is true is that if we go about it the right way, we can take back a lot more than we think we can. If we could all make an effort to let anyone take back anything, if it's in our power to let them take back instead of jumping so greedily at mistakes, we might be able to make life much more pleasant. We might even be able to find a way to go backward in time and patch up what now look like irrevoca-

ble blunders. Letting friends take back chess moves would be
as good a way to start as any.

Sex had never been very carefree or playful between Virginia and me. The events of the past two and half months
were hardly calculated to improve matters. Getting back together was tentative and gingerly. We were two very scared
china dolls. Sex had less than ever to do with biological desire
and was more than ever a garble of symbolic proofs and
deeper needs. It was a desperately important hurdle.

There was so much to say that neither of us said anything.
The first couple of nights we just rubbed and clumsily
hugged each other, pulling back every five minutes or so and
looking into each other's scared, pleading eyes trying to figure
out what if anything was understood between us.

We finally made love. Considering what we had been
through, having any kind of sex was plenty ambitious, but at
the same time having been through all that shit somehow
raised the ante. For it to have been good it had to be much
better than it had been, and it wasn't. In fact it seemed that
nothing had changed at all.

Somehow ten days went by and it was time for me to go
into town and take my immigration physical. Everyone else
had gotten theirs out of the way while I was in the hospital. I
had set up an appointment at the Powell River clinic by
phone just before we came up. Kathy, having set a record of
two months straight on the farm, decided to come with me.

"Are you sure you don't want me to come with you?" Simon asked.

"No, I'll be fine." Was he worried that I'd crack up again?
Did he think he could do something about it if I did? Virginia
asked me the same thing. I responded the same way and had
the same reflections. Had Dr. Dale told them something he
hadn't told me? Did they have special instructions on how to
handle me?

In midafternoon we all tromped down to the lake, list in

hand, a couple of bags of laundry, letters to be sent, library books to be returned. We'd be back the next day, the day after at the most. From the big deal and all the ceremony at the lake, you wouldn't have thought it was such a routine trip. It made me a little nervous, as if there was something I wasn't being let in on. Simon, Virginia, Zeke, Nick, Nootka, Tanga, everyone came down to the lake. Much hugging and excited chatter. Nick had carried the laundry bags down and threw them to me and I caught that look in his eyes again, like there was some special understanding between us. I had a job to do? I wasn't supposed to come back? He would take care of the farm and I would take care of the rest of the world? Nice try, old man, good game, or something? I looked back knowingly. I didn't have the faintest idea of what his look meant, but I could fake it.

Good-by, good-by. You've all been swell. I swallowed the lump in my throat and the tears in my eyes. I'll be back, don't worry. Sleep tight. What bad can happen?

Mark at the helm again. The loader of the boat, the starter of the engine, the regulator of the engine, the navigator, captain in charge of comfort, safety, and peace of mind of my passengers.

Thank God for chores. Something with a beginning and an end. Get the boat and Kathy safely to town. The lake was fairly rough, but she seemed to believe in me completely.

I was into the boat and the waves. Riding them very carefully. Adjusting speed and angles constantly, getting the most out of every crest. It really felt like magic. At the marina, Kathy said that it had been the most enjoyable, worry-free trip she had ever had down the lake.

I started breathing much easier. I was a good captain. I had something to give. I felt a slight giddiness about the whole thing.

Most people who end up in a nut house stay there. People as crazy as I was aren't supposed to get well. Mostly if they do they're cripples one way or another forever. Mostly they never regain joy or competence or the trust of those around them. Here I am. Free. Beautiful and energetic. Returned from the dead and on my way to my long and good life. On my way to my old age, in which I will be a great source of embarrassment and pride to my children and grandchildren. Tough old goat.

The water, the sky, the trees. Life. How nice not to be locked away from it.

We went into the marina for coffee. I was feeling great. Bea was there and said how much better I looked than when she had seen me only ten days ago. "Yes, yes, yes, Bea. It's all on the up now. No more being sick for me. I'm going to get so strong and healthy it'll make you sick." Bea laughed and gave me some free pie. "You still could use a little more weight." What a wonderful mother.

What a wonderful feeling. What a wonderful place to end my generational collage. Going crazy and getting well was just what I needed. I was missing something before. This was just the right twist. A real thing that happened that everyone could agree happened. All that other stuff, all the stuff before the farm and then the farm, was all much more elusive. Head changes and all. It could be argued whether or not they were really happening. But now a real nut house, got my ass shot full of real Thorazine and all that other stuff.

Before maybe I was exaggerating all the bad things, all the villains, all my trials and tribulations. People might not think it was really that bad. Maybe they wouldn't have wanted out of Boston the way I wanted out of Boston. But they'd certainly have wanted out of the nut house the way I wanted out of the nut house.

3
Rounds Two, Three, and Going Home

It's got to be over before you can say,
"That's the best time I ever had."

—S. ADAMS AND H. SMITH

Town Again. "Did you come down for the fight?" One of Bea's kids talking.

"The fight?"

"The heavyweight championship, Ali vs. Frazier."

"No. I didn't even know there was going to be one." Well, one more thing along with the mill, automobiles, the war, that my craziness didn't put a dent in. Haven't people had enough of that shit? How can people get so excited about two men trying to kill each other in a ring?

On to the post office. And for transportation, what else but faithful Car Car, the old Volks that had no right to keep running, great friend of its keeper who had no right to be out of the nut house and so cheerful and spunky to boot. I was cheerful, Kathy was cheerful, Car Car was cheerful.

There were three important pieces of mail—a very nice get-well letter from Genie, one of the few people I had felt close to at Swarthmore, a poster from my father, and a letter from Vincent addressed to "Virginia and the Folks."

The letter from Genie had been forwarded from the hospital. She was sorry I had gone nuts, wondered what it was like, hoped I'd be feeling better soon, plus a few paragraphs of chitchat about various friends. It wasn't a heavy letter but it started me thinking about a heavy question. Why had I put so much distance between myself and the people, places, and things I really loved? How did I end up in the middle of nowhere with a bunch of Swarthmore people I had barely known at all? In a love relationship with so little warmth?

The poster from my father was a spaced-out, apocalyptic, mystic, back-to-the-earth quote. I don't remember that much of it or who said it. "What we are doing is real . . . If we have to go to the headwaters of the Amazon to establish enclaves of civilization . . . return to Caesar's grave . . . Not everyone should go . . . artisans . . ." How did Pa feel about that quote? How did he feel about the farm? How did he feel about my going nuts? But there was no enclosed letter or explanation of any sort, just the goddamned poster.

I hesitated a bit before opening the letter from Vincent, but he'd buggered around in my life enough. I was one of the "folks," wasn't I? Damn the torpedoes.

"Dear People." My mind focused, picking out poor wording, punctuation mistakes, affectations, clumsy constructions. I just barely resisted the impulse to correct it with red pencil and send it back for rewriting.

"Kathy, read this and tell me if I'm out of line thinking it's an unforgivably whiny maudlin pile of shit."

She read it and wasn't as hard on it as I was, but she didn't think I was out of line.

All sorts of memories about Vincent came flooding back. From Swarthmore, the trip to North Carolina, Boston, the farm. I got madder and madder. It felt good. I could get mad without going mad. I wasn't going to say that Vincent wasn't full of shit out of fear that people might put it down to jealousy. Fuck that shit. That's how people end up in nut houses.

My immigration physical was the next day. "They've never seen such health." I was worried some about the questions about ever having been in a mental hospital. I hadn't really figured out how to handle that one. I'd probably tell the truth, what the hell. If they were going to give me shit about it, that was their problem. It was a side issue not really worth thinking about. If I could get myself out of a nut house as quick as I had, I could certainly deal with the Immigration Department.

On to the laundromat. Load up the machines, feed the machines quarters. Make it all clean. A fresh start. By-by old dirt and good riddance. While the machines did their thing, Kathy and I went over to the Marine Inn. The waitress who had given me the Mu tea wasn't there. How nice it was to eat a meal and not have it be the last supper over and over again. I had a steak sandwich just to be tough, on whole-wheat bread just to be healthy. Kathy had one too. We laughed about our sinfulness and agreed the steak sandwich tasted pretty good. We went back and put the clothes in the dryers and went and had a beer. That felt good, too. We had another.

While we were folding clothes, Joe and Mary came in. They had had it with the Powell River area and were about to head for the interior. Land was too expensive here. The De Soto had demised and they'd bought a Microbus. Debts were building up and Joe couldn't get enough work. They were moving on.

They asked us to come to dinner. We were delighted. We hadn't figured out where we were going to stay and they showed up at just the right time and solved everything.

"There's this guy with us who's a big fan of your father's and is dying to meet you. I hope that won't be too big a pain in the ass."

"No," I said, "I should be used to that by now." They gave us a map to their house, the third house they had had in the same number of months.

See how well God takes care of everything? Just one foot in front of the other and everything goes fine. Food, a place to stay, a warm, nice evening with Joe and Mary. What could be better?

We diddled around some more, returning the books, picking out a few to take back up with us, getting a few things we needed at the hardware store. The groceries we figured we'd do the next day, after my physical.

After we had done all the chores we were going to do and since we had all those nice clean clothes, I decided I'd spend seventy-five cents on a shower. It was a sideline of the people who ran the laundromat. They lived above it, and considering the unlimited hot water they had, and all the tourists who camped or came in boats, it made a lot of sense.

So, one foot in front of the other, I walked up the stairs to their front door and rang the bell. It always felt a little strange coming into a strange family's living room and asking to take a shower. This time they seemed flustered. Maybe they had been in the middle of a family argument or something, maybe they were having an early dinner. Anyway, they seemed to be looking at me funny. Maybe they had heard about the hippie who went nuts. Maybe I looked really dirty. Maybe it was the beer on my breath.

"Wait right here. I'll get some new soap." He—their son, I figured—was talking very fast. "We've been having some trouble with the shower. The water doesn't shut off completely. There might be some change in the temperature. My mother's running the washing machine." A mile a minute this guy was going. "I hope everything will be all right."

"Relax, relax, everything's just fine."

Filthy Hippie. "What a perfect place to grow a plague." I was thinking in the shower about my own little body. At the farm we didn't have running cold water, let alone running hot water. That and our inadequate insulation and heating made bathing rare. Occasionally we'd get the stoves roaring, heat up a lot of hot water, and do sponge baths, but it was a lot of hassle and didn't really do the trick anyway. Usually we did without and got pretty filthy. I didn't mind it much. It seemed like a healthy alternative to the spick-and-span neurosis of a shower every day, if not twice, plus underarm deodorant, etc.

I had always figured that if there were a plague that was

going to sweep over the world, it would come out of some citadel of modern medicine, a place where the selective evolutionary pressure was so tough on germs that a superstrain would evolve that sulfuric acid couldn't touch.

But then there was this thing in my crotch. I called it my pet. I had had it off and on for years. I guess it was a fungus of sorts. It didn't do much except itch occasionally. When it got out of hand I'd sock it with a little iodine or Desenex until it straightened out. But for some reason I never killed it off completely. Virginia never picked it up, so I figured it wasn't very contagious. Perhaps I was the only place where this thing could live and I didn't want to add to the long list of things made extinct by man. You could say I was sentimental about it.

Another place I might have bred a nice enough plague was in the mouthpiece of my saxophone. Sometimes it was years between washings. All sorts of cute little things grew there.

I turned on the water as hot as I could stand it and scrubbed and scrubbed and scrubbed. No filthy hippie me. Good-by old dirt, good riddance. A fresh start, a new me. Clean, superclean. How nice to be in the shower and not worry about Auschwitz.

I used up what I figured was my seventy-five cents and got out, dried myself, looked in the mirror, and noted that a little weight was coming back.

Clean, clean, clean. Feeling good, good, good. Clean me, clean clothes. Driving out to good old Joe and Mary's in good old Car Car, taking each hill as it comes, each curve as it comes, in tune with the car and the road as much as with the boat and the lake. One foot in front of the other, simple, so much fun. How many other people ever really drive a car? I mean really drive a car or really steer a boat or really, I mean really, really eat an egg or prune a tree or take a shower or eat a steak sandwich? Lucky, lucky me. What a swell planet.

Up the hill and down the hill, shifting just right, so as not to screw my clutch. It was the clutch more than anything else that made driving Car Car an art. One foot in front of the other, the secret of making my car go. The secret to my getting out of the nut house. It's so simple, such a gas, and it works, works, works. No reason for people to be such jerks, jerks, jerks. No reason for wars, either. If everyone would just catch on to this one foot in front of the other thing maybe the shit would just stop happening. Maybe, maybe, maybe. Who can say? Crest and surge and shift and turn. "There's the VW bus. That must be the place."

Dinner, Etc. I liked staying with Joe and Mary. I usually found an evening with Joe and Mary just the change of pace I needed. I liked it for the same reasons Virginia and some of the others felt uncomfortable there. It was a vacation from hipness.

I didn't feel at home with them as I did with hipper hippies, but there were plenty of times when I didn't feel like feeling at home. There were times when I wanted some hot tea, central heating, electric lights, a nuclear family. Innocence. They would have hated to hear me say that and I never admitted it to myself in so many words. My feelings about Joe and Mary were just one more thing I felt vaguely guilty and defensive about. Getting away from the farm for a bit was nice. It wasn't fear of being cut off, it was just that people, events, weather all mattered so much up there.

I didn't want my life to be a series of evenings with Joe and Mary, I wanted the ups and downs. But it was nice to be with people my life wasn't so hopelessly tangled up with.

If I had been looking for a heavy time, I would have asked Virginia to come to town with me and Joe and Mary's would have been the last place I went. I wasn't looking for a place to get the Eden Express rolling again.

Greetings, greetings.

"Mark, this is David."

"You've probably heard this a million times before, but I've read everything your old man's written and really dig his stuff. I'm really a fan." I just smiled and nodded. Fan seemed like a nice enough kid.

When I met Fan's woman, Becky, I did a double take. She might as well have been Genie, whose letter was in my hip pocket: the body scaled down a touch, but the same sort of face, hair, and sexuality. Wearing a Triumph t-shirt to boot. She was helping Mary do up what looked to be an ace meal. Lots of mashed potatoes, corn, sausage, salad, rolls.

Joe and Mary's new place was quite a change from the previous ones. The others had been in town; this one was about eight miles out toward Lund. Their other places hadn't been what you would call luxurious, but they had a marginal respectability to them, with electricity, indoor plumbing, light fixtures, some furniture. This new place of theirs was more a cabin than a house. It had some electricity, some kerosene lamps, central heating, plumbing—but none of it was very reliable. There was a telephone that didn't work. The place was all crazy-quilt. Nothing fitted together or seemed to follow.

It went so nicely. I was getting exactly the kind of Joe-and-Mary evening I had looked forward to. A good meal. Sitting around afterward talking, playing with Sarah, listening to music, watching Sarah play with Fan's dog. Everyone enjoying everyone else. Worrying about going nuts again was the furthest thing from my mind. I felt so relaxed, so unthreatened, so comfortable. I was on vacation.

In a matter of a couple of hours, maybe less, everything changed. Suddenly my life became inextricably balled up with Joe and Mary's and Fan's and Fan's Becky's and Kathy's. I started caring about what went on there and with those people as much as if not more than I cared about the farm or Virginia or anything else.

Maybe if Fan hadn't asked so many dumb questions about my father. Maybe if we hadn't smoked so goddamned much dope. Maybe if Joe and Mary hadn't said so many dumb things, if they hadn't been so all-fired-up enthusiastic about all the new drugs they had been trying and becoming so hip.

Maybe if there hadn't been so much music, or even if the volume had been a little lower or the music a little lighter.

One way or another, things started happening. At some point what was going on stopped being conversation and started being something else. Getting up and saying "It was a wonderful meal and nice talk. I'm tired. I'll see you in the morning" was no longer possible.

Something real had started happening. Exactly the sort of thing I was trying to avoid by coming to Joe and Mary's.

They'd want something flashy from me, then it would switch around and they were trying to do something for me. The favors in both directions ran the gamut from pedestrian to profound. Who was doing what to whom was never very clear. It was a cosmic orgy of the deaf, dumb, and blind. We were all in over our heads.

I didn't want to help them. I didn't want them to help me. I just wanted to go to bed, take my stupid immigration physical the next day, and go back up to the farm.

A hell of a lot of dope. I remember hoping it would make things better. I remember its making things worse and being unable to stop. I remember wanting to stop.

Fan David was rolling the joints, lots of them. I thought, this kid's got to run out some day, but they kept coming and coming. I'd pretend to be asleep or sometimes really drift off. He'd shake my arm and make sure I never missed a round. It would look funny if I said no or just passed the joint. Maybe they'd think I was going nuts again. When in doubt, do like those around you are doing. Those around me were smoking dope nonstop. I didn't want to make a fuss.

I felt sick to my stomach. It was hot. The air in the room was stale and stuffy. Tobacco smoke, dope smoke, smoke from the furnace in the basement. Had I tried to stand up, I would have passed out.

It was harder and harder to concentrate. That was OK. Attendance wasn't required. Everyone seemed to be drifting in and out of it. Eventually we'd all drift off to sleep. Tomorrow was another day.

Trying to pay attention wasn't very rewarding. It made me feel sicker and there never seemed to be much worth paying attention to. Letting myself drift off seemed to make my stomach feel better.

I was in a drift-off that seemed to go on forever when suddenly a rush of glee seemed to sweep away all the nausea, all the stuffiness, all the fog. Then, "Oh, shit," my heartbeat and the music were going together. Crazy silliness, but such an irrefutable fact that there wasn't much point in arguing with it.

The next song was a little slower. I relaxed and felt much better. But what if it had been faster? All anyone who wants to kill me would have to do is flip that little lever to 78. The perfect crime. What if someone suddenly got it into their head they wanted to hear "Flight of the Bumblebee"? "Please, please. Anything but 'Flight of the Bumblebee'!" But how could I say anything like that without everyone thinking I was nuts again?

All of a sudden I was somewhere without the faintest idea of how I got there. Remembering what a bitch it was philosophically to prove that there was anything but the present if there was even that. Not having the faintest idea what time it was. How long had I blanked? A minute, a day, years, millennia? Maybe I didn't blank at all. Maybe I just think I blanked. But something's out of tune. Either more has happened to here than me or more to me than here. One of us has changed.

When I was able to think at all, I'd go back over the evening, trying to figure out what the fuck had fucked up.

We've been talking about weird things, but lots of people talk about weird things, especially when there's that much dope going around. Astrology, ESP, drugs, hypnotism, schizophrenia, etc., etc. All perfectly standard-issue topics of conversation. Talking about weird things wasn't enough to account for things getting so weird.

I talked less weirdly about the weird things we were talking about. I was the conservative, but conservative with a twist. Fuck me and my goddamned twists. Conservative with a twist, hippie with a twist, artist with a twist, crazy with a twist, everything with a goddamned twist. I couldn't do anything straight to save my twisty life.

Maybe I saw the possibility of taking everyone up on all their weirdness and couldn't resist. "So you like weirdness. Try this one on for size."

Telling them about being in a nut house brought weirdness a couple of light-years closer to home, but how could I resist? This was my first shot at virgins. Everyone else I had talked to already knew about it. They had all had a chance to think about it some. This was my first chance to bring the news. And besides, it fit perfectly into all the other weird things they were talking about. All in all, I had shown great restraint in not bringing it up a lot sooner than I did.

They had so many misconceptions about insanity and seemed so interested I had to try to straighten them out. Maybe I let myself go nuts for the purpose of instruction: Mark's Real Life University course in psychosis.

How much did I tell them about the Eden Express?

One way or another, the ball got rolling. Curiosities were pricked. Lots of private hazy hunches were confirmed and focused all at once. We saw doors we had never seen before and found keys we didn't know we had.

We started off light, doing things like straightening out a kink in Joe's back. Apparently he had been more or less in pain from it for years. It had something to do with his father but that's another story. Then we got into some subtler things, like a kink or two in Joe and Mary's marriage.

It's hard for me to describe, because when I was at my best I wasn't really there at all. We stumbled on some tricks of the exorcism trade and were chucking out the little demons who were mucking up our lives as fast as we could find them.

I remember Mary telling me I didn't have to worry about

any repercussions. The forces of darkness had thrown everything they had at me and I had won. My crackup was like a
vaccination. I had rounded the corner and everything was
going to get better and better for me.

"I sure as hell hope you're right." I remember thinking that
the particular demons and spirits we had dealt with so far
were small-timers and worrying that as soon as word got back
to their big brothers it was going to be shit city again.

"How are we doing this?" Very straightforward question. I
don't remember who asked it.

I wasn't sure, but I had some hunches. "I'm not sure, but I
have some hunches. The potential is always there. You've got
to somehow get a harmony going. It's got to be exact. You
have to have all the parts and nothing left over. Anything we
need is here, as long as we maintain a closed system. Once we
establish that, we can become anything. I know it helps to be
cut off somehow to realize the necessary completeness and
harmony. What we've become is a safety valve. We're letting
a lot of steam escape. Safely."

I think most of the really heavy things happened after my
first attempt to get some sleep and pretend nothing very extraordinary was happening.

Kathy and I had brought our sleeping bags with us. The
room we were supposed to crash in was a little side room. It
might have been an entrance at one point. It was hard to tell,
it was such a crazy building. Crazy plumbing, crazy heating,
crazy basement, crazy everything. There were piles of books
and all sorts of other junk. We stumbled around making separate little nests for ourselves.

Parallels, parallels, parallels. There we were, crashing.

There was Kathy. There was me. Both with the sort of
sleeping bags that could zip together to make a double. I was
feeling a little sick and nervous and lonely and jittery. That
was how it started with Vincent and Virginia. She was feeling
bad and lonely and not able to sleep. Vincent rubbed her
stomach for her and then one thing led to another. Under-

standable, even beautiful. But it never happened with me. I got into these situations where it would be understandable, beautiful, poetic, loving, just what the doctor ordered. It sure would be nice to relax about this sort of crap. It would be a big help toward getting some sleep and feeling more like one of the gang. It made sense in every conceivable way, but I knew it wouldn't happen. It wasn't fair, but I couldn't figure out who was to blame.

A rainstorm had started after dinner and was becoming increasingly violent. I heard someone moving around in the living room. Joe and Mary were saying something was all fucked up with the furnace. I went to use the bathroom just off our little side room. Just as I flushed the toilet, I heard Mary saying, "Don't flush the toilet." I confessed and asked if there was anything I could do to fix it. She said very tiredly it could wait till morning. Everything was falling apart.

In the little room where Kathy and I were crashing, I found a few ink and crayon drawings I had done on some earlier visit with Joe and Mary. They seemed terribly important. I sat there looking at them, trying to figure out their import.

I should have known or someone should have known. Known what? That I was nutty as a fruitcake? Trouble ahead? I should have left Virginia? I should have been a painter instead of doing the farm? The world was going to end soon?

Kathy was looking at them too. "You know, Mark, this sort of thing is much more important and real than the farm."

"Light under bushel burn house down?" I was trying to laugh. It was comforting that if I flunked farm I could be good for something else and that Kathy and others like her would see what I was doing as worthwhile.

Kathy tried to sleep. Her eyes were closed, her mouth slightly open; she was breathing in gulps, the way I sometimes did. Virginia hated the way I breathed. She said it kept her awake and made her nervous. I was being piggy with the oxygen.

Kathy lying there all swaddled in that icy blue. I had always thought she was kind of pretty, but looking at her now she was exquisitely beautiful.

What a bitch Virge was not to like her more. Maybe it was the way she breathed. Kathy wasn't liberated enough or something. The couple thing she and Jack had going didn't pass muster. Come to think of it, I couldn't think of any couple thing Virginia approved of or anything that seemed to turn her on more than a marriage or a long-standing man-woman thing breaking up.

I got in my sleeping bag and tried to go to sleep but it was hopeless. I was wide, wide, wider than wide awake.

Kathy, my stomach feels all screwed up. Could you rub it? No, no. That was all wrong. It was clumsy and stupid. It was what I meant, but somehow there was no way for me to say it.

Was Virginia not thinking about fucking when she asked Vincent to rub her stomach? What a luxury. I couldn't ask anyone for a glass of water without thinking about fucking. Men, women, children, dogs, goats, and on and on. Some part of me somewhere wanted to fuck everything.

And here I was in a situation that wasn't half as kinky as some of my dreams and hallucinations. About my age, single, the opposite sex, someone I had known and liked for a long time. But I wasn't any more sure that I really wanted to sleep with Kathy than I was that I didn't want to hump alder trees.

Maybe if she rubbed my stomach she'd want to sleep with me and I wouldn't want to sleep with her. And if we did make love, weren't things complicated enough at the farm already? It would be doing to Jack what Vincent did to me or doing to Kathy what Vincent had done to Virge or doing to Virge what Virge had done to me and on and on. Not that those things had been bad. In fact it might be doing us all a world of good, but maybe it would be a good idea to let the smoke clear from round one before firing off round two.

Maybe a good toss in bed would do the trick. According to
Freud, sexual repression was the root of mental illness. The
sexual content of my hallucinations made it clear my crotch
was somehow involved. If I wasn't such an uptight, hung-up,
sexual prig, if I could just let myself go go go . . . but where
would it stop stop stop?

If I gave in to all my sexual impulses, I wouldn't have time
for much else. Maybe Warren was right about lust being my
big sin. Maybe I should be put away for the public good. If
the choice was between spending my life in a padded cell and
giving in to every sexual impulse, I'd just as soon one as the
other and I could hardly blame the powers that be if they
decided on the padded cell.

A possible alternative suggested by Jesus didn't appeal
much either. If your left hand offends you, cut it off. If your
right eye causes you to sin, pluck it out.

The person I least wanted to know about my sexuality was
Virginia. She might put it all together and figure out that my
being monogamous with her was the sexual equivalent of
what I wanted from an evening with Mary and Joe. I wasn't
following my "heart." Had I followed my heart, I would have
ended up exhausted and with some pretty strange bedfel-
lows.

So there I was, going nuts again and pretty sure I was going
nuts again. The voices were getting clearer and more insistent. The crazy taste was in the back of my mouth. Things
were starting to glow and shimmer again. Thinking maybe if I
could make love with someone it would defuse this whole
damn thing, but it becomes too late too fast. As soon as it
starts happening people are scared to death just to talk with
you. For someone to be able to get into all the tenderness and
unguardedness of nakedness and lovemaking with someone
on the verge of a breakdown, they'd have to be either awfully
brave or so dumb they didn't realize what was happening.

What if I just laid it on the line? Kathy, I'm starting to
crack up again. If you will just hold me and maybe make love
with me, maybe everything will be all right.

What if she said yes and we made love and I still cracked up? She might figure there was something more she could have done and just be one more person feeling guilty and helpless. Even if it worked, I'd spend the rest of my life wondering if I had cried wolf just to get laid.

If it worked, did that mean I had to go through life with this awful threat over my head? If I didn't get laid every two days or so I'd go crazy? Maybe the problem would get more serious. It would get to be once a day and then once every twelve hours and so on till someone had to invent a twenty-four-hour-a-day fucking machine just for me.

Maybe the object of my affections would work the same way. Now I could stay out of the nut house by giving in to my sexual impulses toward Kathy, later I wouldn't be able to resist chickens and get away with it.

I was supposed to take my immigration physical the next day, the same goddamned physical I was supposed to take when I went bonkers the last time. What is it with me and this physical, anyway?

Just a few hours earlier it was nothing to worry about. Just another dumb thing. Nothing very exciting one way or another could happen. But now all that was changed. My body was all fucked up again. I was hot when others were cold, cold when others were hot. I was going into faints and shakes bordering on convulsions. My heartbeat seemed all wrong. What would happen if I blanked and ran amuck or whatever it was I did in those blanks? My voice was unrecognizable and words were getting out of place.

Was the prospect of an immigration physical screwing me up this bad? What would happen if anything serious came up?

No matter what it was that was cracking me, there would always be fans, Joe and Marys, rain and wind and smoke in the air. There would always be weird conversations and immigration physicals and sexual confusion and all the other kinds of confusion. What bothered me wasn't so much the shit, but my low and getting-lower shit tolerance.

I got up and talked with Kathy. I got up and tried to read. I got up and found myself talking with Joe and Mary. Did push-ups, trying to exhaust myself. I tried yoga, meditation, drawing, writing, anything I could get my hands on, and then tried to sleep and then got up again.

I heard voices in the living room. There was light coming under the door. It was Joe, Mary, and Fan talking but their voices sounded strange. I tried to go to sleep.

Very low and wispy, like wind: "Mark, Mark, Mark." Being polite, I got up and went into the living room. Mary was wearing some priestess-type outfit. She told me to sit down in a voice too low to be hers or anyone else's for that matter. Her legs were spread and her crotch was glowing smoky Day-Glo orange.

Why couldn't it be her fingers or something else? Why her crotch? What the hell is that supposed to mean? Don't I have enough problems without Day-Glo crotches? I tried not to stare. It seemed an unnecessary touch. I wasn't about to argue that whatever my problem was, there was a lot of sex involved. Day-Glo crotches seemed to be rubbing it in.

"Do we have time to move to higher ground?" There was that voice that wasn't Mary's coming from Mary again.

"Huh? Come again?" I had heard but was stalling for a little time.

"Do we have to move to higher ground?" She sounded impatient. The storm outside took on a new meaning, or rather a meaning I had been trying to push out of my mind.

"Higher ground?" I looked at her, trying to catch a glimpse of humor. There was no movement in her face.

"Higher ground is within." It seemed to be the right thing to say. There was a long, long silence.

Well, these people need a prophet and I guess, times being what they are, short notice and all, I'm the best they could do. They seemed to think I knew something they didn't, that I had access to cosmic truths. So I started talking. I started teaching. I started preparing them and me for what we were going through. How to deal with the end of the world and how to deal with being crazy. There were plenty of parallels. "The first lesson is about time. 'Cause time is what you're about to run out of. The first lesson is no matter how little or how much actual clock-calendar time remains to you, there is enough. Enough to get done whatever you have to get done. So don't panic. Even if it's only a minute or even just a second, there is time. There is enough time."

Back under my sleeping bag. Shaking, not knowing whether I was too cold or too hot. Cut off. The storm was raging. The fire was out. The heat I had was all there was. There was no way to move. I just lay there groaning trying not to. Way out at the end of Highway 101. A broken phone, broken plumbing, a broken furnace. Were the others dead? Why couldn't I move? How long had I been lying there? Cabin fever. Jack London. The waiting, lying, trying to hold on to whatever so there would be something for them to save when they got there. Oh, shit, why did I ever leave Massachusetts? Trade the friendly, nicely scaled hills and plants for these monster trees, monster mountains, monster beauty where man didn't really belong? Barnstable Harbor for Powell Lake? A rotten trade. Rock and water, no mud. I'd give anything for a little mud. Cut off. Shit, fuck, cunt, bitch, whore. Remember old rock songs and old friends to pass the time. Wait for the inevitable, the earth claiming back what was hers. The antibody systems of Mother Earth wiping me out. It made such sense. It was just surprising it hadn't happened earlier. How long did I think I could get away with it? Stupid stupid stupid. I'd so much rather die in the Barnstable marsh instead of British Columbia. Why, when I got out, didn't I head home? Talk about being willfully dense. Talk about being Taurus. Talk about being perverse. I'm sorry again, too late again.

* * *

When I was a child I fell thirty feet from a tree onto my
head. I realized I was dying but wasn't really very upset about
it. I was dreaming, drifting back through my life like a cloud,
and everything made perfect sense. The dream had given me
promise that pleasant enough things were ahead, so I kept
sinking back into that dream world. Why get sore? But gradually I wasn't able to sink into the peace as deeply as I had
before. I kept coming back to the very real pain. The pain
became stronger, the dream weaker, and I realized I was
going to live after all.

Darwinian explanation of why your life flashes before you
just before you die is impossible. Evolution has no use for
dying things. Since it can't be an evolutionary thing, probably
all organisms experience something similar. More complicated entities like friendships, love affairs, cultures and institutions seem to go through a comparable process. There's
something in consciousness that seems to favor neat endings.

I knew something was ending. The voices, the dreams, the
visions and other wild things were all clues to what was dying, but I couldn't put it all together.

"Let me go, Mark. Please let me go." It was my father
again, begging me, pleading with me, trying to explain, trying
again to make me hate him. Again I got the feeling he wanted
to kill himself.

"Don't you see I'm responsible for all this pain you're going
through? How can you not hate me?"

"If you weren't the fifteenth joker through here in the last
few hours trying to claim responsibility for the hell I'm in, I
might be able to take you more seriously. I admit you've got a
better case than most. A lot of what's going on certainly has
your flavor to it, but there are plenty of others who have a
reasonable case. Virge is pretty sure she did it. Mother certainly had her hand in it. Bob Dylan, believe it or not, was just
through to apologize and try to make it all better. He figured
the whole thing was his fault. I told him to tell you that.

Tolstoy was sorry I had taken his work so seriously. Said he was awfully sorry, he just couldn't have known what would happen but all the same he's glad to know how it turned out. Jesus said he'd do what he could but I could tell by the look on his face he wasn't sure he could be of much help.

"The thing I'm telling them and want to tell you too is that it's not all that bad. I've really had an awfully good life and don't feel sore at anyone. I have a feeling that I'm somehow where all you big deals were afraid to go. Where you all drew the line and chickened out. That may sound grandiose but it certainly feels like that's what's happening. You all feel shitty because you figure that where I am must be unbelievably awful and that things you did steered me to this. It's true I never would have gotten here without you, but it's not all that bad. I'm finding out lots of interesting stuff. Doing lots of things I've always wanted to do.

"Every time I say something like that you get this unbeliev-able look of horror. How could I possibly be digging this? Like you're afraid I'm going to drag you into it. What would it take for me not to dig something? Well, I'll admit this is hell. I mean, if I was going to try to really do the worst possible thing I could do to someone, this would be it. Whoever set this up is some sort of a genius. But maybe that's what I dig about it. This is awful, the worst thing I could imagine and it's happened. I've taken whoever the fuck is against us's worst punch and I still chuckle a bit about this and that. Isn't that good news?"

Miracle. In the morning the trees were green again. Some-how the destruction had been reversed, the earth reprieved. There was still time.

"Joe and Mary, quick! Pack your stuff, grab your kid. Get in your bus and split. Get to wherever you want to get to quick." I was so happy. Maybe everyone could make it to wherever home was for them. Or maybe just enough time to say "Good-by, I loved you" to a few more people.

"I'm going to step outside, check the weather, get a little

fresh air." They looked at me as if opening the door would let death inside. Mary had been so adamant about my not opening the door the night before.

"Are you sure you want to do that, Mark?"

"Yes, my God, yes. Do you think that if there's a prayer of getting out of here I'm going to pass it up? How long will this break last?"

No one had the energy to stop me. I opened the door. It was still raining pretty hard but the wind had calmed. I breathed shallowly, just tasting it to make sure it wasn't death. The world smelled like it was still alive. "See, I can breathe, nothing bad happening." They looked at me worriedly.

"We can make it, don't be so afraid. Come on, get with it. Wake up! This is our chance."

They just kept looking at me. "What about your physical, Mark?"

"My physical?" How could anybody think that was relevant to anything? I had a hard enough time taking that shit seriously before the apocalypse, shit storms, and eternal truths. "My physical?"

"We very much want you to pass." Why was it so important to them that I pass? It didn't mean diddly to me. Their tone of voice seemed to say that if I took my physical I'd flunk.

"Are you going to tell them about your crackup or not?"

Questions, questions, questions. "I really haven't figured it out."

"Well, Mark, you know it's only physical," Kathy said very meaningfully. The whole sex thing came tumbling down about my head. Why did it have to be Kathy who said that? Like she knew that I knew that she knew that everyone knew the whole thing was sex? Why did she have to look so beautiful? Why hadn't we made love the night before?

Joe and Mary talked about some nice doctor who had taken care of something for them. Said he was an awfully nice guy and that he'd probably be willing to help out. I guess they made a phone call. Anyway, they had it all arranged for me to see him later that same morning.

"You want some coffee?"

"No, thanks, why don't we set out now? I mean, just in case the car breaks down or something. We can have coffee at the marina with Bea. That would be nice. I really want to make sure I don't fuck up this appointment. Let's get moving."

Joe drove. I sat in the front passenger seat. Kathy and Mary were in the back. The bus started. Thank God, thank German mechanics, we're going to make it. Hot shit, I'm not going to die in this shit hole. Gush bump gurgle slop, the bus worked its way up the dirt driveway and climbed up onto the good old solid pavement of Highway 101. Just outside the driveway there was a road crew at work. Thank God for the salt-of-the-earth workers keeping this road in shape. The storm had destroyed it but they had gotten up bright and early to repair our link with the rest of the world. Thank you, thank you, thank you. Everyone's so wonderful. I waved at them with tears of gratitude streaming down my face. They waved back.

"Mark, are you all right?" Joe asked.

"Ya, Joe, I'm fine. It's just that everyone's so wonderful. I never really appreciated it before. I've been terribly blind, I think."

"It's all right, Mark. Just relax. We'll be there in a few minutes."

Things looked none the worse for that dreadful storm. A few branches had come down but that was about it. Then the sun came out and everything got bright, too bright. The whole bus was shaking. The road was shaking and everything on it started to fall apart. Oh, shit, oh, shit. Just hold on. Make like it's not happening. By force of will I kept the road from breaking up, the sun from exploding, the bus from falling apart, and Joe alive and seeing and keeping the bus on the road.

Trying to induce a leisureliness, a lack of urgency, I reminded them about the marina. "Well, let's go have our coffee with Bea."

"Are you sure you want to do that, Mark?"

"Yes yes yes. I'm in no hurry to see the doctor. It's not like this is an emergency or anything. I'd like to have a cup of Bea's coffee." So we stopped.

One foot in front of the other into the little snack bar. "Hi, Bea." She looked worried. Paul, her youngest son, was crying. "Don't worry, Paul, please don't worry. Everything's going to come out fine. Just you wait and see."

There was no one else there. That was usual. Except for us, they didn't really have much business. All for us. Sam and Bea must be losing their shirts in this business and these self-indulgent punks come down from the lake once a month or so, buy a tank of gas, and give them shit about eating meat.

Joe all of a sudden said to me very meaningfully, "You're in. You've made it. Relax, you're in." It seemed like a strange thing to say. I was in where? Mary had spent the past day or so telling me I was out. I looked at Bea. She looked perplexed. Maybe she thought Joe was nuts and dangerous or something.

"Well, OK, if you say so, Joe," I said, sort of winking to Bea. I rolled a cigarette, sipped at my coffee, and talked about the weather some. Yes, it was a strange spring. No, Bea could never remember another that had been like this. Just what I thought, just what I was afraid of. Something had fucked up. What good did being "in" or "out" do me if the earth was dying?

"Well, we'll be seeing you soon, Bea. Give everyone my love," and off we went.

As soon as we got in the car, Joe turned to me and said pleadingly, "Mark, I sure as hell hope you believe in faith healing. I don't think you realize half how many people are behind you." It sounded more like a threat than anything else. If I didn't pull through I would be taking a lot of good people down with me. Bea, all her children, Joe and Mary and Sarah and millions more were all counting on me. The pressure was on. Everyone I cared about had bet their lives on my recovering, whatever that meant.

What kind of quackery show was this going to be? Was some joker going to put his hands on my head and say "In the name of Jesus Christ, be well"?

"I swear to you, Joe, I'll do my best. I'm trying, I'm trying, I'm trying. I'll see the doctor. I'll do anything he asks. Shit, Joe, I'll try to walk on water if you think it will help."

Keep putting one foot in front of the other and hope everything comes out all right. Ride on tough. I didn't see any alternative except maybe . . . maybe the going backward in time thing would work.

"Joe, there's a way for you to get out of this mess. Take from me anything that's yours and run. Take me and leave me by the water where you met me. Do it all backward. Pretend you never met me. There's got to be a way around this. I don't want my not getting well to fuck you up. Just leave me by the water. Faith will meet me by the water."

Joe pulled into the hospital. The big red sign, EMERGENCY ENTRANCE. The dam was right alongside of me now. Oh, shit, the bomb is going to blow. "Keep driving, Mac. I said we had to meet faith by the water. This isn't where you met me."

"Come on, Mark," Joe said apologetically, "we have an appointment."

"OK," I said, scared to death, trying to steady myself for whatever was ahead. I couldn't move. It was awful. It was over.

Joe came around to my side of the bus and opened the door and took my arm. "Come on, Mark. I'll go with you. This won't be so bad."

I was clutching my "important papers." My birth certificate, immigration forms, passport, etc.

"OK," I said weakly, and let Joe lead me out of the car into the hospital. "Did we have to come to the emergency entrance?"

"Relax, Mark, relax."

Joe left me in a chair. I didn't look around. I was too

scared. He went and talked to a nurse in a low voice I couldn't quite catch. It was all arranged. It's not up to me any more. If it ever was, it's not now. Joe and the nurse came over and they led me to a little curtained-off place with a bed on rollers. The nurse left Joe and me there for a bit.

"Now, Mark, this isn't going to hurt. Whatever happens, everything is going to be all right." I just kept looking at him pleadingly. Why hadn't he taken me to the camp site, to the beach, like I had asked? He had betrayed me.

"I don't know what your problem is, Mark, but I'm sure it's bigger than mine," he said, gesturing vulgarly at his crotch. It seemed like a joke in questionable taste.

"Here, Joe, take this," I said, giving him all my identification. "I want you to have it." He looked puzzled.

"Are you sure, Mark?"

"Yes, I'm sure. Take it."

"The doctor will be here in just a little bit," Joe said, and he left.

I sat there for what seemed like years, trying to figure out what the hell was going on. Were they going to operate on me? Cancer? Sterilization? Lobotomy? I couldn't get anywhere with it. So I just sat there and waited.

"Hi, I'm Dr. Miller." There didn't seem to be anything unusual about him. Was he a faith healer? Did he know what my problem was? Was he going to do something about it? What had Joe and Mary told him?

"What seems to be the problem?" Good question. Here I was in the emergency ward, just what was the problem? Why hadn't someone asked me that before? It seemed so straightforward. What was the problem?

"Well, I think my friends are worried about me." It sounded stupid as soon as I said it. I had to be able to do better than that. He just sort of nodded knowlingly. "They're worried about me not passing my immigration physical." That seemed even sillier. Why should they be worried or not worried about my passing my immigration physical? What was the problem?

Stainless steel, gleaming lights, plastic curtains, iridescent floor tiles. One foot in front of the other, counting out nothing, doing my best to answer the questions. Doing my best to make sense to the doctor. One foot in front of the other, on my own power, avoiding looking at anyone. Following my imaginary trail of crumbs. Past all the sick and dying, the coughing, the pale, crippled, confused faces. "Sorry, sorry, sorry."

One way or the other I found myself back in the front seat of the Microbus. Relieved, breathing a little easier. But all was still not well in Mark land. The sky still threatened destruction. There was still a tenseness in me and the people around me. I guess more was required than just seeing Dr. Miller. There was a little piece of paper. It was a prescription for pills I was supposed to take "if the going gets rough." I think I put Kathy in charge of that. How was I supposed to tell when the going got rough? Cyanide to take before I got into the wrong hands? What were right hands, what were wrong hands? Where did the Royal Canadian Mounties stand on all this? The faith healing thing Joe had said on the way still bothered me. Were they going to turn me over to Oral Roberts? Fly me to Israel for a special part in an Easter pageant? The fact that Joe and this Dr. Miller were somehow in cahoots was both comforting and disturbing.

While we were in the drugstore parking lot the wind and rain picked up some. Everything looked dead. Kathy got the pills.

We were just a few blocks from where I was supposed to take my physical. There was maybe about forty-five minutes before my appointment. All the lonely, sick, unhappy people. The sky was crying. Everyone was dragging, stumbling through life. A fat girl went into the drugstore, a limping woman came out. Cars were choking along. The wind and rain slashed through everything, biting and cold, and here I was, safe inside the bus.

I started crying. It was just too awful what life had done to these people. Limping along in their death-spewing automobiles, trying to do chores of one sort or another, and they were all going to die. "It's all right, Mark. You're on the outside." Mary's words. On the outside? The suffering I was seeing wasn't really going on? It was just being projected on the windshield?

"You've got to worry about yourself. Just worry about what you have to do. Your tears won't do them any good now."

So just worry about myself, be tough, keep truckin'. It seems so cruel to not cry, seeing all that terrible stuff. But it wasn't real or didn't matter. Was Virginia inside or out? Ma and Pa and Zeke and all the others? But get tough; worrying about myself is the best way to help! Remember Lot's wife.

The physical? Had Dr. Miller diagnosed something? Was it imperative that I not see some doctor who hadn't been clued in? I left the decision up to the others. They decided the physical wasn't such a hot idea.

Errands done. Pills in hand in case things got rough. Still blacking out from time to time, body not in much control, voices talking up a storm. Back to Joe and Mary's cabin. Back to Fan David and Becky and Sarah and David's dog. Everybody seemed to be all right.

See, what did I tell you? Nothing bad happened. How lucky I am to have friends who are fearless and loving enough. to let me stay on the loose, instead of being petty about the whole thing and having someone locked away the minute they get a little out of line.

Somewhere in there I started calling Fan David Tom. He looked a little like Tom, an old friend from prep school, and Tom was one of the people I wanted around. I needed someone who could understand a lot of these images. Tom could play the piano, which came in handy, and he was one of the first people I ever talked seriously with. He and I had shared a lot.

I remember getting a certain amount of resistance. "No, Mark. That's David, not Tom."

I stuck to my gust. "You're Tom and you play the piano."

Fan David's was the most persistent "Far out, that's cool," etc., I have ever run into. I remember how I finally shook him up. I went into the room where he was sleeping. He started up, per usual, being enthusiastic about how far out I was. His dog was lying next to his bed. I reached over and jacked his dog off. Fan got very upset. I guess everyone has a limit.

Little by little, person by person, the mood switched over from the thrill of having a real live prophet guru to worry about my pain and what to do with me. Even in the beginning there was some worry about me and even in the end there was some feeling that I was on to something very important and real. It was never all or nothing.

A Walk with Fan. I must have been gritting my teeth or shaking or something. It was a pretty rough time just about sunset of the second day. David came up to me. He put his hand on my shoulder and said, "Come on, brother, don't hold it all in. Let some of that energy go. There are lots of people who could use some of it."

"No one wants this shit."

"No, you're wrong. It's just that you've got too much. Give some to me."

"You really want it?" I was incredulous. "I really don't want to put anyone through this shit."

"No, really. I could use it. Give it to me."

I wasn't real sure how to go about it, but my religion-major days weren't for nothing. I put both my hands on his head. "OK, you want it? Here it comes."

What exactly went on, who can say? But I felt something pass from me to him. I felt a rush of relief as something went from my hands into his head. He stepped back; his eyes were wide. "Wow, you're not just fucking around, are you?"

I just sort of nodded and shook my head all at once. Like so much else, that something real had happened was both frightening and comforting.

I said, "Let's go for a walk."

"Sure," he said, half in a daze, and we headed down a little two-rut dirt road that ran toward the woods behind the cabin.

"I think I'm starting to catch on," he said.

"Well, it's a funny thing. Once you start to get it, you won't be able to figure out why you never saw it before. It's really so simple."

"Has your father been here?"

"No, I don't think so. But he knows or strongly suspects it's here. For some reason he couldn't make it or didn't want to. He sort of decided to send me instead."

It was the first rational conversation I had had in a long time. Actually just about a day or so, but it seemed much longer. I felt relaxed and not half so lonely. Fan was catching on. There was someone to talk to. I started crying softly.

"What's wrong, Mark?"

"Nothing's wrong, really. I just sort of wish he was here. I wish I could talk to him here like this. I mean with his body here like mine. I mean, I can talk to him like this now, but if he were here, if he brought his body along, all we'd be able to talk about would be Mickey Mantle or something neither of us really gives a shit about."

"You mean he's here now?"

"Yes. Dad, we know you're here. Why don't you bring your body along sometime?"

"Hi, Mark."

"Hi, Pop."

"Hey, Mark, did you ever think that maybe I'm writing this script?"

"Hey, Pop, did you ever think that maybe you're not?"

"I mean, Mark, did you think that maybe I'm a good enough writer to write what you're going through?"

"Frankly not, Pop. I don't think anyone could."

"Well, Mark, you're probably right. I couldn't begin to write what you're living, not even begin. But you know there were guys who were really good. It's really incredible some of the things people have written."

"You mean like Tolstoy and Dostoyevsky?"

"Ya, and there were some others, too."

"Well, Pop, guess what your college-educated son just happened to pick up for light reading fresh out of the nut house? I just happen to have a copy of *The Brothers Karamazov* right here in my pocket."

"Oh, shit, Mark, was that ever a mistake. But what a beautiful one. I mean, really, first thing you picked up when you got out?"

"Yup, Dad, you guessed it."

"Well, Mark, let that book fall open." I let the book open. About halfway down on the right-hand page, one sentence stood out, glowing from the rest of the print: THE END OF TIME WILL BE MARKED BY ACTS OF UNFATHOMABLE COMPASSION.

"Thanks, Dad." Then I started to laugh in spite of myself just a slight chuckle.

"What's funny, Mark?"

"Not much, Dad. I was just thinking what shit I would have gotten if I had *Cat's Cradle* or something instead."

"You don't have to rub it in. There's just one thing I'd like to ask you, Mark."

"Fire away, Pop."

"Well, Mark, just how exactly did you get here anyway?"

"Well, Dad, that was the one thing I thought you probably knew. After all, it was something I sort of picked up from you. It's really amazingly simple. Just never turn down an invitation."

"By, Mark."

"By, Dad. See you around and thanks for dropping by."

Sarah. There was something about Joe and Mary's kid Sarah. Evil? Sexy? She wasn't your standard three-year-old. You got the feeling that she knew things she shouldn't know, being three and all. It was a lack of innocence. I know what it was now—the lack of innocence that comes from a calcium deficiency. She had rickets, but nobody knew that then.

When did she start calling me Daniel? And I called her

Lion or Fire as the mood took me. Why wasn't she in bed like good little three-year-olds would have been at that hour? But what hour was it? Chronology wasn't my strong point. And she was the only person I could communicate with. She was overjoyed to find someone her age to play with. When times gets funny, age gets funny.

Her being young was the whole point. She was the hope, the future. If I could somehow get her to know all I knew about art, about life, about religion, about craziness, then maybe it wouldn't be lost. Someone had tagged me, so I had to find someone else to tag with all this stuff as quick as I could. If they came to get us, the cops or someone, and destroy us as the carriers of some awful truth, surely they would spare the child. Who, even among the hardest-hearted cops, could resist that kid's smile? Who would suspect that even most perverse Mark would stoop to hiding the goodies in a three-year-old girl?

Patience. Waiting for Easter was all right but maybe this bitch, whatever it was, would go on past Easter. I set my goals ahead a bit more, so as not to come up for air too quickly. I was waiting for Sarah to grow up, so we could live happily ever after as man and wife and have lots of nice kids and all. If I'm willing to sit here and wait for Sarah to grow up, you don't have to run around like a chicken with its head cut off. Time to move to higher ground? Relax. As soon as Sarah is eighteen or so we'll think about it.

She was such a bright, attractive kid, Joe and Mary must have been doing something right, but the way they treated Sarah was one of the things that hip folk put them down for. YOU DON'T HIT KIDS. Not that they really clobbered the kid, but she came in for some pretty healthy whacks now and then. I couldn't help wincing when Sarah screamed and Joe hit and Sarah screamed louder and Joe hit harder and Sarah screamed like the end of the world and Joe hit harder.

I had never heard Sarah screaming so loud. I couldn't stand it. My face must have been contorted in agony. I started crying. "It's all right, Mark. Children recuperate quickly." That was Mary.

"Oh, my God. What have they done to her?" More bloody murder, screaming, piercing. Maybe I was responsible. Was my condition contagious? Had I ordered the demon or whatever that was in me to take her over? Or maybe in one of my blanks I had told Joe and Mary that Sarah was somehow tainted and had recommended some sort of exorcism rite which they were putting her through.

The screaming subsided into pathetic sobs and then stopped altogether. I sank into utter despair, drifting nowhere, just the other side of consciousness. I felt Joe's hand on my shoulder. I looked up with tears in my eyes. His face was very somber.

"Want half of my sandwich, Mark?" Oh, my God, how could they? How could he? Tears started pouring out of my eyes. "Here, Mark, help me eat this."

"Shit. This has gone too far." Joe had shown faith. I'm a bigger bastard than God. If only I had known, maybe I could have said something like, "Hold it, Joe, there's some bologna caught in the brambles."

"Here, Mark, eat this." Joe was still holding the sandwich in front of me. His look was insistent. I took a bite. Gagging and choking, I couldn't swallow. My mouth and throat just froze up solid. I couldn't move a muscle. I couldn't hear. I couldn't see.

But I could still think and vow. Vow I did. "God, if that child doesn't recover! I don't know what's wrong with her. I don't know what Joe did to her. I don't know what I passed on to her. But, God, if anything happens bad to that kid I am going to kick Your ass all over heaven. I'm not sure how, but I'm catching on to You little by little. You can put me through hell for as long as You like, shock treatment, padded cells, the works. But I'll remember You, cocksucker. Kick my ass around all You like, but if You start fucking around with Sarah, and Joe and Mary, I'll find a way to make You very sorry. Her mother said she'd recuperate quickly and You damn well better make her mother right."

The Arts. "Mark, I've never read much." Joe talking. It was part apology, part regret, part accusation. The talk got pretty heavy into literature now and then. I remember Kathy saying things like, "Don't worry, Mark, just think of this as *Lear* backward without the script." I was talking to Tolstoy and Dostoyevsky and lots of other guys. Fan was heavy into my father's stuff. Joe must have felt left out by the whole thing. "I never read anything by your father."

Apology—maybe if he had read more, paid attention to that sort of thing, he might have been able to understand more of the things I was saying. Regret that he had missed something. Accusation that we, the upper middle class, the intellectual elite, were leaving him out. If the secret of life, the real goodies of one sort or another, depend on a liberal arts education, if little parts of the puzzle were squirreled away in *War and Peace,* Shakespeare, here and there in a combination that only someone like me would have a chance of coming upon, it wasn't very fair.

"My father never read anything. He had an eighth-grade education."

My answer to Joe on all counts was a crash course.

"Well, old man," I said affectionately, putting my arm around him, and started reciting *Moby Dick* from memory. It seemed like as good a place to start as any.

I had only read *Moby Dick* once and hadn't made any effort to memorize it. I had been going on for about five minutes before I realized what I was doing. "Incredible, I'm reciting *Moby Dick* from memory. How can this be?" But there it was, and the more I relaxed, the more it came.

It was a stall. I wanted a story that took a while to finish. The length of *Moby Dick* was a big point in its favor. I had already done "The Charge of the Light Brigade," but that went too fast. Somehow I figured the world would keep going or I would keep going as long as I had things to do.

War and Peace wouldn't have held his attention as well. I could get to it later depending on how *Moby Dick* went. Too much history and other background stuff was necessary for *War and Peace.*

I remembered Mary, a few months before, rapping on drunkenly, "Why do I love this lout? It's not just that he has a cock that stretches from here to here," she said, stretching her arms as if telling a fish story. *Moby Dick* was just right in lots of ways.

So I took Joe to the chapel and we listened to the sermon. We went on board and set out in search of whales and adventure. We lived through tempests in the hold with sperm lamps flickering. The smell of ropes and salt and tar. We breathed the close air of the holds and the brisk salt air on the deck. We sailed through the tropics to the Arctic Circle. We slaughtered whales, thrilled to the chase, thrilled to the dangers. Wept together over dead friends. Bitched about the food and the captain. Dreamed about what we'd do with our pay. We'd be rich men some day, owning land and boats. Mansions and big families on Nantucket. Telling whaling stories to our grandchildren and great-grandchildren. It was a good life. He lost a finger in the ropes. I lost three toes to a harpoon. In the end, we drowned in each other's arms when the *Pequod* went down.

Some was done with gesture, some with words, some was done in ways that can only be called psychic.

I remember feeling his hand on my arm, shaking me. And then, slowly, the sea and the *Pequod* went away and we were back in his cabin. "I think I understand, Mark. Thank you. No one's ever done anything like that for me before." There were tears in his eyes and in mine too.

"But I can't let you go on. I'm afraid of what it's doing to you. Take this." He handed me one of the pills that Dr. Miller had prescribed if things got rough.

"Well, so this is it. It's all right, Joe, I understand you have to do it." I recognized the pill. It was exactly like one a greaser hippie in Philly had laid on me a couple of years earlier. I had thrown the damn thing away. "Yes," I said, looking at it. "I was supposed to take this a long time ago. I hope no one minds too much that I overstayed my welcome. I guess I just didn't want to leave. Good-by, Joe. No blame."

"Good night, Mark. No blame."

The pill went down easily and took effect quickly. My breathing, my pulse, my heart all became softer and softer and softer until there was nothing. "Everyone was swell." My last breath, last whisper, and I lost consciousness.

If someone had told me that at the end of the world I would be reciting *Moby Dick* from memory to a guy like Joe, if someone had told me that what I would really feel was worth passing on to someone who might survive me were things about art, I would have thought them utterly insane and totally misreading who I was. But they would have been right.

A lot of why the arts became so all-important to me was tied up with the limitations of my situation, both real and imagined. I was cut off. Cut off physically and otherwise from friends, from life, from civilization, from all sorts of things. In the real world I was less than useless. I was a liability. In the imagination it was another story. As a carpenter, a farmer, even a dishwasher, I was a dead loss. But I could still move people deeply. I could still be an artist. That was what was gorgeous about the arts. That was what I had never understood about the arts before.

A baseball glove. How the hell did this get here? Pounding my fist in it. "Pitch it in, Pop. Chuck it in there. Wop wop wop. Sock sock sock." It was an old, huge pancake mitt, no stringing between the fingers. Overstuffed with whatever they stuff them with. Impossible to move the fingers, no pocket. If you were good, maybe you could use it to knock down a few balls, but it certainly wasn't designed to catch anything.

In junior high I used to dream that I was walking down the hall or sitting in class with that dumb baseball glove on. What a jerky thing. What the hell am I doing with a baseball glove?

It alternated with dreams of being in school and finding out
all of a sudden that I had no pants on.

"Wop wop, pitch it in, Pop. Wop wop wop, sock sock sock.
Fuck 'em. There are worse things than having a baseball
glove in class. At least I ain't napalming babies."

"Wop wop. No time for Italian jokes. No telling where
Gentile might be."

"Wop wop." It was just like the glove Mike Levin had given
me when I was five or six. "Wop wop Jew."

"No time for Jew jokes either. They seem to have ways of
finding out." Mike Levin. He had a lot to do with things. He
gave me my first chess set, the one I had learned to play with.
The set that was still at the Barnstable house, if the Barnstable house was still there. He had an ESP thing with my
mother. Whenever she was in a tight situation Mike would
call up out of the blue and say, "OK, Jane, what is it?" According to her, he never missed. My mother loves ESP stuff.
Can't get enough of it. My father's not so hot for it any more.
I think he's about had his fill. You would think everyone in
our family would have.

So here it was, just before the heavyweight championship
fight. Frazier vs. Ali. "OK, Pop, so who do you want to bop?"
We had the machine, the father and son team he had
dreamed about, he had worked on me with things like the
match game. "Who do we bop? Who do we buzz? I'm supposed to go back to Caesar's grave, huh? OK, ready when you
are, Pop, I'm as much there as anywhere else. How about a
little job on Maharishi and then Billy Graham? Those fuckers
thought they had a touch of cosmic clout. They're gonna shit
their pants when they see our show."

"Billy."

"Who's that?"

"Who do you think, Billy."

"No."

"Billy, who taught St. Vitus how to dance?"

"Mark." Joe was tapping on my shoulder.

"What is it, Pops?"

"Mark, you've had a relapse!"

"Relapse, synapse, Pop. Snap crackle fizzle, Pop. I'm fine. Don't worry about me, Pops. Go find some higher ground. I'll be fine. I came through this once. I'll come through it again. Those fuckers want to fight, they don't have the faintest idea who they're fucking with."

"Mark, OK, Mark, you've had a relapse. Listen to me. We're going to have to take you back."

"Back to my little room? Back to Dr. Dale?"

"Yes, Mark. But you'll get out again just like you did before."

"Have I hurt anyone? Am I dangerous to myself and others?"

"No, it's just that you have to go back."

"And after I get out again will I have to keep going back and keep going back over and over again? Mary said that I had already been down as far as I could go. Why would she lie to me?"

"It's OK, Mark. It'll be all right. You'll get out again. You'll get well again."

"Promise?"

"Yes, I promise, Mark. A lot of people love you and are behind you. No matter what's wrong, we'll find a way out. When this is all over I'll come and get you."

"And we'll go fishing and play some chess."

"Well, I'm not much of a chess player, Mark. But, yes, I'll take you to some of my kind of country and we'll fish as much as you want. I'll take you fishing up in the Kootenays."

"Can't I come with you now? Can't you take me with you now?"

"No, Mark. I'm sorry. I can't explain it all now. But as soon as things get straightened out I'll come get you and we'll go fishing."

"OK, Pop, I'll go back. It's not really so bad. Easter break is coming up pretty soon. I have a feeling this is going to be one hell of an Easter."

* * *

Mary made me tea now and then or a sandwich or gave me paper and crayon to play with. She was terse with me but not unloving, just a harried mother with a big problem son. Trying to keep me out from underfoot. Trying to reason with me on an adult level wasn't very rewarding.

If Daddy knew that Marky wanted to fuck Mommy, Daddy probably wouldn't like it much. If Daddy knew that Marky wanted to fuck his sister, Daddy would most likely not approve. If Daddy knew that Marky wanted to fuck the little doggy, he might think his son a little weird. He maybe might think that Marky should have an operation. He might be right. Isn't there anything I can do to it? I don't want an operation, Daddy. Please, Daddy, don't be so square. There's nothing to be afraid of. Daddy, now really, a big strong man like you afraid of a thing that maybe weighs three ounces? Now really, Daddy, let's get serious. How can something so small be so much trouble? Isn't this the sort of thing daddies are supposed to clue little boys like me in to? Come on, Pops, give it to me straight. Daddy, stop fidgeting.

One way or another, I found myself in Powell River Hospital again. Nurses and doctors would come say inane things and give me all sorts of shots. An old girl friend brought a baby she had had by me that I never knew about. I had a good view of the parking lot and you wouldn't believe some of the people who came to pay their respects. Jackie Kennedy dropped by. Everything was terribly confusing, but I had told everyone everything I could. It was all up to others now. I just sat around or danced or sang or did acrobatics, and several hundred dollars' worth of property damage, waiting for whoever was in charge to tell me what I should do next.

Simon and Virginia came to visit me. Virginia said something about my needing energy. She hugged me and then went limp in my arms. I guess she thought that was how you gave someone energy. She was probably just trying to keep from getting crushed.

*   *   *

A cop on either side of me. Half holding me up, half holding me down. Virginia and Peter behind me. Virginia saying,
"Walk, Mark."

"What the fuck you think I'm trying to do, bitch?" That's
the last thing I remember for quite a while.

There's a whole day, maybe more, that's just completely
gone. I've looked pretty hard but can't find any of it.

Apparently we went to the airport and the two cops and
Simon flew me down to Vancouver. They put a straitjacket on
me and kept me in a cell for a while and then took me to
Hollywood Hospital. I remember nothing. Simon says I was
alert and pretty chipper on the flight. I kept patting the youngest, most uptight cop on the thigh and Simon kept having to
talk him out of clubbing me.

The End. At this point the last few threads between my
reality and that of others snapped. Throughout most of my
insanity I had been responding, albeit bizarrely, to external
events. My perceptions of those events had been bizarre and
there was much else going on, but now what was really happening stopped happening altogether. It was the end.

I didn't mind its being the end. Ending it there gave things
a pleasing full-circle aesthetic balance. In terms of cosmic
brawls, religious quests, and even life on the planet earth, I
felt I came off rather well ending there, maybe even heroically.

Earthquake. Sun too bright. The sky looking like no sky I
had ever seen. Noises, deafening roar. Everything quaking,
trembling. The foul stench everywhere. Harder and harder to
breathe. Rush upon rush, summing it all up.

"How far did you get?"

"I think it was somewhere round 1971."

"1971! I don't think I ever heard of someone making it that
far. It must be some sort of record. You must have been about
the only one left. Most of us gave up a long time ago. There

didn't seem to be much point in sticking around. It was all over."

"There seemed to be others."

"Think about it a minute. If there really were others around, what are you doing here? You must have had your suspicions that something was going on. Weren't they more and more just reflections of yourself? It got lonely and so you decided to hang it up? That's the way I figure it works. I don't know for sure. I'm still trying to find out."

"From time to time I figured something like that might be going on. I just thought it would be bad manners to call them on it."

"1971? Jesus, are you sure about that?"

"Pretty sure."

"That's amazing. I thought I was something making it to '54."

"I guess I was just trying to be polite."

"I'm pretty sure there really wasn't much of anybody left when you split. There was just about no one when I finally hung it up. Just a bunch of bodies people left around that sat around reflecting you in funny ways. Like I say, I'm not sure of that. It's just how I figure it. They leave their bodies with just enough vitality to make a half-passable show and just sit around giggling, waiting and wondering how long it will be till you figure it out. Giving more and more hints that they're not really there, making you curious about where the hell they went."

The last thing I wanted was to be a mental patient again. To be dragged through all that shit. To face the prospect of a later but less pleasing ending. The last thing I wanted was to identify in any way with a body again, especially the one I had at times called me.

It would have been such a nice ending, but little by little, against every fiber of my will, my heroic marble features became more and more like putty, putty I was reluctantly forced to admit I could partly control. Little by little I became a mental patient again.

Hollywood, Take Two. "The first time you were in here you were the Father. Now you're the Son. Next time you'll be the Holy Ghost and you won't need me and my keys any more." It was said affectionately. It was an orderly bringing me some food.

"Oh boy," I said slowly, just shaking my head. "Oh boy, I've fucked up again." Shrug.

"Oh boy," he said, agreeing, nodding as he left.

"Oh boy, oh boy, oh boy." I ate slowly. I didn't have the faintest idea how I had gotten there but I knew where I was.

And then I wouldn't know where I was or wouldn't care or the place was some elaborate hoax or sinister plot, and back and forth several times a day for about a week.

Dr. Dale came into my little windowless seclusion room one day and asked if I'd like to see my mother. I figured he was just asking to torment me. Of course I wanted to see my mother, but even if I wasn't dead and in hell or being kidnaped by Martians, even if I was a real patient in a real mental hospital, my mother was in Jamaica. And then alakazam he materialized my mother and she was hugging me and we were both sobbing and sobbing under Dale's tight satanic grin. "That guy really is the devil."

Our first few visits were fairly disjointed. I tried to explain what I thought was being done to me. They were draining my blood and replacing it with something else and changing the lines on my palms and . . .

My mother didn't argue with any of my crazy notions and even elaborated a bit on the milder ones involving astrology and palmistry. My mother is one of the world's greatest empathetic suspenders of disbelief. If there's a thread of sense woven into a vast tapestry of nonsense, my mother will find it. And even if there's not, she'll spend forever and a day looking, always assuming that it's her denseness and not any lack of sense.

Just after I recovered I thought my mother's attitude and behavior had been a big mistake. "Ma, the first time you visit someone in a seclusion room, you don't read their palm." But the more I think about it, the less I think it was a mistake. Arguing with them wouldn't have made the crazy ideas go away, and being willing to talk about them gave me a chance to get them all out where I could look at them. It made at least part of my insanity a lot less hellishly lonely.

She talked Dr. Dale into letting Virginia visit me and they'd show up together like clockwork every afternoon. They spent lots of time together talking over their visits and plotting my recovery. They were an ideal visiting team.

When I recovered enough to care about where I was, my first reaction was to be pissed off at the hospital. If only they had given me a few pills to take along, this whole thing could have been avoided.

If anything, I was less patient than before. There wasn't much magic about pills three times a day. What did I need all these jokers for? Why don't they just give me the fucking pills and let me the fuck out of here?

Then they seemed to loosen up a little. Dale told me about what he thought was wrong with me, what could be done about it, what the pills did. What I had was schizophrenia. It was probably genetic. It was biochemical. It was curable. It might have something to do with adrenaline metabolism. There were dietary adjustments I could make that might help. Dope wasn't such a hot idea for someone like me.

I was skeptical about some of what he said, but I accepted much of it and was glad to at last be told something. All the same, I was still angry. Why hadn't they told me any of this earlier, the first time I was here? I still didn't think of the hospital as a good place to spend much time, but I gained at least a marginal faith that they were trying to help me and a glimmer of hope that they might know what they were doing.

I also found out that my legal situation was quite a bit more complicated than it had been last time around. My first stay I was, technically at least, a voluntary patient. This time I had arrived in a straitjacket accompanied by four Royal Canadian Mounties armed with, among other things, commitment papers signed by three doctors. They could lock me away for years. I decided to work on patience again.

I doubt if the staff would believe how hard I worked at being patient or that I worked at it at all. They steadily maintained that I was the least patient patient they had ever seen. "Look at Mary. She's been here for years. She's not jumping to get out of here." Somehow I didn't find Mary a very attractive model.

Impatience was a symptom, so I did my best not to mention anything about getting out or thinking that maybe I was ready for grounds privileges or that I was anything but tickled to be a patient at Hollywood Hospital. I read a lot of novels, wrote a lot of letters, drew a lot of pictures, played the old piano as often as I could, tried to develop relationships with patients and staff, all the time saying over and over to myself, "Patient, patient, patient." I used it like a mantra in meditation. Very careful to keep it quiet and make sure my lips weren't moving. "Patient, patient, patient."

Poor Dr. McNice. Hollywood Hospital's saving grace. The man who allowed us to salvage a bit of dignity.

No hippie, to be sure. But at least he didn't drive Cadillacs and wear baby-blue alligator shoes. There wasn't much chance of his actively joining our quest, but we knew he had sympathy and understanding and hope for what we were doing. He had in his eyes a vague apology for not being more like us, an ever-so-faint hint of self-contempt for an even vaguer cowardice.

Poor Dr. McNice. He had tried to be a good doctor much the same way I had tried to be a good hippie. He had acted reasonably and compassionately. He honored noble precepts.

Now he averted his eyes whenever we passed in the hall. He avoided me, my parents and friends as politely as he could. When cornered, he was evasive.

We figured that Dale must have given him hell for letting me get away, and then when I returned a few weeks later in even worse shape than I had been on my first admission, McNice was lucky to still have a job. Dale must have given him strict orders to have nothing whatsoever to do with my case.

And it was my fault. Poor me. In spite of myself, I was the most telling argument against all that he and I and all my friends and humanitarians everywhere wanted to be true.

I looked in a mirror. "Mark, you're the best argument fascism ever had."

I had worked my way out of the locked wards. Even had all my own clothes back. I was in one of the best rooms. I had been supergood for what seemed like an awfully long time. The doctors said I was doing well. The nurses and orderlies thought likewise. The patients all thought I was OK. My mother and Virginia seemed to think I was OK.

All Dale would say when I hinted about getting out was that we'd talk about it later. He started getting stingy with his information again. Maybe he just didn't have any more. It was back to "You've been a very sick boy. We don't have all the answers."

I found myself sobbing uncontrollably, scared to death they were going to catch me at it and lock me up in that little room again.

I was crying because, among other things, I was doubtful that they were ever going to let me out. They were very much "them" and I was cracking under the strain of trying so hard to be patient and not knowing how long I'd have to keep it up. Sure enough they caught me at it. "I suppose it's not manly to cry. I suppose this means I'm nuts." But they didn't zap me into the little room. The nurse even sat down and comforted me some and said crying was OK. It didn't mean I was crazy. It didn't mean I wasn't a man. I cried with her holding my hand for a while.

Then Ray showed up. I think the nurse asked me if I'd be more comfortable talking with a man.

I had seen Ray around the hospital before but never really talked with him. He looked maybe a couple of years older than I. He was my version of what I would have been had it not been for the war, dope, the draft, America, Virginia, whatever this biological condition was that they kept talking about, and a few other things. I too would have been a bright, earnest, clean-shaven young man, very possibly a clinical psychologist. My feelings toward him were a mixture of envy and superiority. He seemed so naïve. I didn't know whether to thank or hate whatever it was that had me turn out differently from him.

"A whole lot of shit happened to me all at once."

The talk I had with Ray wasn't all that extraordinary except that it was the first time I had talked about things in a down-to-earth way. He was the first person whose attitudes toward what I was going through seemed remotely related to mine. I felt that he liked me. It was the first time I had felt that in a long time, too. I didn't feel threatened or abused or greatly misunderstood.

"My woman went off and balled another man . . . My parents are breaking up . . .

"A whole lot of shit happened all at once," was what it all boiled down to.

I talked some about the hospital and not understanding at all how the score was being kept. What sort of things did I do that were considered crazy? What sort of things did I have to do to be considered well?

I talked about feeling horny and wishing there was some way to get laid. I talked about there being nothing to do and wishing I could at least take some long walks. I asked him why they had held me down and shaved off my beard and cut my hair. Wasn't that maybe not such a hot thing to do to someone who was having a hard enough time identifying with his body and trying to believe this wasn't a repressive institution, hostile to everything that had ever meant anything to me?

He offered to take me on a walk the next day. It was a nice walk. We talked about a lot of things. I loosened up and felt much better.

After my walk and talk with Ray, I was given unlimited afternoon and evening visitor privileges, and allowed to go out with friends for whole afternoons. Simon, Kathy, Jack and André from Stevens Street all dropped in from time to time, never more than two or three at once. Sometimes I'd go on a picnic with Virginia and whoever else was visiting. I was still feeling shaky but less and less so, and I was more and more eager to get the hell out of the hospital.

My mother went to visit an ailing uncle in California. She and I agreed that I was in good enough shape that she didn't really need to hang around any more. We were all just waiting for that slowpoke Dale to realize I was OK and let me go.

And then, seemingly out of nowhere, all hell broke loose again and I was back in that fucking little room. No visitors, no clothes, no one would even talk to me through the little hole, no nothing.

McNice came in one day with three of the meanest orderlies. I had been utterly alone for days.

"I think I'm dead, I'm dead, aren't I?" pleading and grasping for his arm.

"Yes, I know you feel like that." He left quickly. The orderlies held me down and jabbed another needle in my ass.

The third crackup was different from the first two. In lots of ways it was the worst.

Not much fun or funny happened the third time I cracked. Maybe it was because I cracked in the hospital and there was no running room, no slack, no chance for the Eden Express to get up a decent head of steam.

Maybe it was because I really didn't want to go crazy then. I really tried to stop it and couldn't. Both other times there had seemed to be some point in it.

I was running out of excuses. My father hadn't committed suicide. Virginia was OK. My mother was OK. Spring was on schedule. Life seemed to be going on. I had taken all those silly little pills. I hadn't touched anything remotely dopelike. I had followed all doctor's orders faithfully and here I was back in that fucking little room again.

Maybe it was just the repetitiveness of it. Once was an accident, twice a coincidence, but three? A habit. Three strikes. Three points define a circle. A closing one. There had been a few weeks between cracks one and two and just a little over a week between two and three. This was how I was going to spend my life.

My suicide attempts became more frequent, more pathetic, and more sincere. Before I had danced with death, loved death, hated death, teased death, been teased by death. Now I was rolling on the floor in my own shit, clumsily trying to strangle myself. Before there had been elements of hope and nobility. By dying I could help others live, bring back the sun, teach some truth. Now I just wanted to die.

I was running out of material. I had been back and forth over my life so often and so thoroughly there was nothing left. I had been Hitler, Napoleon, Lincoln, Jesus, Joan of Arc, Bob Dylan, Billy the Kid, Bach, Wagner, Shakespeare, and Nietzsche, to name a few. I had been through every novel I had ever read and a few I hadn't at least twice. Movies likewise. I had said everything I ever wanted to say to everyone I wanted to say it to. I had made love to everyone and everything and been made love to in turn and fucked and been fucked. Longings I hadn't dreamed of had been fulfilled. I had no more unfinished business.

Power. Just before my third crack-up, I learned that Joe had landed in a nut house and was going through electroshock. It was another hint that "delusions of grandeur" was at least partly a misnomer. I remembered that Warren, the aspiring guru, had also wound up in a nut house shortly after his encounter with me. I felt shitty as hell about Joe being in the hospital. Warren, I felt, had it coming.

Both had played somewhat similar roles in my crack-ups. They were both primary males. Each had been some strange combination of father, devil, and God. Both had tried to cure me. I had had the feeling that these guys were both trying to use cosmic clout. My reaction in both cases was the same: No hard feelings, fellas, but this time you've bitten off more than you can chew.

Uncanny feats of memory, physical strength, spiritual power, agility: I'd be inclined to dismiss them if there weren't so many instances supported by people who were there. In fact, I'd feel much more comfortable about the whole thing if I could dismiss all the spooky stuff as delusions.

Maybe it was just that I was able to create an atmosphere which destroyed people's customary expectations, an atmosphere in which miracles could flourish. Anyway, it spooked the hell out of me. I even managed to spook a few doctors and nurses. That's impressive spooking, considering the extensive spookproofing those people go through and all the antispook drugs they pumped me full of.

Somehow I managed to stumble onto some tricks of the holy-man trade. Call it cosmic disability compensation, a bonus dividend accruable on ego disinvestiture.

I doubt that I had much to do one way or another with the California earthquake or what was being broadcast on the TV or any of the numberless other things I felt responsible for. But I wouldn't have taken such bizarre notions as seriously as I did if it hadn't been for the smaller-scale miracles that were undeniably real. My notions of what I was and was not capable of were blown to smithereens.

I had some help from my friends. In folie à deux a crazy person is able to convince another person of his bizarre notions. Why not folie à cinq, six, sept, huit? My smaller-scale miracles worked on those around me much the same way they worked on me. When I started acting like I could control the weather or raise the dead, they couldn't rule it out.

I hate to think I've come this far, carefully nourishing my credibility every inch of the way, only to blow it this close to the end. But if I were asked to swear on all that's holy that I had no extraordinary powers, I could not do it. As uncomfortable as it made me, I had extraordinary powers.

I have no such powers now. I hope I never have them again. I'm glad there isn't very much concrete evidence to back up the contention that I had such powers then. Mostly there are just some eyewitness accounts a good cross-examiner could make look pretty silly.

The worst thing about the powers was how little control I had over them. They coincided with the blanks. The more rational control I had, the less power I had. So the powers were to me a powerlessness. I didn't have the faintest idea of what went on in those blanks. I'd come out of them and by the way people were looking at me and the questions they asked, I got bits and pieces of it. The bits and pieces added up to power, power I doubt that I would have trusted myself with even if I had been able to control it.

The power phenomenon had a neat, almost ceremonious ending which sets it apart from other things. The voices, visions, misperceptions, irrationality, bizarre behavior all faded fuzzily, much the way they had come. Milder versions still come to visit occasionally. I'd just as soon they didn't, but as long as the powers stay away, I don't mind too much.

It was a few days before Easter. I was in the little windowless room. Why I was there, when I was allowed to go to the bathroom, when food came, when pills came, were all a complete mystery. I had lost any hope that anything nice was going to happen. No one had come to visit me forever. No nurse, orderly, doctor, patient, no nobody wanted anything to do with me. I was hopeless.

But then a miracle. The door opened.

"Bring him in here." A voice that can open doors. A voice that people with keys pay attention to. It was a lot more than could be said for my voice. And what's more, a voice that seemed interested in me.

I was taken into the room diagonally across the corridor. It had windows, curtains, flowers, paintings, books, paper, pens. It was all anyone could ever ask for.

To whom do I owe this honor, this reprieve from windowless, everything elseless nothingness?

I owed this honor to Wally.

"Sit down, Mark." I sat down. "My name's Walter. Call me Wally."

"Wally? Wally? My roommate in prep school was called Wally. His last name was Walters. His father fell six stories onto a sidewalk but came out OK except for one leg being shorter than the other which gave him a limp."

Wally seemed to know all this and a lot more. I didn't get a chance to find out how he knew all these things. I couldn't get a word in edgewise. But he was answering so many questions there didn't seem to be much reason to get a word in edgewise anyway.

Most of what he said wouldn't have made much sense to anyone but me. It would have been just another poor crazy person raving his brains out. What it boiled down to was that I was being divested of my power.

"You're not the conductor any more. Someone else is in charge of the train." He seemed to be congratulating me for having done my part well and saying that now I could relax. He filled me in on lots of the places, people, and things I had been worried about. Told me that for the most part I had caught on beautifully, far better than anyone expected.

He must have been listening to my ravings for the past few days. Maybe he just wanted me to shut up so he could get some sleep. He knew all the key words, all the themes, key players, etc., and how to put them together. It worked like a charm. I don't think I did any raving after that. I felt great relief. My prayers had been answered. I had no more power. I could not be just one of the fellas.

Meals started coming more regularly. Orderlies and nurses

stopped beating me up and sticking needles in my ass. They let me out of the little room more and more. And then my mother showed up and then Virginia.

Wally was gone the day after our visit. I tried to find out more about him but no one seemed to know much. According to the nurses he was just another patient.

Easter morning I was sitting just outside the little room rolling a cigarette, still trying to put together some of the things Wally had said and who the hell he was.

A breeze came through the ward. It smelled like spring. It was the first smell I had noticed in months that hadn't been death.

Something was saying good-by to me.

"You're still smoking cigarettes." It wasn't the voices exactly.

It wanted me to notice more than the fact that I still smoked cigarettes. It wanted me to recognize myself.

"Cigarettes? Sportsman? Export? Tobacco? Papers?" It was chuckling, almost laughing, feigning amazed disbelief, making sure there were no hard feelings. I almost felt an arm around my shoulder.

"Good-by, sport. Who would ever guess?" And it was gone.

Tears started streaming down my face. They tasted sweet. I sat there smoking through the tears, tasting them both, and how good they were.

Two nurses came up and asked if I was all right.

"Yes," I said. "Yes, yes. Everything is going to be OK from now on."

They seemed to believe me. They seemed as relieved as I was and on the verge of tears themselves. They offered me some tea and hot cross buns. I accepted.

Biochemistry. At first my friends and I were doubtful that there was any medical problem. It was all politics and philosophy. The hospital bit was just grasping at straws when all else failed.

It took quite a bit to convince us that anything as pedestrian as biochemistry was relevant to something as profound and poetic as what I was going through. For me to admit the possibility that I might not have gone nuts again had they given me pills when I left was a tremendous concession.

It's such a poetic affliction from inside and out, it's not hard to see how people have assumed that schizophrenia must have poetic causes and that any therapy would have to be poetic as well. A lot of my despair of ever getting well was based on the improbability of finding a poet good enough to deal with all that had happened to me. It's hard to say when I accepted the notion that the problem was biochemical, it went so hard against everything I had been taught about mental illness. At the farm we were coming more and more to seeing physical illness as psychological. A cold or slipping with a hammer and smashing a finger was psychological. Schizophrenia was biochemical?

But the idea had a lot to recommend it. The hopelessness of dealing with it on a poetic level was the start. The doctor who had apparently been able to bring me out of it was working from a biochemical model. According to most authorities who believed in this or that poetic theory, my case was hopeless. The biochemists said otherwise. The poets in the business gave little hope and huge bills. The chemists fixed me up with embarrassingly inexpensive, simple nonprescription pills. Vitamins mostly. The biochemists said no one was to blame. The poets all had notions that required someone's having made some mistake.

The AMA had no particular affection for megavitamin therapy. That was something. Anything the AMA hated couldn't be all bad.

The more research I studied, the more impressed I was. I remain converted.

It's impossible to say whether full insight and understanding would help a schizophrenic or not. We all have vastly greater capacities for experience than for understanding. A hundred of the best shrinks in the world working day and night for years would be doing well to scratch the surface of a day in anyone's life. Schizophrenia multiplies the problem manyfold and disability makes the problem more pressing. Since there is always so much more to be understood and dealt with, the notion that understanding will clear up the problem can't be tested.

They used electroshock on me. There was nothing I or my parents or any of my friends could do to stop them. I was scared to death of it. It probably did me some good.

I was given no advance warning about it. One morning my breakfast tray didn't show up and I knew what that meant. The rationality of my efforts to avoid it is the best proof I have that I was already in pretty good shape. I talked to the nurses perfectly logically. I remembered phone numbers and talked with my mother and then Virginia, trying to get them to do something about it. I think it was another case of hierarchy lag. The nurses knew I was OK, the orderlies knew I was OK, but the doctors who gave orders for such things hadn't caught on. They were several days behind.

I thought the purpose of it was to make me forget things that were bothering me. I composed a series of ten rhyming couplets that included all the most awful things that had ever happened to me and scratched the first letter of each line in the wall behind my mattress. For the experience itself, I was knocked out with sodium pentothal. Just before I went under I remember saying to the doctor in charge that I didn't think this was such a good idea. When I came to, about fifteen minutes later, I was disoriented for a bit but remembered my ten rhyming couplets without having to look at the wall. Except for a bitch of a headache, I felt fine.

I think that maybe a lot of the horror people feel about shock comes from confusing its effects with those of mental illness itself, or some of the other medications often used. The dull, glazed look, the amnesia and confusion found in mental patients may be caused by a number of things, but electroshock is what people usually blame because it sounds so awful.

If I found myself going under again, I'd choose electroshock ahead of a lot of things. My only complaint is that they made no attempt to clear up my misconceptions about it and that they didn't use it earlier. I really didn't need it by the time they got around to using it. This isn't to say that shock isn't grossly misused in some situations.

Getting Out Right. "This time we're going to do it right." Virginia said it so often I started thinking there might be some sort of hidden meaning or message. "This time we're going to do it right. We're not going to make the mistakes we made last time."

I, for one, wasn't all that sure we had made mistakes. They were the ones who blew it. If they had given me a little more information and some pills, everything would have been fine.

If we had just listened to Dr. Dale, everything would have been OK. That was certainly the version he and lots of the other staff were trying to put over. He never came out and said it in so many words. He didn't have to. We all felt it hanging over our heads.

When I was finally released from the hospital, I bore little resemblance to the dynamo of assertion I had been on my first release. I had nothing but a feeling of extreme fragility and vulnerability and a little hope that some day things would be different.

I didn't adjust well to being fragile and vulnerable. Virginia or my parents or anyone else could break me inadvertently. Just a slight bit of human clumsiness and *snap*.

I was once again completely financially dependent on my parents. There were the hospital bills, and the prospects of my being able to handle any sort of job in the near future seemed slim. Dale said at least a year.

I was cramping Virginia's style, the farm's style, everyone's style. And for what were all these people going out of their way? A hollow, shaky shell that didn't know what to think about anything.

We got a little apartment in Vancouver. Dale said it wasn't such a hot idea to just head right back up to the farm. Virginia still kept saying, "This time we're going to do it right."

My mother and Virginia took care of most of the arrangements. I just sort of dragged along.

Taking Thorazine was part of doing things right. I hated Thorazine but tried not to talk about hating it. Hating Thorazine probably wasn't a healthy sign. But Thorazine has lots of unpleasant side effects. It makes you groggy, lowers your blood pressure, making you dizzy and faint when you stand up too quickly. If you go out in the sun your skin gets red and hurts like hell. It makes muscles rigid and twitchy.

The side effects were bad enough, but I liked what the drug was supposed to do even less. It's supposed to keep you calm, dull, uninterested and uninteresting. No doctor or nurse ever came out and said so in so many words, but what it was was an antihero drug. Dale kept saying to me, "You mustn't try to be a hero." Thorazine made heroics impossible.

What the drug is supposed to do is keep away hallucinations. What I think it does is just fog up your mind so badly you don't notice the hallucinations or much else.

My father sent me an article in *Psychology Today* on an experiment with schizophrenics to evaluate the effectiveness of Thorazine. The conclusion was that patients who before their illness had been well socialized, able to make friends and function effectively on a social level, actually recovered more quickly without Thorazine than with it. People who had been all fucked up before their illness benefited from Thorazine.

I was so fucked up on Thorazine at the time that I had a great deal of difficulty figuring out to which group I belonged, but I knew I hated Thorazine.

I managed to cheat on the Thorazine some. Very whimpy unheroic cheating. I deliberately misinterpreted what some nurse had said and skipped a few days. I felt great. My mother and Virginia both remarked on how fast I was recovering and how chipper I was getting. The spirit of our little apartment jumped a hundredfold. I wasn't cramping anyone's style any more. I even got chipper enough to tell them why I was so chipper. They were a little worried about that, but I was so obviously in a good state of mind they almost started questioning Dale's judgment.

When I went to see Dale that week it was far and away the nicest visit we'd ever had. He said I was making a remarkable recovery, I was putting on much-needed weight, color was coming back into my face, I was in better shape than he had ever seen me. If I just stuck with his regimen and kept improving, I could maybe visit the farm for a few days in a couple of weeks.

He was so pleased. I was so pleased. Virginia and my mother and all my friends were so pleased. In this atmosphere of seemingly unanimous, universal pleasedness, I told him I didn't need so much Thorazine. I told him, in fact, that at least part of the reason everyone was so pleased was that I had stopped taking it and I was sure I could recover much more quickly without it.

He became a lot less pleased and came on with his antiheroics theme again. I showed him the article my father had clipped from *Psychology Today*. He wasn't impressed.

He called my mother and Virginia into the office. He explained that under no circumstances was he going to take any chances with my health. "Remember what happened last time?" Blah, blah, blah, etc.

So I was back on Thorazine again.

On Thorazine everything's a bore. Not a bore, exactly. Boredom implies impatience. You can read comic books and *Reader's Digest* forever. You can tolerate talking to jerks forever. Babble, babble, babble. The weather is dull, the flowers are dull, nothing's very impressive. Muzak, Bach, Beatles, Lolly and the Yum-Yums, Rolling Stones. It doesn't make any difference.

When I did manage to get excited about some things, impatient with some things, interested in some things, it still didn't have the old zing to it. I knew that Dostoyevsky was more interesting than comic books, or, more accurately, I remembered that he had been. I cared about what happened at the farm, but it was more remembering caring than really caring.

After I had been out of the hospital a few weeks, Dale said it would be OK for me to go up to the farm for a weekend. Jack was down visiting us so I went up with him for a few days.

Jack came into his own after I went nuts. His approach was very much no bullshit. He analyzed pretty accurately how the hospital worked and we talked about what parts of it could be incorporated into the farm. There was no mysticism from Jack, no flashy cosmic theories of why I had gone nuts or flashy any-other-kind of theories either. He didn't think I needed spiritual guidance or T-groups. He didn't want to love or teach the craziness out of me. For him it was a simple engineering problem. He was ready to build a padded cell. We even talked about it some. If electroshock worked, he was ready to price the equipment and learn how to use it.

He didn't like the idea of depending on a man who drove Cadillacs and wore baby-blue alligator shoes. If we needed a mini-mental hospital to be independent, he'd build one.

Jack became a dynamo of energy. He took on leadership roles left and right. I loved it. I didn't have much energy myself and felt I could sort of glide along behind and let this hot knife cut the butter. Jack was saying lots of things that I wanted to say but for various reasons couldn't. Energy, vested interests, who listens to former psychotics anyway?

The thrust of Jack's thrusts was that we had a farm and not Eden or some half-baked hippie summer camp. Further, that we really didn't have a farm but a rather pathetic little vegetable garden and a lot of land that needed lots of work. Our house was a bad joke, our goats were shitty goats. All the dogs except Zeke were less than worthless.

The trip to the farm was fairly uneventful, although without Jack's dynamism it might have been otherwise. The farm had been going through a decidedly strange phase. There had been a lot of visitors, four of whom were toying with the idea of becoming permanent. Not much work was getting done. The original crew and the visitors were all suffering from various forms of the heavies. A couple of the newcomers, and even Simon, were pretty sure they saw ghosts. There was tension in the air and a lot of talk about it. Maybe the whole problem was sexual repression, lots of talk about that. There were some stabs at novel couplings, straight mate swaps, homosexuality, three- and four-somes, and lots of talk about that and wondering why not everyone in a big heap. Then there were the old faithful heavies of "Why'd Mark go nuts?" and "What kind of a place is this farm going to be anyway?"

Jack filled me in on what had been going on in a very matter-of-fact way. Without his briefing, Simon's version of the news probably would have given me the hoodoos.

". . . Heavy changes . . . getting it on . . . coming together . . . ghosts . . . heavy vibes . . . ghosts . . ." It could have meant almost anything, but knowing who had done what with whom and how it had turned out helped keep my imagination within bounds.

How it had turned out was all the newcomers scattering to the winds and the old-timers coming down to town to catch their breath. Jack had come to visit Virge and me while Simon and Kathy hung out at Prior Road. John Eastman took care of the animals for a few days.

After our brief visit with Simon, Kathy, and the folks at Prior Road, Jack and I headed up the lake to relieve John.

We told the ghosts to get the fuck away from us if they knew what was good for them, and walked around talking about the various things we had to do to get this place in shape.

After three very down-to-earth pleasant days at the farm, planning and good talks with Jack, playing with Zeke, as noble and beautiful as ever, Jack and I headed back to Powell

River. He took Kathy and Simon back up the lake and I hitched down to Vancouver.

When I told Dale about visiting the farm, he chided me. I was supposed to have gone for only two days and I was supposed to have had Virginia with me. He accused me of trying to play hero again.

I apologized without knowing what I was apologizing for and warned myself about trying to make any sense of it. I wasn't supposed to think. I was just supposed to follow doctor's orders.

We left the apartment and moved back up to the farm toward the end of June. It was OK with Dale as long as I promised to come to see him every two weeks.

It was hard to be graceful. I felt weak and burned-out. I was being watched. I was being treated with kid gloves. I needed it. I hated it.

There was no way for things to be right. I needed time. Everyone around me needed time. Time to get stronger. Time for everyone to relax.

Balancing. Too much pressure, I'd crack. Too little, I'd never get any strength. One day I'd feel tough as nails, fed to the teeth with people tiptoeing around. The next day I'd find myself shaking, holding my knees, ready to hang it up and check myself back into the nut house.

When I went back to the farm, I don't think I had any real hope of making it my life any more. It was more like I owed myself and everyone else there a graceful exit. It was like getting back up on a horse after you've been thrown. It was like a lot of things, but it wasn't much like Eden. It was the best of a lot of lousy alternatives.

Getting well outside the hospital seemed a lot like getting well inside. The dos and don'ts made no sense. My friends' judgments of what were good and bad signs were as ridiculous as the hospital's. There was no percentage in trying to get people to understand. It probably wasn't possible and it seemed like what had gotten me into trouble in the first place.

I went back to the farm because I knew it. I knew the hopelessness of my heroism there. The farm knew the hopelessness of my heroism back. There was nothing I'd be tempted to try there. I had tried it all. I had been burned. It had been burned.

Other places, other people would tempt me and me them.

The experiments of spring had all the makings of a superhippie summer.

It was a nothing summer. Thank God it was a nothing summer. Thank Simon, Kathy, Jack, and Virginia that it was a nothing summer. Thank me.

I did to the farm what Thorazine was doing to me. I was a down.

Clay Foot was my new private name for myself. Ol' Clay Foot don't go around saying stop that shit or I run amuck. Ol' Clay Foot he just walk into a room not sayin' much at all and everybody be cool. Just like that. Ol' Clay Foot he don't have to say nothin'.

There was a moratorium on heaviness. Everyone went back to sleeping with whoever they had slept with before I went nuts. New visitors weren't exactly discouraged, but we weren't out recruiting either.

Three months of nothing later I headed East. I was feeling pretty strong. The trip had Dale's blessing. He said I had made remarkable progress but I still had to avoid being a hero, I still had to keep taking Thorazine, I ought to see a shrink now and then; but all in all he thought I was out of the worst of it.

Three months of nothing isn't quite fair. After the dynamism and pitched battles of being crazy, it would have been hard for anything to move me much.

I started writing. I built a chicken coop. I had a few minor fights with Virge. Things happened, but nothing that called me out. There were some visitors and guests, but they were all reasonable, relatives or close friends mostly. No out-of-the-blue wanderers. No superfreaks. No cosmic messengers or extraordinary chess players.

I left saying I'd be back in a couple of months. I knew it wasn't true and I suspect everyone else knew it too. I wasn't fleeing painful memories or friends and a way of life that I feared might drive me nuts again. I felt and still feel that without the farm and those friends I would have cracked sooner and healed more slowly than otherwise. I was leaving because I was well.

I felt strong in a way I had never felt before. I was curious about this new strength and there wasn't enough variety at the farm to give it a thorough testing out.

It seemed that virtue was no longer compulsory. I had spent a lot of my life trying to figure out what "good" was and trying to do it. It had seemed that my state of mind, mental health, was directly tied to how much "good" was in my life, which would have been fine if the process hadn't been such a progressively demanding, implacable one.

In the beginning I couldn't take physical violence. In the end I couldn't cut firewood. I didn't want to move or breathe for fear of harming microbes. My life became more and more an instant-karma replay. There was no way to be good enough. My friends had gradually become as monstrous as the SS, and the farm as hectic and frightening as New York City. I had had a certain amount of hope in this process. I assumed it was happening to everyone and that, sooner or later, the same feelings that made me incapable of handling rush-hour traffic would render the Air Force incapable of dropping bombs.

I was so convinced of the connection between my mental health and "goodness" that something's upsetting me was enough to make it evil. The world's sinfulness and horror matched step with my ever deteriorating shit tolerance.

Looking back at those changes in my life I can now see

much more than the "good" I saw at the time. Along with all my new sensitivities and deep concerns came a peculiar immunity to love that my family, friends, and lovers had for me. I thought about, talked about, and needed love very much, but whenever I got it, it touched me less and less. Which led me to assume that it wasn't really love. If I had ever come to see that Virginia really loved me, which I see very clearly now, I doubtless would have found some excuse to put several thousand miles between us.

Because they made me feel better, trusting nature, letting it be, etc., were all part of being good.

But nature had apparently intended me to spend the rest of my life chained to a wall, or, barring intervention, to rave my brains out and starve to death. Philosophical niceties were swept aside. Biochemistry and these funny men calling themselves orthomolecular psychiatrists were my new buddies. The more the vitamins took hold, the less my mental health depended on being good and the more curious I became about what life out there would be like this way.

I'm pretty sure I could live in a plastic condominium with a wife I didn't love and lots of bratty kids, drive six hours a day in rush-hour traffic to work at a boring meaningless job, and mutilate cuddly little puppies in my spare time without its putting much of a dent in my mental health. I wouldn't like it but it wouldn't drive me nuts.

Before, nearly everything I did was to nurture my mental health. Becoming a religion major, politics, hippiedom, the farm, all made me feel a little less shaky. The ironic thing is that my big theme as a religion major had been the crassness and other drawbacks of morality under threat of damnation. Insightfulness, honesty, etc., under threat of mental illness is much the same game. As much as I value the experiences and lessons of both the mild and decidedly unmild parts of my travels with schizophrenia, it's nice to be back on my own. In any event, my mental health doesn't give me many clues about how to act any more.

Another reason for leaving was that it was time for Virge and me to go our separate ways. It wasn't so much that I had changed as that we had been through so much together and knew each other so thoroughly. Ideally a couple reaches that degree of emotional fullness and exhaustion with the general exhaustion of old age. We were an eighty-year-old couple stuck in bodies in their early twenties.

Leaving Zeke behind was the toughest part of coming East, but there wasn't any way around it. He was healthy, safe, and happy being king of the farm. There would have been all that traumatic traveling and I didn't have the faintest idea where the hell I'd end up living. Virginia, Simon, Kathy, and Jack had all come to respect and love him as much as I did. They would have squawked like hell if I tried to take him with me. Besides, he wasn't a pup any more, he was getting sort of set in his ways. I had put Zeke through odysseys aplenty. He had found his niche, it was time for me to go find mine. If it turned out to be one where he could be half as healthy, safe, and happy as he was at the farm, I'd be back to get him in a flash.

The farm went on. Jack dropped out about six months after I did and went down to Los Angeles to become a carpenter. Kathy lasted a few months beyond his leaving and then became a schoolteacher in Vancouver. Simon and Virge turned out to be the true diehards. They kept the place going with various newcomers through another two winters.

By the time they left, the house was warm and tight and had running water, a much expanded, productive garden replaced our pathetic first efforts, funky Blue Marcel was replaced by a very fast, dependable inboard, a big beautiful barn was nearing completion, and a tractor did much of the work we had once done by hand.

There have been many plans and a few stabs at making the farm a full-time operation again, but nothing that's amounted to much. Now it's mostly a pleasant retreat for Simon and his Vancouver friends. It's hard to say what happened in between our all being so sure we had found some forever and our recent talks about signing the place over to some free school. The apocalyptic visions that drove us there softened as time failed to bear them out. As soon as the newness and challenge that made it fun wore off, the impact of being so isolated set in. Add that we could each expect to live another fifty years or so and you've got some powerful incentive to transcend the doubts about whether or not you could hack it out there. I'm just guessing. It was probably different things at different times for each of us. The one thing I'm sure of is that none of us was driven away by the hardness of the life. It really wasn't very hard, and if any of the things we feared were happening ever do happen, it's nice to know it's there.

Myself. I came East, kept writing, got more and more disgustingly healthy, did substitute teaching and masonry, went back to school to learn more about the biochemistry I was suddenly so enthusiastic about, danced around love a bit before falling, and am now trying to get into medical school.

Zeke became Virginia's dog. He managed to survive several stays in Powell River, but in September 1974, after a car-free summer at the farm, Zeke was struck and killed by a car his first day back in town. Farewell, noble, beautiful, true true friend.

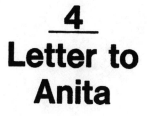

4
Letter to
Anita

I doubt if there will ever be anything with the eloquence and simplicity of an arm in a cast. And while more and more is known every day, what are appropriate allowances and what is the best medical help are much more difficult questions for schizophrenia than for most diseases.

I myself was a Laing-Szasz fan and didn't believe there was really any such thing as schizophrenia. I thought it was just a convenient label for patients whom doctors were confused about. I even worked in a mental hospital for several months without being convinced otherwise.

All that's beside the point. The point is that there's overwhelming evidence that there is a very real disease called schizophrenia (actually probably several very real diseases with overlapping symptoms), and, as you yourself suspect, it's very possibly what you're suffering from. There's no percentage in your wasting energy wondering whether or not you're crying wolf, Anita. What you're suffering from is very real.

Krishna Murti said, "It's no measure of health to be well adjusted to a profoundly sick society." Laing has called schizophrenia a reasonable response to an insane world. While there is certainly plenty to be upset about in these strange times, and as much as I tried to place the blame there when I went under, there is precious little evidence that our troubled world can be realistically blamed for schizophrenia. Schizophrenia occurs in all cultures in all times, displaying a remarkable consistency. What this means is that while some people at some times may have better reasons for going nuts, about the same number go nuts regardless. Translated to your situation: your mental health is not dependent on the moral, sociopolitical health of the world. Thank God for little things like that. It also means that getting well doesn't involve selling out or becoming any less angry with things as they are.

World-mess theories are only the beginning. You've doubtless already run into several theories of what is causing your problems and will run into many more. Everyone has a field day explaining schizophrenia. It's your parents, your childhood, your love life, your religion, your life style, and on and on. Usually each theory will contain just enough truth to make it irritating, but the vast majority of these theories end up giving you explanations of why you are sick rather than clues about how to get well. Besides which, most theories on this level have only poetic attractiveness and scanty, if any, objective evidence backing them up.

Love, insight, talking about your feelings, creative expression are all valuable commodities in their own right, Anita, but don't expect them to make you well or let anyone con you into believing that some lack of these is responsible for your troubles. Freud himself said that psychotherapy wasn't of any value in schizophrenia and all subsequent studies have borne him out. Case histories that seem to show the opposite are more than likely a reflection of the fact that a great number of schizophrenics—approximately a third—improve without any treatment. Whatever shrink happens to be standing around when such remissions occur is usually willing to assume credit.

A more serious problem with most psychological theories and therapies is that they usually involve placing blame. According to their model, your parents or your friends or you yourself or someone else has screwed up. The fact is, there is no blame. You haven't done anything horribly wrong and neither have your parents or anyone else. Everybody's just sort of bumbling along and everyone makes mistakes. But mistakes aren't the reason you're having trouble. Anita, I'd be all for making someone feel lousy and guilty, even wrongly, if there was the slightest evidence it helped schizophrenics, but there isn't. More often it just further terrifies and alienates those who most want to help you.

If you fail to benefit from psychotherapy, you stand a better than even chance of being accused of "resisting therapy." As if things weren't bad enough already, you are now accused of subconsciously or even consciously wanting them that way.

If on the other hand you do recover while under psychotherapy you may come away feeling that honesty and other forms of virtue were at the root of your problem and that if you and those around you are not always wise and pure, you'll go nuts again. Truth and beauty are wonderful things, but I want to assure you that, once recovered, a schizophrenic can lie, cheat, and be dense with consequences no more dire than those faced by anyone else.

Doctors, family, and friends will inevitably get into figuring out which parts of what you do and say are "crazy" and which are sane. It would be a harmless enough diversion if it weren't such an irritating distraction from the real problems. It's impossible to sort out the sanity of any given thought or action. Every fantasy and hallucination has at least a germ of truth and often more. Everything I did, even at my craziest, was "appropriate" with a little imagination. The dead-end route I kept traveling was working hard on figuring out exactly how my thoughts and actions made sense and then trying to get others to see it. Since I was acting "appropriately," there was nothing wrong.

What I finally caught on to was that there was something very wrong and that whether or not my thoughts and actions were "appropriate" had very little to do with it. What was wrong was that I had lost control of my life, and not just because I had been locked up. The simplest way to describe it is that my stress tolerance had been whittled down to nothing in a process that went back far beyond the time when everyone got so interested in the appropriateness of my actions. Appropriate shmappropriate, the problem is that schizophrenia makes you so goddamed fragile. I was reacting appropriately but to so many different things, so strongly, and in such a personal way that it didn't look that way to anyone else. More important, my being that fragile and reactive meant I couldn't do many things I wanted to do. I was so distractible that even very simple tasks were impossible to complete, so sensitive that the slightest hint of negativity was utterly crushing, so wired that no one could relax around me.

Like you, Anita, I cracked in very hip surroundings. While it has advantages in terms of people being willing to go the extra mile, having more respect and sympathy for the terrors you're going through, it can also add some new problems. I was often afraid to tell my friends what was going on, not so much because they'd think I was nuts, but more because it might sound like bragging. Many of the things that were happening to me were things I was supposed to like: ego death, communicating with the supernatural, hypersensitivity of all sorts. If there's anything worse than bragging about such things, it's not liking them.

It's been suggested by many that a schizophrenics is a failed mystic. The same thing happens to both, but in the face of God, infinity, or whatever, mystics keep their cool but schizophrenics end up in such rotten shape because they cling to their egos, refuse to accept their own insignificance, or some such sin. Let me say this: It seems more than likely that there's a relationship between the two, but what sets them apart is far more a matter of degree and circumstance than wisdom and virtue.

Most descriptions of mystic states, while they include feelings of timelessness, actually cover very little clock time. For the schizophrenic it's a twenty-four-hour day, seven days a week. Realizing the transient nature of material things helps for a while, but it's got its limits.

There's no denying that much of the content of my experience came from childhood experiences, my sexuality, my culture and situation within that culture, and so on. The content of hallucinations and fantasies is so fascinating it's easy to overlook the question of how the frame of mind came about in the first place. People suffering from high fevers also sometimes suffer from hallucinations and delirious thinking, but I have yet to hear anyone suggest that understanding the content of such delirium could bring down the fever.

There's also no doubt that psychologically traumatic events often trigger off a schizophrenic episode. Just prior to my crackup, my parents were splitting up, the woman I had been virtually married to took off with another man, my father was becoming more and more outlandishly famous. But these things and much worse happen to lots of people who never go crazy, and I doubt very much that maturity, insight, or understanding is the missing ingredient. Working out these "traumas" had nothing to do with my recovery. To tell you the truth, Anita, all three issues and lots else still puzzle the hell out of me.

So what is it that's different about me and possibly you? The only decent answers I've been able to come up with are biochemical ones. Admittedly biochemistry is boring as mud next to psychology, religion, and politics, but the objective evidence for schizophrenia's being biochemical is overwhelming. The literature I sent you via Headly is a good introduction if you're interested in the details.

Simply realizing that the problem is biochemical can be enormously helpful. That in itself can cut much of the pain and frustration for you and your friends. No one's to blame. Psychological heroics are not required to improve things. But beyond this the biochemical model gives you many helpful clues about how to get better. ‚

As poetic as schizophrenia is, I know of very few cases in which poetry was of much help. It's unlikely that any understanding you can reach, or love that anyone else can give you, will have much effect on how things go. As irrelevant as it may seem, what you eat, how much sleep you get, and similarly pedestrian factors are what matters.

While schizophrenia makes keeping any sort of schedule difficult, try to eat and sleep regularly even if you don't feel like it. I got it into my head that I had attained enlightenment that made me above eating and sleeping. That was no help. My diet before I cracked up probably contributed to my problems. I was more or less vegetarian-macrobiotic for economic-political-religious reasons all mixed in together. While some people thrive on such a diet, it's a disaster for me and many schizophrenics. A high-protein diet with a minimum of starches and sugars is generally best, though there are exceptions. Simply be aware that what you eat or don't eat can be terribly important and try to notice which foods are helpful and which are harmful.

Coffee is nearly always bad for schizophrenics. Grass, hash, and especially the hallucinogens and speed can be real trouble. Good old alcohol, interestingly enough, can be helpful in a pinch. A good many alcoholics are probably schizophrenics who drink to keep schizophrenia away. Don't depend on it too much, however, as there are better ways and you could end up with two problems instead of one.

There is nothing permanent about any of these restrictions. As soon as you get yourself together, you can do whatever you like. I now have coffee occasionally, and could probably eat tons of sugar and smoke lots of dope with no worse effects than anyone else. But for now, give yourself every break you can.

Some of the literature I've sent you deals with orthomolecular therapy. It's a cumbersome phrase which simply means restoring normal brain chemistry with high doses of vitamins and minerals, dietary adjustments, and, more recently, allergy desensitization. This approach focuses on making "normal" behavior possible rather than the usual attempts to make "crazy" behavior impossible.

Unfortunately, an up-to-date, comprehensive book on the subject does not exist. This is mostly attributable to rapid changes within the field and is usual for any new medical approach. But I think you would find these two books interesting:

How to Live with Schizophrenia, by Abram Hoffer and Humphry Osmond (University Books, New Hyde Park, N. Y., 1966), may be hard to find but is well worth the effort. It is an excellent introduction to the field even though some of the technical information is out of date. The therapy available today has become considerably more sophisticated and individualized than the simple niacin and vitamin C regimen it describes.

The Schizophrenias, Yours and Mine, by Carl C. Pfieffer (Pyramid Books, New York, 1970) contains some of the more recent work and is also very helpful.

There are a number of organizations that may be helpful. There are chapters of the American Schizophrenia Association in many states. The Huxley Institute, 1114 First Avenue, New York, N.Y. 10021, is an excellent source of information. Many of its pamphlets and reprints are quite good. The Institute will also be able to tell you what organizations are available in your area.

More and more doctors and clinics are using the orthomolecular approach, but they are still, especially the good ones, few and far between. Most of them are overworked and are booked solid for months in advance. At the moment, finding good orthomolecular treatment is a matter of patience, luck, and hard work. I hope that this will change soon.

Orthomolecular therapy is considered controversial by many doctors, but you have nothing to lose and possibly a great deal to gain by trying it. Many schizophrenics and many doctors have found vitamins highly effective, and the worst that critics have been able to say is that they don't work. They don't cost much, which means the worst you could do is waste a little money. The vitamins used are all water-soluble substances that your body is well accustomed to. The dangers are very limited, as you will simply piss away anything you don't need.

There are several problems with the vitamin approach, the principal ones being that it doesn't work for every schizophrenic, and that with many of those it does work for the results are long in coming. I responded positively in a matter of weeks, and so do many others, but six months to a year for positive results is not uncommon. Many doctors involved with vitamin therapy freely admit that their treatment is far from what they wish it were, but it happens to be the best thing going at this point. Much more research is needed before we have any fast, easy answers to schizophrenia. Doctors using vitamin therapy don't do so to the exclusion of other approaches. They are generally experts in drugs and other therapies and don't hesitate to use them when called for.

While I very likely owe my life to Thorazine, I doubt if I will ever develop much affection for it or similar tranquilizers. They act very quickly and are invaluable in many situations, but have numerous unpleasant side effects. I don't see them as an attractive long-term solution but more as a way to buy time for the vitamin, dietary, and other less coercive approaches. The heavy drugs can make your illness somewhat less troublesome to yourself and a lot less troublesome to others, but what I like so much about the vitamin approach is its utter lack of coerciveness. If your body doesn't feel the need for a vitamin, it simply gets rid of it. Things aren't so simple with substances like Thorazine, which it's unaccustomed to. There is no way the vitamins can be an infringement on your individuality. They simply make sure your body gets whatever raw materials it wants.

Suicide is a very real danger. It may sometimes seem like a rational choice. I tried to kill myself a number of times, but was luckily so screwed up I couldn't do a decent job of it. I had heard that schizophrenia was incurable, which is most definitely untrue. I would much prefer death over life with my head in such desperately bad shape. It's very possible to recover, and you must try very hard not to lose sight of that.

Anita, I'm not sure what your financial shape is at this point, but if your parents are in a position to help you, this is no time to get proud. Your primary responsibility at this point is getting well. Most jobs involve anxiety, which can very easily set you back. Any short-term money you might make just isn't worth the risk. The best way to insure your not being a financial burden is to accept the fact that you can't support yourself now and concentrate on getting well.

Part of why I cracked as often and as hard as I did was my refusal to give myself many breaks. Every time my head cleared for as much as ten minutes, I believed myself completely cured and ready to take on the world. I found the notion of being recuperative or giving myself any special allowances abhorrent. A lot of that is due to the deceptive nature of schizophrenia. One day you're fine, the next you're clutching your knees trying to hold on. And there's no simple reminder of what you can and can't do, like that arm in a cast. The best general advice in terms of diet, social activity, or whatever is simply to notice what affects you badly, and to be utterly unabashed about avoiding it.

Friends and family can be enormously helpful as long as they understand what's going on. Here again the biochemical model is invaluable. Instead of tiptoeing around, afraid of saying the wrong thing, dreading that they somehow drove you crazy, making feeble stabs at amateur psychotherapy, nervously checking out everything you do or say to see if it's "crazy," friends and family who understand that the problem is a medical one usually become excellent allies. Besides companionship, they can help you keep to good eating and sleeping habits, protect you from unwanted stimulation, and look out for your interests in countless other ways.

As well as being one of the worst things that can happen to a human being, schizophrenia can also be one of the richest learning and humanizing experiences life offers. Although it won't do much toward improving your condition, the ins and outs of your bout with schizophrenia are well worth figuring out. But if you concentrate on getting well for now, and come back to puzzling things out later, I guarantee you'll do a better job of it. Being crazy and being mistaken are not at all the same. The things in life that are upsetting you are more than likely things well worth being upset about. It is, however, possible to be upset without being crippled, and even to act effectively against those things.

There are great insights to be gained from schizophrenia,

but remember that they won't do you or anyone else much good unless you recover.

**Take care,
Mark**

Afterword

The events described in this book took place nearly twenty years ago. Some things have changed. The notion that mental illness has a large biochemical component is no longer very radical. Things have come full circle to the point where it's unusual to hear anyone say that mental illness is all mental. The view that going crazy is caused by bad events in childhood and that talk and understanding offer the best hope for a cure seems very out-of-date. This is a change for the better, though it has by no means brought an end to the shame, blame, and guilt that continue to compound the suffering of the mentally ill and their families.

The clinical definition of schizophrenia has been changed. Under the old definitions there was considerable ambiguity about what to call people like me. Under the new definitions I would be classified as manic depressive rather than schizophrenic. I wasn't sick for very long and I didn't follow a downhill course, both of which are required by the new definitions to diagnose someone as schizophrenic. While it's tempting to dismiss this as an insignificant change in labels and be more than a little irritated that they went and changed the rules after I built a book around the old definitions, I have to admit that this, too, is probably a positive change. It should mean that fewer people with acute breakdowns will be written off as hopeless. Eventually someone will develop a simple blood test that will sort out who has what disease and what treatments should work. In the meantime we're stuck with arguing about labels and indirect evidence as the best way we have of approaching useful truths about how to help people.

There are probably a dozen or so separate diseases responsible for what we now call schizophrenia and manic depression. Until the definitive work is done, many things are plausible and almost anything is possible. This lack of certainty makes mental illness wonderful ground for intellectual speculation and absolute hell for patients and their families.

At the time I wrote my book I felt that the large doses of vitamins with which I was treated, along with more conventional approaches, had a great deal to do with my recovery. It was my hope that many people diagnosed as schizophrenic would get better if only their doctors would become more open-minded and treat them with vitamins. Since that time I've seen people with breakdowns like mine recover every bit as completely as I did without vitamin therapy. I've seen many cases where vitamin therapy didn't make any difference and a lot of cases like mine where it's hard to say exactly what did what.

I continue to feel a great deal of affection for the doctors who treated me. They were good doctors, with or without vitamins, which they saw mostly as something that couldn't hurt and might help. I continue to feel that the debate over whether or not vitamins might have a role in the treatment of some forms of mental illness has been miserably handled by both sides.

What I can no longer continue to do is to maintain that the vitamins played a major role in my recovery. I have not changed the text of my book because I think it should stand as I wrote it. I remain very proud of the book but if I could have one line back I'd delete "The more the vitamins took hold . . ." (p. 257). I'd also drop the paragraphs dealing with how to find out more about the vitamin therapy in the postscript.

Life has been good to me. I made it into and through medical school and managed to enjoy myself most of the time. I'm a pediatrician and I continue to find it very congenial, rewarding work. I have two healthy sons and am still in love with my wife. I'm surprised how much I care about the Red Sox.

I still think a fair amount about the sixties and trying to be a good hippie. I'm under no illusion that I understand exactly what was going on back then, but there are a few things that need saying. We were not the spaced-out, flaky, self-absorbed, wimpy, whiney flower children depicted in movies and TV shows alleging to depict the times. It's true that we were too young, too inexperienced, and in the end too vulnerable to bad advice from middle-aged sociopathic gurus. Things eventually went bad, but before they went bad hippies did a lot of good. Brave, honest, and true, they paid a price. I'm sure no one will ever study it, but my guess is that there are as many disabled and deeply scarred ex-hippies as there are Vietnam Vets.

When all is said and done, the times were out of joint. Adults as much as said they didn't have a clue as to what should be done and that it was up to us: the best, bravest, brightest children ever to fix things up. We gave it our best shot, and I'm glad I was there.

Printed in the United States
by Baker & Taylor Publisher Services